Teachers Teaching Nonviolence

Christian A. Bracho and Danita Dodson (editors)

ISBN 978-1-64504-052-1 (Paperback)
ISBN 978-1-64504-053-8 (Hardback)
ISBN 978-1-64504-054-5 (E-Book)

Library of Congress Control Number: 2020938952

Printed on acid-free paper

© DIO Press Inc, New York
https://www.diopress.com

This book is part of the *Liberating Education, Liberating Educators* Series
Series Editor: Andrew T. Kemp

"*Teachers Teaching Nonviolence* offers examples of peace education in action from educators across the United States who have attended a formative bi-annual summer institute on nonviolence. Through this institute, educators deepen their conceptual understanding of nonviolence, and then create action plans and curricula to infuse lessons and practices of dignity, justice, and empathy in their classrooms. The authors and editors of this book offer ground breaking practical insights on how to inspire students, deepen our self-reflection as educators, and teach for a more just world."

Monisha Bajaj
Professor, International & Multicultural Education
University of San Francisco

"Advocates for reimagining education for the 21st century have often overlooked a discussion of how the purpose of education needs to evolve with explicit understanding that human and ecological well-being are intertwined. The profound wisdom of *ahimsa* is that it advocates well-being for all. Applying this to education is a vital ingredient for transforming education. The educators who have shared their experience and practice of *ahimsa* in *Teachers Teaching Nonviolence* eloquently illustrate that the mindset and practice of nonviolence can enhance individual, community, and global well-being."

Catherine O'Brien, PhD
Senior Scholar, Cape Breton University

For all those who seek the path of nonviolence

In Memory of Shalom Mary Montgomery

TABLE OF CONTENTS

Section 2: Integrating Mindfulness and Compassion

Section 3: Subverting Curriculum through Nonviolence

Foreword

By Tara Sethia

> Just as pain is not agreeable to you, it is so with others. Knowing this principle
> of equality of all beings, treat all with respect and compassion.[1]

The need for education about nonviolence is relevant and urgent in our
current context. News reports are full of cases of road rage, sky rage, and
sideline rage, not to mention the increasing instances of terror, unending
stories of horror about wars, and growing global conflicts leading to death
and destruction. All around us we see discord and divisions deepening,
inequalities increasing, and animosity rising. Violence is pervading all walks
of our lives—homes, schools, colleges, airports, streets, game fields, and
workplaces. Most disturbing, however, is the rising trend of violence in
schools, which does not bode well for the future of humanity. The sad truth
is that our youngsters are growing up seeing violence not only as normal
but also necessary and, in some cases, even "cool."

Violence in schools occurs in various forms, ranging from bullying to
killing. Schools, in turn, respond with a variety of "anti-violence"
interventions. While it is important that we move away from violence, it is
even more important to devise ways for creating and sustaining a culture of
nonviolence. This is particularly desirable as the data shows empathy has
been in decline since 1980 and even more so since the dawn of this century.[2]
Therefore, we need to expose students to the knowledge and
understanding of nonviolence vs. violence. They must know why the choice
of nonviolence is important for their future and the wellbeing of humanity
at large.

Nonviolence is not merely the absence of violence. Nonviolence and
violence are, in fact, very different in terms of their premises, goals,
modalities of action, and outcomes.

Nonviolence is rooted in unity, in oneness, in the integrity of the whole.
This sense of unity applies to the individual, to the mind-body harmony, and
to the unity of thought and action. On a larger scale, it applies to the
indivisibility of all existence, signifying not only the oneness of all humanity
but also the oneness of humans and nature. Violence, in contrast, is rooted
in separation, in divisions. These divisions can be within oneself—as in

C. A. Bracho and D. Dodson (eds.), *Teachers Teaching Nonviolence*, xi–xv.

between one's thought and actions, or between the self and others—as in "us" vs. "them," or between humans and nature.

Nonviolence seeks to transform hearts, to change minds, and to cultivate a sense of care and compassion. In contrast, violence aims to defeat and exploit, coerce and control, and does so by causing hurt and harm.

Violence is often committed unconsciously, and many violent actions occur with a sense of suspended judgment, if not altogether without thought and reflection. We witness and speak of violence inflicted on unsuspecting subjects. In contrast, nonviolence cannot be "inflicted" on others. Nonviolence involves conscious and mindful choices.

Nonviolence always assigns primacy to individual responsibility. It is worth noting that Gandhi felt highly sceptical about the idea of inventing "a system so perfect that nobody had to be good." Therefore, Gandhi was emphatic in regarding individual transformation as a precondition for social transformation. History offers us numerous instances of collective and institutionalized violent action, and of structural violence evident in inequitable social arrangements such as slavery and serfdom. In all such instances, the dominant locus of decision-making is the system or the structure, and any kind of individual responsibility is generally diffused and negligible.

Nonviolence regards every individual as part of the whole. In the dignity of one lies the dignity of all, and the loss of one is the loss of the whole. Nonviolence is desirable not only because it is a defining element of a good life but, more importantly, because it is an integral part of the quality of life.

Violence undermines the essential dignity of human being. It is harmful for both the victims and the perpetrators. To the victims, violence denies human dignity and justice. The perpetrators, who depend on violence, are drawn to it by anger and hatred and live a life without peace and happiness. Moreover, for them violence becomes habitual. Then it spreads like a virus, infects others, and becomes a norm.[3] In this way, violence diminishes the quality of life.

Choosing nonviolence means to be in the state of empathy and love. It means to have compassion and gratitude. It requires humility and thrives on forgiveness. As such, nonviolence is a key for sustaining peace and for building harmonious relationships among individuals, communities, and nations. The choice of nonviolence—love, compassion, kindness, generosity—as a pragmatic approach to human relations and as the creation of positive change is one of the greatest gifts we can give to our children and youth. The question is what can we do, and where do we begin to expose children and youth to the ethics of nonviolence?

Education is an important vehicle for fostering a culture of nonviolence. At the dawn of this century, I began to explore the possibility of creating a forum for nonviolence education on our campus. Subsequent efforts led to the establishment at Cal Poly Pomona of the Ahimsa Center in 2003-2004. Since then the Center has launched various educational initiatives for creating a culture of nonviolence.[4] The Center's approach encompasses both the domain of "thought"—drawing upon philosophical and religious traditions of nonviolence from around the world—and the domain of "action"—the political and social movements genuinely committed to nonviolence as demonstrated by the life and work of historical figures such as Mohandas K. Gandhi, Martin Luther King Jr., and César Chávez.

One of the Center's major initiatives has been a fellowship program for K-12 teacher-leadership in nonviolence education. Open to educators nationwide, these two-week intensive institutes brought together K-12 teachers from across the country for a deeper study of nonviolence. In conceptualizing and directing these institutes, the goal was to expose these educators to the life and movements of exemplars of nonviolent social change; to provide a rare opportunity to interact with internationally acclaimed scholars and experts featured during lectures and seminars; and to facilitate the development of curriculum in nonviolence education through collaboration in peer-led curriculum workshops.

Accordingly, in 2005 the Center started hosting biannually a summer institute for K-12 teachers. In the institutes, these "Ahimsa Fellows" learn about the nonviolence in religious and philosophical traditions and the histories of nonviolent social change. They are introduced to the exemplars of nonviolence through primary and interpretative texts. This allows them to situate historical figures in their contexts, examine the challenges they faced, and study the approach and methods they devised for dealing with their challenges to assess how they used nonviolence in leading social change. Through an in-depth learning about historical exemplars of nonviolence and their movements for nonviolent social and political change, teachers gain not just the content knowledge, but also derive pedagogies and methods of individual and social transformation. For instance, by learning about Gandhi's journey to nonviolence or by understanding King's pilgrimage to nonviolence, these educators also learn about what it takes to evolve and transform themselves, and how and why that may be necessary for transforming others.

The Ahimsa Center Summer Institutes train teacher-leaders with both the knowledge and skills needed to bring a cultural shift within their schools. These teacher-leaders have both the capacity and the opportunity to transform their students and classrooms. They can act as agents of change by modeling the change themselves. By not only teaching about nonviolence but also integrating nonviolence in their pedagogies and interactions with students, teachers are poised to inspire, create, and sustain a culture of peace in their schools and communities.

The institutes serve as catalysts for building a "fellowship of the future,"[5] binding groups of educators who collectively share a commitment for advancing education about nonviolence and for creating a culture of compassion and kindness in schools. Driven by the collective intellectual rigor and vigor of the ahimsa institutes, the educators bond as a professional community. They feel inspired by what they learn from experts, read in primary sources, see in documentaries and hear in conversations with one another. In their analysis of violence and conflict, they learn to delve below the surface and attempt to find and address the root causes. They know that true nonviolence finds expression in compassion, caring, empathy, love, generosity, and forgiveness. They become equipped with ideas and strategies to solve conflicts and to make a difference in their classrooms and schools by planting and nurturing among their students and peers an understanding about the role of nonviolence in a free society that upholds equality of all, and amity among all peoples irrespective of gender, race, religious or national backgrounds.

The fellows from these programs are playing a leadership role in nonviolence-centered curricular innovations for the benefit of students from elementary to high school level.[6] This collection of essays is a testament to their collective commitment to contribute their insights and share their respective journeys. The essays demonstrate wide-ranging experiments with both content and pedagogies to implement education about nonviolence.

A couple of years ago, we discussed an idea of publishing these as a volume on teaching nonviolence. The editors— Drs. Christian Bracho and Danita Dodson, both former ahimsa fellows and teacher-leaders— have not only taken this idea to heart, but have thoughtfully compiled these essays in a volume, perhaps the first of its kind. I hope it will inspire future teacher-leaders in further advancing education about nonviolence and nonviolent social change.

Tara Sethia, Ph.D.
December 7, 2019
Founder and Director, Ahimsa Center
California State Polytechnic University, Pomona

notes

1   Varni, J. (1999). *Saman Suttam* (T. K. Tukul and K. K. Dixit, Trans.). Delhi, p. 150.
2   Zaki, J. (2011, January). What, me care? Young are less empathetic. *Scientific American.* https://www.scientificamerican.com/article/what-me-care/. Retrieved December 1, 2019.

3 Sethia, T. (2012). *Gandhi: Pioneer of nonviolent social change*. New York: Pearson, p. 4.

4 These include (1) an interdisciplinary minor in nonviolence studies on our campus open to students in all majors; (2) a teacher-leadership program in nonviolence and nonviolent social change; and (3) a variety of public programs, such as conferences, symposia, lectures, dialogues and workshops. Through such educational initiatives, the Center is fostering a vision in which each individual is an important player in building and sustaining a culture of nonviolence.

5 A term coined by Mihaly Csikszentmihalyi (1994), a pioneer of positive psychology. This fellowship brings together "a group of kindred spirits dedicated to supporting trends that move in the direction of greater harmony...." See his book, *The evolving self*. New York: Harper Perennial, pp. 281-289.

6 The lessons created by the fellows are wide-ranging and aimed at K-12 students. The curriculum they create on nonviolence education benefits them and their students, and, by making it available as an open source on the Center's web site, it also benefits others.

https://www.cpp.edu/~ahimsacenter/k12/

Introduction

Nonviolence Education Is Real Education

By Christian A. Bracho

In the December 1, 1937, issue of the newspaper *Harijan*, Mohandas K. Gandhi wrote, "Real education consists in drawing the best out of yourself. What better book can there be than the book of humanity?" This collection of essays, *Teachers Teaching Nonviolence*, takes Gandhi's message to heart, integrating the narratives of 18 teachers from all over the United States as they tell their stories of learning about and teaching nonviolence. In each narrative, the teachers explore their own humanity as they explain how learning about nonviolence through an intensive, two-week experience at the Ahimsa Center for Nonviolence at California State Polytechnic University, Pomona cultivated their capacities to "be the change," serving as exemplars and agents of nonviolence by working within and across various contexts: from their classrooms to their schools, from their cities to their states, from their country to the world at large. Through acts both small and large, in their relationships with students, colleagues, families, and members of their communities, the teachers demonstrate how learning about nonviolence can galvanize their capacities to act as agents of nonviolent social change.

American schools need to integrate education about nonviolence in response to a culture of violence that has deepened in scope and terror since the 1990s. While the Columbine shooting in 1999 turned out to be the advent of school shootings as a normal aspect of life in the United States, American schools continue to operate as historical sites of physical and symbolic violence, where students face bullying, racism, homophobia, and gender discrimination, as well as violence not only in formal curriculum (e.g., in textbooks) but also in the hidden curriculum (Apple, 1971) of active shooter drills or the presence of campus "peace officers" armed with guns and batons. Public schools encounter major divestment at local and national levels of government, increasing pressure on teachers to use their own resources to pay for classroom materials, and mobilizing teachers' unions all over the country to resist reforms that would increase the influence of privatization lobbyists in K-12 schools and higher education. Movements like Black Lives Matter have raised awareness about police brutality and everyday racism and have pointed to the ongoing effects of African-American slavery and Jim Crow laws, while the separation of families at the Mexican border has reminded some of the internment of Japanese-Americans in the U.S. and of Jews in Germany. Social media in the current political era has encouraged vicious bullying, given legitimacy to fringe groups, and stoked partisan divisions that threaten societal cohesion and interpersonal understanding. In the wake of the Stoneman-Douglass shooting in 2018, which spurred a nationwide student movement demanding reform and legislation around gun ownership, the National Rifle Association and the U.S. President responded by calling for teachers to be armed with weapons, an idea so absurd and alarming it had to be heard to be believed.

The teachers in this volume, who teach everything from English to science, Spanish to economics, kindergarten to 12th grade, have all witnessed violence in their schools and communities. Their stories ask us to consider how teachers might contribute to a culture of peace by learning about nonviolence and practicing it in their schools and classrooms, in the tradition of teachers in the United States serving as peace educators, activists, and ethical professionals with great power to affect change. Via these 18 narratives, we make the case that the way to respond to violence is not to arm teachers with guns, but to arm them with nonviolence, which Gandhi termed "the weapon of the strong." Through innovative approaches to curriculum and pedagogy, through revitalized relationships with others, and through personal transformation that spirals outward, the teachers' narratives show how learning about nonviolence equipped them to act forcefully in their local contexts, calling on satyagraha (truth-force or soul-force) and a commitment to ahimsa (nonviolence in thoughts, word, and deeds).

In this introduction, I will narrate my own journey toward nonviolence and explain my collaborations with nearly 200 teachers trained at the Ahimsa Center K-12 Institutes. I will argue that nonviolence education has a place within the larger field of peace education, and I will suggest that we must extend more opportunities for teachers to *learn* nonviolence so that they may effectively teach it to others. My hope is that this book can compel people both within and outside the worlds of K-12 and higher education to draw on principles of nonviolence, and the exemplary lives of such nonviolent figures as Gandhi, Martin Luther King, César Chávez, and Nelson

Mandela, as they design programs and initiatives aimed at cultivating a culture of peace.

A Journey to Nonviolence

My personal journey toward nonviolence began in 2005, when I was employed as a high school English teacher in the San Gabriel Valley suburbs outside Los Angeles, California. I was in my fifth year as an educator and overwhelmed by a sense of powerlessness as the country deepened its military engagements in Afghanistan and Iraq in response to the 9/11 attacks in 2001. Over the three years since that horrific event, I witnessed my students utter calumnies about Islam and people of Arabic and Middle Eastern descent, and I saw how they attacked peers who expressed dissent. My daily encounters with students across five hour-long periods made me realize that my students were parroting national conversations about foreign and domestic policies, filtered through the partisan lenses of networks such as CNN and FOX News. At that time in the early 2000s, expressing any critique of the President or of American wars could lead to accusations of betrayal or treason and assertions that one should "just leave this country if you don't like it." Social norms shifted toward the sense that patriotism meant not questioning our leaders or policies, that it was turncoat to discuss the number of Iraqi civilian deaths or remind others that no weapons of mass destruction were ever found. At the local level, my district banned films like Al Gore's *An Inconvenient Truth* and circulated a memo reminding teachers to lead students in the Pledge of Allegiance, a policy that had never been enforced prior to 9/11. As a public schoolteacher, I struggled with how to navigate my response to the racist and militarist language and beliefs I heard in my classroom, and in uncomfortable conversations with colleagues about the culture wars in America, around topics like gay marriage and immigrant rights. With the war spiraling out of control, and the horrific torture at Abu Ghraib coming to light, I wondered: What is my role as a teacher at a time of crisis? To simply follow a curriculum and avoid any discussions of present-day politics, or to guide students toward critical thinking that might lead to deeper empathy for the Other? The sense that I could do nothing meaningful shook me; like many early-career teachers, I even considered leaving the profession.

This changed in 2005, the day I received a flyer in my faculty mailbox for a two-week professional development institute for K-12 teachers at Cal Poly Pomona, where Professor Tara Sethia founded the Ahimsa Center in

2003. The Center's Mission spoke to me: "Through its educational programs and outreach activities, the Ahimsa Center fosters synergistic interactions among students, scholars, educators and the community at large." Dr. Sethia's first K-12 institute, entitled "Nonviolence and Social Change," offered teachers a two-week fellowship where they would engage scholars and practitioners of nonviolence and produce curriculum grounded in what was learned. As I read the announcement over and over again, I sensed that the institute announcement had been sent to me for a purpose and that the experience could provide something essential to my survival, to my growth as a high school teacher, and, indeed, to my whole being. I encouraged two English department colleagues also to submit applications, and the three of us were accepted into the inaugural cohort of Ahimsa Fellows. At the first meeting in April, the cohort met with civil rights leader Dolores Huerta on what was her 75th birthday. She encouraged our group of teachers to not be afraid to engage in civil disobedience, or to get arrested if necessary as she had dozens of times. I remember my colleague Shalom Montgomery glanced at me during Ms. Huerta's speech and shared a knowing look: We are meant to be here. We are meant to do the work of nonviolence.

Attending the institute was the transformative experience I imagined it would be, and more. Our group of two dozen educators, mostly from California, examined nonviolence in the tradition of Gandhi, emphasizing the way that *ahimsa, satyagraha,* and *swaraj* (self-rule) operated as fundamental concepts in his philosophy and practice. We studied his autobiography, *The Story of My Experiments with Truth,* to discover Gandhi's campaigns in South Africa and India, and we explored how Dr. Martin Luther King inspired participants in the Civil Rights Movement to use nonviolence as an active moral force to combat systemic racism in the American South. We learned about the use of nonviolence at national scales, such as in South Africa, where nonviolence has been a mechanism to mobilize forgiveness and reconciliation once societal truths have been voiced and legitimized. Through dialogue with scholars, educators, and practitioners, our cohort of educators grappled with how to translate nonviolence into a meaningful curriculum for our own students, be they kindergarteners or seniors in high school, and helped each other have the courage to experiment with nonviolence in our lives. My curricular project at the end of the Institute integrated various texts into an interdisciplinary unit on African-American slavery, emphasizing the ways slaves resisted dehumanization; I recognized later that my actual goal was to encourage students to acknowledge the humanity of others in both the U.S. and the Middle East, and to understand how systems of violence—such as slavery and war—can make us complicit in the oppression of others. It was not a perfect lesson, but it was my first experiment with truth. My first step on a long journey to nonviolence.

The experience at the institute fulfilled a desire to feel like an active agent in my work as a teacher and as a human being. I developed what Rossatto (2005) has called "transformative optimism," a term that critical peace education scholar Monisha Bajaj (2008) included in an analysis of peace education. Bajaj cites Rossatto's definition of transformative optimism: when an individual "sees himself or herself as a necessary and viable participant in the collective process of social change" (Rossatto, 2005, p. 81). In the context of a War on Terror that was killing thousands of people all over the globe and affording political cover to abandon long-standing international statutes designed to protect the dignity of human life, the Institute provided me symbolic and material resources which I could regularly return to and draw upon as fuel to cultivate nonviolence in my personal and professional spheres of influence. Texts like King's "Pilgrimage to Nonviolence" and Gandhi's Hind Swaraj empowered me to dialogue with others about the violence occurring locally and globally, and I found myself thinking of new and creative strategies to integrate ahimsa into my classroom. For example, I experimented with mindfulness by incorporating 30 seconds of silence to begin my 56-minute class periods, an effort that revealed to me how hungry students were for even a few moments of contemplation and quiet. When I ended up teaching my African-American slavery unit, I modified the unit to include discussions of reparations and forgiveness, and I homed in on Frederick Douglass's letter to his former master as an illustration of how dialogue with the oppressor is necessary to achieve moral transformation.

Following the 2005 institute, I began to volunteer at the Center, and Dr. Sethia later asked me to become a workshop facilitator at five subsequent institutes over the next ten years. Starting in 2007, the institute became a residential program with a national recruitment strategy, a shift that enabled teachers from all over the country to come to Cal Poly Pomona to live and work together as they immersed themselves in nonviolence. In my role, I worked directly with those 200 "Ahimsa Fellows" who hailed from states like Washington, Oregon, Nevada, Oklahoma, Texas, Tennessee, Florida, Massachusetts, New York, New Jersey, Wisconsin, New Hampshire, Maryland, Pennsylvania, Colorado, Hawaii, Alaska, Wyoming, New Mexico, Virginia, and Illinois. The teachers represented all grades across the K-12 spectrum, and those in middle or high schools from various disciplines; while the majority worked in social studies and English departments, many of them taught science, math, Spanish, art, music, and physical education. Though they embodied unique cultural and ethnic communities, embraced diverse gender and sexual identities, and belonged to a range of socioeconomic backgrounds, they shared a common desire to learn about nonviolence in the hope that it could make a difference in the lives of their students.

At the five institutes that I served as a facilitator, I lived in the dorms with the teachers over the course of the two weeks, attending seminars and dialogues, participating in informal conversations at mealtimes, and meditating on tough themes via long walks around the campus. With each Institute, I deepened my own understanding of and commitment to nonviolence, and I experienced the wonder of watching the K-12 educators begin their own journeys, experimenting with it as a philosophy and practice. The institute themes were:

2007 Gandhi, Nonviolence, and 21st Century Curriculum

2009 Journeys of Nonviolence: Gandhi and King

2011 Journeys of Nonviolence: Gandhi and Chávez

2013 Gandhi, Sustainability, and Happiness

2015 Journeys of Nonviolence: Gandhi and Mandela

Across the five institutes, which varied thematically, Gandhi's story was central to the study of nonviolence and how one can become an ahimsaka— a practitioner of nonviolence—through sustained commitment to ahimsa. Indeed, the idea of a "journey" of nonviolence took on special resonance at the 2009 institute, and I observed how that metaphor helped teachers release a sense that nonviolence was "too hard" or "too idealistic" to manifest in their personal or professional lives. The immersive nature of the Institute also allowed teachers to deeply examine how nonviolence can manifest at micro and macro scales in response to violence felt in particular historical and contemporary contexts. Teachers explored Gandhi's work to dismantle structural racism and colonial domination; King's efforts to challenge structural violence against Black people, and mobilize against the Vietnam War; Chávez's commitment to nonviolence as a method to demand economic and social justice for farm workers, often immigrants or children of Filipino and Mexican descent in California; and Mandela's embrace of Ubuntu and national reconciliation trials as a tactic for healing a post-apartheid South Africa. Alongside the primary texts from these leaders, teachers also read texts about happiness, flow, positive psychology, sustainability, mindfulness, and nonviolent communication; watched media content such as *Doing Time, Doing Vipassana*, a documentary about a large Indian prison that implemented 10-day meditation retreats attended by both prisoners and guards; and analyzed books like *The Buddha and the Terrorist* by Satish Kumar.

Over the years, along with teachers Susan Milan, Peggy Sia, and Michele Milner, I co-facilitated workshops that guided teachers toward curriculum development and/or pedagogical innovations rooted in principles of nonviolence. In early iterations of the Institute, we also helped them create digital stories that combined visual and audio content to relay nonviolent concepts and narratives. My co-facilitators and I discovered how important it was for teachers to personally grapple with the violence they witnessed in their own classrooms and communities, and we helped them construct images and narratives of nonviolence in examples that made sense for their individual environments. Some teachers were inspired to address bullying, especially in the early 2010s as the country saw a dramatic rise in suicide within the LGBTQ community, while others focused on economic inequality in the wake of the 2008 recession that exposed the weaknesses of the global capitalist system and raised questions about "modern civilization." Teachers in the primary grades developed lessons that aimed to teach young children concepts like ahimsa at developmentally appropriate levels, while others endeavored to make kids aware of local issues related to food justice or environmental degradation. Math teachers connected concepts like "The Power of One" to their algebra classes, and social studies teachers revamped curriculum to focus less on militarism and historical battles and more on social movements and individual contributions by activists and leaders. In each lesson that the teachers produced, they grounded their work in the material they studied, and they made nonviolence tangible and meaningful for themselves, their students, and, in some cases, their colleagues or the families they served.

In the 15 years since I attended my first Institute, I taught my unit on African-American slavery several times, but I also developed new lessons that I taught in my own classroom and as a guest teacher for colleagues. The most significant was a two-part lesson that first asked high school English students to explore nonviolence in thoughts, words, and actions, followed by a discussion of the key vocabulary words ahimsa and satyagraha, as defined by Gandhi and King. The unifying goal was to afford students opportunities to describe what nonviolence could look or sound like in concrete action, grounded in the firm and eloquent statements by leaders who used nonviolence to mobilize massive social change. One year, after guest teaching the second part of the lesson to students, I was amazed to learn that only a few days later, they decided to organize an "ahimsa protest" on campus when a school dance was canceled in response to a spate of fights in the week prior to the event. My colleague Nicole Meylor, who also attended the Institute, worked with her students to activate what they had learned about nonviolence, and she encouraged them to consider nonviolent means to express their discontent toward the administration and the student community-at-large. The students met outside of school to create posters and t-shirts, and they lobbied their friends to participate in a peaceful march during lunch that culminated in a silent demonstration in the main quad. The images of the students marching, protesting, and standing in silent solidarity resonate in my mind to this day.

What I have learned from my experience teaching about nonviolence is that both students and teachers need only a little vocabulary about it in order to stimulate their personal capacity to practice nonviolence in everyday life. Teaching nonviolence affirms for me that human beings are starved for this kind of knowledge, for opportunities to wield their power nonviolently and act in ways that humanize themselves and others. I remember one year, when I guest taught in the classroom of my colleague Esteban Hernandez, a student asked, "Why is it that I'm 16 years old and have never heard about nonviolence?" It's that question that compels me to keep doing this work and underlines the value of this volume.

Developing Peace Educators

Peace education has a long history in both the United States and abroad; a wide body of literature examines how it has been applied to address problems at local, regional, national, and global scales. This volume is in dialogue with that literature, but it aims to emphasize the concept of "nonviolence education" as a unique approach in its own right, in which teachers learn nonviolence so that they can effectively serve as peace educators, implementing a pedagogy of nonviolence in their professional settings.

Peace education has origins in the 19th century, but it grew in scope after World War II as nations all over the globe attempted to unify groups of people and resolve conflicts through programs and initiatives focused on reconciliation, dialogue, and peacebuilding. While these efforts focused primarily on avoiding further conflicts, peace research and peace education have evolved to more critically examine systems of violence such as war, poverty, and patriarchy (Harris, 2004; Hantzopoulous & Williams, 2017). The end of the 20th century saw peace education efforts grow alongside subfields such as human rights education, environmental education, and multiculturalism (Bajaj & Chiu, 2009). Within peace education circles, rich dialogues continued about the differences between negative and positive peace, or the contrasts of "education for peace" versus "peace education." Rather than simply define peace as the absence of violence or peace education as the mere study of peace, peace educators articulate the need to foster a culture of peace through direct confrontation with forms of structural violence in society (Agnihotri, 2017; Hantzopoulos & Williams, 2017). In other words, we might define peace education as "problem-posing education that attempts to build in every person the universal values and behaviors on which a culture of peace is predicated, including the development of non-violent conflict resolution skills and a commitment to working together to realize a shared and preferred future" (Kester, 2010, p. 2).

Global institutions such as UNESCO have dedicated considerable resources to peace education in the interest of building a future that recognizes human rights for all, cultural diversity, and environmental sustainability (Reardon, 2012). In a 2011 article, Bajaj and Brantmaier call for a critical peace education in which individuals exercise "transformative agency and participatory citizenship" (p. 221) to promote a culture of peace, keeping in mind global or universal dimensions of violence but meaningfully situating them in local or particular contexts. Hantzopoulous and Williams (2017) assert, "At the core of critical peace education is an intensified analysis of power; it re-centers the interrogative gaze on structural inequality, deepened in the most recent epochs of globalization...balancing the tensions inherent to fueling a planetary consciousness without localized realities being subsumed into a blur" (p. 6). The shift toward the local indicates the need for individuals (such as students and teachers) to identify what is going on in their own communities and neighborhoods and to work within them to affect change, acknowledging that, while macro-level forces such as capitalism, militarism, and nationalism do shape local realities, actions at the micro-level can have immediate consequence as well as long-reaching impact.

What is the place of nonviolent exemplars in peace education? Reardon (2012) argues that nonviolence in the vein of Gandhi and King has been included in peace education as a curricular topic to be explored, but its value as a political strategy and form of advocacy has been avoided. Bajaj (2010) invites greater dialogue between peace education scholars and those within Gandhian studies (a field largely found in India), arguing that U.S. peace education would benefit from the critical analysis of social and economic inequality manifest in Gandhi's works. Bilimoria (2015) likewise calls on education practitioners to attend deeply to Gandhi so that education might better integrate strategies for resolving conflicts, elevate the significance of truth-telling, highlight local realities and challenges, and cultivate nonviolence as an "inner disposition" (p. 15). These scholars suggest that nonviolence, especially as conceptualized and practiced by Gandhi, must be elevated within peace education so that individuals might develop a personal sense of agency and a greater empathy for the plight of others (Schmidt, 1984). Activating such power and compassion can inspire individuals to develop a culture of peace "rooted in the reality of suffering and the need for change and transformation" (Magro, 2014, p. 141), through the use of nonviolent approaches and tactics to identify structural inequalities felt in local settings.

The Significance of Teachers

Peace education research clearly illuminates how students and societies can benefit from initiatives focused on themes such as conflict resolution, reconciliation, and forgiveness, amongst many others. Yet little attention has been paid to how teachers might *learn* nonviolence so that they can effectively serve as peace educators or implement a pedagogy of nonviolence in their professional worlds. To effectively nurture peace and nonviolence in the hearts and minds of students, we must look to teachers, the individuals entrusted with the intellectual, emotional, and social development of young people. Teachers are nested in and work with many groups of people, and they possess considerable creative power and agency (Prinz, 2000); their interconnectedness makes them well-suited to create nonviolent curriculum and practice peaceful pedagogy appropriate to the social and cultural communities they serve. Recognizing this, the United Nations has called for "training [that enables] adults to create environments that not only teach about a culture of peace, but model it in the policies and practices of the classroom, the school and other learning environments" (UN, 2000). When teachers learn and practice nonviolence in their own lives, they foster their own sense of compassion and love, emotions that can change their students' lives. Lunenberg (2011) proposes that when "teachers are supportive, encouraging, and caring about students' futures, students report less social tension and violence in their schools" (p. 3).

If teachers can learn to both teach and act nonviolently, they can facilitate opportunities for students to interact with adults peacefully, and practice the kinds of pro-social behaviors that foster community and empathy. For example, in Northern Ireland, continued conflict between Catholics and Protestants, who have long been educated apart, led the Department of Education to create integrated schools that would bring the two groups together in the interest of desegregation. In these schools, teachers played decisive roles in modeling for students an "ethos of tolerance and respect for diversity" that is essential to cultivating peaceful coexistence between these two religious groups (Donnelly, 2004). Likewise, in war-torn societies like Iraq, teachers help students return to a sense of normalcy in the wake of serious conflict; Vongalis-Macrow (2006) believes that the return of teachers to work "is a positive signal that peace-building and restoration are beginning. The work of educators is critical for the return to stability and social reconstruction" (p. 106). While in Northern Ireland teachers worked to bring together traditionally opposed groups and model nonviolent attitudes, in Iraq teachers helped students come back to school, where nonviolent interactions might counter the traumas experienced as a result of the war.

In a comparative study of schools in New Zealand and the United States, Cavanagh (2008) argued that the school culture at most sites favors punishment, adversarial relationships, control, and inequitable power relationships between groups. Yet Cavanagh argues that most schools also demonstrate sincere efforts to create a culture of peace and nonviolence. In his ethnographic fieldwork, Cavanagh noticed how teachers tried to model respectful and healing relationships and respect the cultural diversity of their students. Similar findings emerged in a study of peace educators in the United States in the decade following the September 11, 2001, attacks on New York City and Washington, D.C. The authors found that many teachers, even those who do not explicitly consider themselves "peace educators," worked to promote "peace, nonviolence, or social action" in their classrooms and schools. Some modeled peacemaking activities, like dialogue circles intended to resolve classroom conflicts, while others taught about human rights activists, to help students see how people in the real-world use nonviolence as a means to achieve social change. Some teachers did extensive community-building activities at the start of the school year aimed at building empathy and understanding, and others taught explicitly anti-war curriculum to challenge American foreign policy in the Middle East and Central Asia. The study concludes that "the question of how educators infuse a discourse of nonviolence into schools by teaching a pedagogy of peace has become ever more important" (Joseph & Duss, 2005, p. 205).

In sum, studies in this realm point to teachers' considerable capacity to address the complex structures of violence that they and their students experience. Although the particular psychological, emotional, and spiritual dimensions of violence will differ across locations, teachers are uniquely situated to offer and model nonviolent alternatives. Though some teachers intuitively attempt to cultivate peace in their classrooms, peace education programs can present educators with an extensive repertoire of content and pedagogy to draw on as they work with children all over the world. Ideally, teacher education programs would incorporate these elements as pre-service educators learn about the profession; Tony Jenkins (2007), former director of the Peace Education Center at Teachers College, maintains that "Training in such methods can help educators stir up collective social imagination through critically challenging worldviews about violence and security" (p. 368). When teacher education programs incorporate peace education and help teacher candidates "imagine" nonviolent alternatives in everyday life, teachers are more likely to transfer these ideas into their teaching practice.

Defining Nonviolence Education

Only recently have some scholars articulated a vision of nonviolence education or a pedagogy of nonviolence; over the last ten years, Hongyu Wang most definitively elaborated how nonviolence education can be constructed and shared with teachers (2010, 2013, 2014, 2019). Wang's specific vision of a pedagogy of nonviolence draws on Buddhist and Taoist traditions, as well as the South African concept of ubuntu, to explore "relational dynamics of differing for one another, inner peace as the basis for outer peace, and the necessity of nonviolent means" (2013, p. 502). Wang's research interrogates how teachers can learn to adopt a nonviolent lens as they encounter various forms of violence in their classrooms and schools, and she finds that teachers who learn about nonviolence can be better equipped to build "organic, interconnected, and nonviolent relationships... in all scales of community in the long term" (2010, p. 4). After traveling to India to learn about nonviolence in the Jain tradition, as part of a summer program for teachers, Rubin (2018) came to see the concept of *ahimsa* as a guiding principle for her teaching, "fostering students' affective awareness and supporting their growing understandings of, and capabilities for action toward, many kinds of justice, care, and peace" (p. 337). Chubbuck and Zembylas (2011) echo similar themes, defining *critical pedagogy for nonviolence* as "a holistic integration of nonviolent attitudes and practices, a transformative use of power relations in the context of inequitable structures, and a utilization of the constitutive power of emotion to resist and transform unjust structures—[which] can form an action-oriented pedagogical approach" (p. 263). Like others, Chubbuck and Zembylas articulate an educational vision grounded in interconnectedness and unity, stirring individuals to take action as a result of confronting and analyzing violence, inequity, and abuses of power. Together, this nascent body of research suggests that nonviolence education can aid individuals to develop intrapersonal capacities for introspection and self-transformation, which can then lead to more caring relationships rooted in a desire to humanize one another (Jenkins, 2007; Bolliger &Wang, 2013). When teachers and students learn about nonviolence, they can meaningfully contribute to building a culture of peace through their sustained commitment to such values as *ahimsa, ubuntu, satyagraha, agape,* and *swaraj.*

The vision of nonviolence education presented in this book operates on the principle that individuals must learn and practice nonviolence personally, and that their experiments with nonviolence radiate outward and forward through time and space. The teachers' stories offer persuasive evidence that immersive professional development, grounded in a culture of caring and collaboration with fellow, like-minded educators interested in cultivating a culture of nonviolence and challenging the culture of violence, can activate teachers' transformative optimism and galvanize their willingness to create change in a variety of spaces and situations. Indeed, as they move about their personal and professional worlds, teachers possess strong agentic capacities for teaching nonviolence; the nature of their roles can put teachers in contact with hundreds of students a year—often thousands over a career—as well as numerous colleagues, parents, guardians, and professional staff.

In reflecting on the impact of their training, Ahimsa Fellows impart intriguing insights into what nonviolence education can look like, and its potential impact. Most significantly, teachers described a need to respond nonviolently to the immediate violence they observed locally. Many teachers expressed a sense that their schools were poorly equipped to address violence occurring in local neighborhoods or within the school setting. Others felt that school structures themselves propagated violence through harsh disciplinary practices that left little room for restoration. A teacher from Massachusetts indicated that the rise of suicide attempts amongst LGBTQ youth in the United States compelled her to combat that sort of self-violence, while another teacher from Texas, who worked at a school with 99% Latino students, explained, "there was a lot of border violence in my community due to drug-related issues," and she felt the institute on César Chávez could help her integrate stories of Latino role models into her curriculum. This teacher, like many others, knew of the concept of social justice but felt that she needed explicit professional development that would give her tools to actually teach from that perspective.

In regard to the training, many teachers affirmed the value of living and working with other educators from all around the United States. The residential component allowed teachers to build community and engage in tough conversations about the violence they witnessed and their personal desires to be agents of change. Through sustained conversations about how nonviolence can look and what it can feel like, teachers felt prepared to design lessons that made sense for their own local contexts and within their own disciplinary fields. Below is a small sample of the kinds of lessons teachers developed as a result of their study of nonviolence; more curriculum can be found at https://www.cpp.edu/~ahimsacenter/k12/:

- Ahimsa in the Real World: Truth, Love, Restorative Justice (6th Grade Humanities)
- King, Gandhi, and Nonviolence in Indian Art (High School Visual Arts)
- Breaking the Unjust Law (High School Government)
- Distance Formula and the Power of Nonviolent Marches (High School Math)
- Following Chávez: The "Wrath of Grapes" Today (4th Grade Science)
- Food Chains (4th-6th Grade)
- Gandhi and Montessori (Kingergarten-3rd grade)
- Gandhi's Influence on Mandela (7th Grade History)
- Gandhi's View of Women (High School English)
- Gandhian principles of Unity (Algebra)
- Interculturalism and Immigration: A Nonviolent Approach (K-8 Spanish)
- Is Modern Civilization Civilized? (Middle School Humanities)
- Muhammad Ali and Nonviolent Resistance (High School English and Social Studies)
- Nonviolence as a Way of Life (Art)
- Satyagraha in Daily Life (8th grade Social Studies)
- Sustainable Communities and Gandhi's Ashrams (Environmental Science)
- Sustaining Happy Genes through Epigenetics (High School Biology)
- The Popular Bully (5th grade)
- Writing as Nonviolent Resistance (8th Grade English)

Although these represent only a handful of the hundreds of lessons teachers have developed over the Institutes, they illustrate how teachers who learn about nonviolence can translate their new knowledge into meaningful curriculum for their students.

Beyond curricular development, the Ahimsa Fellows stated other means for moving their learning into the classroom. Some say they adopted an ethos of nonviolent communication with students, grounded in a personal understanding of ahimsa or agape. One teacher noted, "I think fundamentally it changed my attitude and understanding of my students, and how to create an environment that is as nonviolent as possible in thought and action." Another teacher believed that the training "helped in using the affective domain that can give greater purpose in a lesson; one student may take time to contemplate. This has also helped me to achieve a greater sense of personal ahimsa that allows for better communication and reactions." Teachers also said they felt a greater sense of inner peace upon leaving the Institute, and they also felt encouraged to operate from a new perspective of empathy and compassion: "I am much more conscious of how I interact with students and treating them with more humanity and working to maintain a positive relationship, even in the face of negative behaviors." Another teacher noted, "The institute helped me to look at a student who is acting out and see a wounded soul who deserves my empathy rather than my condemnation." Multiple teachers affirmed that the Institute induced them to incorporate mindfulness activities into their teaching practice, sometimes through sustained moments of silence to start class or as a "break" in order to re-center the classroom. These comments all illustrate that nonviolence education is not just about innovative curriculum, but also about helping teachers consider different pedagogies that can encourage relationships grounded in ahimsa. This ethos can also extend beyond the classroom; some teachers discussed seeking out opportunities to deliver nonviolence workshops or distribute resources to colleagues in the hopes that a spark will ignite. In their own families, some teachers found themselves in the position to manifest nonviolence as they confronted interpersonal conflicts, drawing on a personal sense of *satyagraha* to engage lovingly but firmly. As one teacher put it,

> The institute was a transformational experience for me, not only as an educator, but as a parent, daughter, sibling, colleague, and citizen. I no longer view authority as something above and beyond me. Instead, studying Gandhi helped me see that the authority rests in ourselves, and if we truly do not agree with the status quo, we have the power to change it.

Overview of the Volume

We believe that teachers' stories are essential to an understanding of what a pedagogy of nonviolence can look and feel like, and such stories are critical counternarratives that challenge standardized conceptualizations of the profession. The narratives in this volume highlight how teachers all over the United States embrace the moral and ethical dimensions of the teacher's role in society, using nonviolence as a guiding or foundational principle to resist being complicit with the culture of violence felt at micro, meso, and macro levels. The stories document how teachers contend with the culture of violence and seize opportunities to wield nonviolence in response.

In the first section, "Learning and Practicing Ahimsa," five teachers from Tennessee, Florida, California, Oregon, and Maine narrate their personal journey learning about ahimsa and finding pathways to practice it in their respective environments. The teachers describe the kinds of violence they have observed in their personal and professional lives, and how this prompted them to learn about nonviolence as a tool to create change. Fundamental to this learning was the concept of ahimsa: doing no harm to self or others, grounded in a sense of unity and humanity. The teachers in this section discuss the strategies they employed to enact a pedagogy of nonviolence with young people both in and outside of schools and with adults in teacher training settings. In their journeys, the narrators suggest that the seed of ahimsa planted at the institutes eventually blossomed beyond their initial imaginings, touching the lives of hundreds of students and colleagues to cultivate a culture of nonviolence.

In the second section, "Integrating Mindfulness and Compassion," four narratives by educators in California, Maryland, and Oregon illuminate their journeys creating curriculum and pedagogy that emphasized the nonviolent values of mindfulness and compassion. At a time of high stress in American schools, and society more generally, it is no wonder that schools have finally seen the value of mindfulness education, and have reconsidered the importance of character education, in the wake of sweeping educational reforms such as No Child Left Behind and Race to the Top. Teachers and students alike have become fatigued by standardized curriculum, constant assessments by local, state, and national bodies, and a militarized school culture wherein metal detectors, active shooter drills, and on-campus military recruiters are normative aspects of everyday life. The educators in this section convey how teaching students and teachers about mindfulness, and having them practice it, can lead toward greater compassion toward the self and others—which are essential to combating a culture of violence.

In the third section, "Subverting Curriculum through Nonviolence," four educators from Colorado, California, and New Mexico explain how they activated their sense of agency to challenge normative practices in education. The teachers affirm how a personal sense of satyagraha enabled them to identify injustices or inequities and act upon them rather than accept them or become complicit. As in the second section, the teachers' narratives show how making changes, both big and small, with nonviolence in mind can meaningfully challenge standardized and traditional education models that propagate violence or undermine students' humanity. This can mean redesigning entire units with nonviolence as the primary lens or underlying principle, or using digital technologies to give students opportunities to tell their personal stories and accounts of survival. Such innovations inspire students to consider their own agency and their potential to contribute to a culture of peace.

The last section, "Students and Teachers Making Change," includes narratives by teachers in Washington, Oregon, South Carolina, and California, who further the notion that nonviolence education leads individuals to create change in their lives and in the lives of others. Learning about nonviolence compelled the educators in this section to act forcefully, with ahimsa and satyagraha in their hearts, as they practiced nonviolence and shared it with others. The narratives suggest that nonviolence education instills a sense of personal responsibility for the wellbeing of others, or by the belief in ubuntu, the term Mandela used to encourage reconciliation in South Africa: "I am because we are." With that principle in mind, two teachers describe creating clubs at elementary and middle school levels focused on students becoming "changemakers" or "change agents" in their communities, while others tell how they created change through self-transformation and efforts to foster community with others. In modeling nonviolent social change, and encouraging others to do so as well, the teachers in this section illustrate how a culture of nonviolence is built locally, and how such change radiates outward into the world and into the future.

We feel this volume contributes significantly to the field of nonviolence education, not so much by proposing a theory of how it works, but by providing empirical accounts of what it looks like in real life. Indeed, Dr. King himself, in his seminal work "Pilgrimage to Nonviolence" (1960), noted that it was not until he entered the situation in Birmingham that he fully understood the power of nonviolence:

> As the days unfolded, I came to see the power of nonviolence more and more. Living through the actual experience of the protest, nonviolence became more than a method to which I gave intellectual assent; it became a commitment to a way of life. Many of the things I had not cleared up intellectually concerning nonviolence were now solved in the sphere of practical action. (p. 101)

This volume thus represents how teachers all over the United States have committed themselves to nonviolence as a way of life, and it reveals how they apply it in the sphere of practical action in a wide range of educational settings. Equipped with two weeks of specific content, and feeling buttressed by the sense of community built at the Institutes and afterward, the teachers in this book offer up their own humanizing journeys, bringing out the best of themselves as they experimented with nonviolence as "real education."

References

Agnihotri, S. (2017). Critical reflection on the role of education as a catalyst of peace-building and peaceful coexistence. *Universal Journal of Educational Research, 5*(6), 911-917.

Apple, M. W. (1971). The hidden curriculum and the nature of conflict. *Interchange, 2*(4), 27-40.

Bajaj, M. (2008). Introduction. *Encyclopedia of peace education.* https://www.tc.columbia. edu/epe/epe-entries/Bajaj_ch1_22feb08.pdf

Bajaj, M. (2010). Conjectures on peace education and Gandhian studies: Method, institutional development and globalization. *Journal of Peace Education, 7*(1), 47-63.

Bajaj, M., & Brantmeier, E. J. (2011). The politics, praxis, and possibilities of critical peace education. *Journal of Peace Education, 8*(3), 221-224.

Bajaj, M., & Chiu, B. (2009). Education for sustainable development as peace education. *Peace & Change, 34*(4), 441-455.

Bilimoria, P. (2015). Gandhi on nonviolence in action and education. Satyagraha Foundation for Nonviolence Studies. http://www.satyagrahafoundation.org/gandhi-on-nonviolence-in-action-and-education/

Bolliger, L., & Wang, H. (2013). Pedagogy of nonviolence. *Journal of Curriculum and Pedagogy, 10*(2), 112-114.

Cavanagh, T. (2008). Creating schools of peace and nonviolence in a time of war and violence. *Journal of School Violence, 8*(1), 64-80.

Chubbuck, S. M., & Zembylas, M. (2011). Toward a critical pedagogy for nonviolence in urban school contexts. *Journal of Peace Education, 8*(3), 259-275.

Donnelly, C. (2004). What price harmony? Teachers' methods of delivering an ethos of tolerance and respect for diversity in an integrated school in Northern Ireland. *Educational Research, 46*(1), 3-16.

Hantzopoulos, M., & Williams, H. (2017). Peace education as a field. *Encyclopedia of Educational Philosophy and Theory.* https://hakimwilliams.files.wordpress.com/2014/10/ hantzopoulos-williams_2017_p-e-as-a-field_publ.pdf

Harris, I. (2004). Peace education theory. *Journal of Peace Education, 1*(1), 5-20.

Harris, I. (2008). History of peace education. *Encyclopedia of peace education.* https://www.tc.columbia.edu/epe/epe-entries/Harris_ch2_22feb08.pdf

Jenkins, T. (2007). Rethinking the unimaginable: The need for teacher education in peace education. *Harvard Educational Review, 77*(3), 366-9.

Joseph, P., & Duss, L. (2009). Teaching a pedagogy of peace: a study of peace educators in United States schools in the aftermath of September 11. *Journal of Peace Education, 6*(2), 189-207.

Kester, K. (2010). Education for peace: Content, form and structure: Mobilizing youths for civic education. *The Peace and Conflict Review, 4*(2), 1-10.

King, M. L. (1958). *Stride Toward Freedom: The Montgomery Story.* New York: Harper & Row.

Lunenburg, F. (2011). School violence in America's schools. *Focus on Colleges, Universities, and Schools, 4*(1), 1-6.

Magro, K. (2015). Teaching for social justice and peace education: Promising pathways for transformative learning. *Peace Research,* 109-141.

Prinz, R. (2000). Research-based prevention of school violence and youth antisocial behavior: A developmental and educational perspective. In *Preventing School Violence: Plenary Papers of the 1999 Conference on Criminal Justice Research and Evaluation.* National Institute of Justice. < https://www.ncjrs.gov/pdffiles1/nij/180972.pdf>

Reardon, B. A. (2012). Education for sustainable peace: Practices, problems and possibilities. In *Psychological components of sustainable peace* (pp. 325-352). New York: Springer.

Rossatto, C. A. (2004). *Engaging Paulo Freire's pedagogy of possibility: From blind to transformative optimism.* Rowman & Littlefield Publishers.

Rubin, J. C. (2018). Rethinking literacy and responsibility: A diffractive engagement with posthumanist education and Jain nonviolence. *Literacy Research: Theory, Method, and Practice, 67*(1), 327-342.

Schmidt, P. (1984). Peace is our profession: Teaching nonviolence in the schools. https://files.eric.ed.gov/fulltext/ED248154.pdf

United Nations Secretary General. (2000). International decade for a culture of peace and non-violence for the children of the world. <http://www.culture-of-peace.info/annexes/A-55-377.pdf>

Vongalis-Macrow, A. (2006). Rebuilding regimes or rebuilding community? Teachers' agency for social reconstruction in Iraq. *Journal of Peace Education, 3*(1), 99-113.

Wang, H. (2010). A zero space of nonviolence. *Journal of Curriculum Theorizing, 26*(1), 1-8.

Wang, H. (2013). A nonviolent approach to social justice education. *Educational Studies, 49*(6), 485-503.

Wang, H. (2014). *Nonviolence and education: Cross-cultural pathways.* New York: Routledge.

Wang, H. (2019). An integrative psychic life, nonviolent relations, and curriculum dynamics in teacher education. *Studies in Philosophy and Education, 38*(4), 377-395.

SECTION I

Learning and Practicing *Ahimsa*

Section Overview

Learning and Practicing Ahimsa

By Danita Dodson

Nonviolence education, as practiced by the Ahimsa Center Institute Fellows, is moored in an awareness of the amalgamation of the two parts of the Sanskrit word *ahimsa* to create a transformative signification: *a* indicating *non*, and *himsa*, connoting *violence*. Tara Sethia (2015) asserts that ahimsa, or nonviolence, is not simply the antithesis or the nonexistence of violence—it has fundamentally different aims, premises, modalities, sources of power, and outcomes. As Hongyu Wang (2018) likewise suggests in her qualitative study of nonviolent principles in teacher education, *violence* and *nonviolence* should not be positioned as binary terms. Instead, for the future of our nation and globe, it is critical that nonviolence be elevated, taught, and lived as a daily commitment to unlearn violence and to promote nonviolent relationships.

This first section of the book elucidates the idea that the active renunciation of violence requires an informed awareness of the various ways that today's youngsters experience it. Growing up in an era of recurrent school shootings and institutionalized aggression, all of which are socially motivated and overtly visible in the media, school-aged youth often begin each day with disquiet and distress. This reality is confirmed by the American Psychological Association (2018) in its recent survey *Stress in America: Generation Z*, which reveals that 75% of youth claim that fear of mass shooting is a significant source of stress. When we live in a nation where school names like Columbine, Sandy Hook, and Parkland have become synonymous with the jaded acceptance of violence as a norm, pedagogy must aspire to build a culture of nonviolence that is transformative and sustainable. In addition to gun violence in schools, it has also been shown that rising suicide rates, sexual harassment, migrant family separation, political turmoil, and social media judgment have inundated

C. A. Bracho and D. Dodson (eds.), *Teachers Teaching Nonviolence*, 21–25.

young people with daily feelings of angst (American Psychological Association, 2018). Therefore, it is unequivocally urgent that educators and educational systems consciously strive to "reculture" schools (Joseph, Mikel, & Windschitl, 2011) and to construct loving landscapes that are radical antidotes to harm, defeat, disempowerment, exploitation, and coercion—the aims of violence (Sethia, 2015).

This vision of a nation of recultured schools can become a reality through the learning and teaching of ahimsa, which is anchored in a belief in oneness that motivates what Gandhi called "love in action." The narratives in this section all illustrate that nonviolence education imagines a learning community based on a recognition of the interdependence of all existence, operating in an earnest acceptance of the essential self of others. Working from the objective to transform the minds and the hearts of others and to encourage collaboration, these writings reveal that an emphasis upon nonviolence can elevate youth in constructive ways that lead to optimistic negotiations, creative solutions, explorations of mutuality, and transformation of the roots of conflict and injustice. As a daily pragmatic strategy, nonviolence education can dishevel longstanding cycles of violence, promote understanding, cultivate compassion and dialogue, and create apertures to lasting happiness and positive change (Sethia, 2015).

Dedication to this pragmatic strategy is a process that does not happen overnight. As the following educators will show, to teach nonviolence, one must first learn it. The Ahimsa Center Institutes have exposed teachers to the creative learning experiences of ahimsa and have encouraged life-altering lessons anchored in the historical studies of Gandhi's worldview. This worldview is centered upon four kindred concepts of ahimsa: sarvodaya (the well-being of all), swaraj (self-rule), swadeshi (self-reliance), satyagraha (truth force). Exemplars such as Gandhi, Martin Luther King, Jr., César Chávez, and Nelson Mandela demonstrate to educator-practitioners that the rhetoric of nonviolence activates a moral purpose and has the transformative power to encourage young people to be compassionate, collaborative, reflective, and constructive citizens of tomorrow.

As teachers experience and learn nonviolence as a daily practice, they become more equipped to envision a future of hope, creatively applying the lessons that can change society and the environment positively through its youth. Nonviolence as content, training, and professional development can lead educators to better help students, other teachers, and their communities attain a sense of *swaraj*, which involves both individual and social transformation. During the moment of India's national independence, Gandhi wrote one of his last statements, the Talisman, to inspire a widespread moral regeneration. While working to lead the poor to liberation, he also cared for those who might be able to effect change.

Educators are ideally in the position to see students as faces and hearts who can be empowered, liberated by love, quickened by knowledge, and dedicated to the "uplift of all." This section includes narratives that explain how the educators' integration of *ahimsa* in their curriculum, pedagogies, and communities prove the possibilities that nonviolence education can engender in the lives of students *and* teachers as they navigate schools vexed by physical violence and regimes of standardized curricula and assessments. The authors discuss pioneering strategies to create educational opportunities that are anchored in empathy, self-awareness, constructive work, dialogue-based instruction, youth engagement, and revitalized teacher leadership training.

In Chapter 2, "Gandhi's Talisman: Inspiration for Cultivating Lessons in Empathy," Danita Dodson explores her curricular applications of Gandhi's compassionate response to the faces of the poorest and the weakest as he created justice for the oppressed, as evidenced by his poignant Talisman. She illustrates how pedagogies that raise similar mindfulness of suffering can foster empathy and nonviolent social action in today's youth. Providing examples of student voices from her 12th-grade English classroom in Tennessee, Dr. Dodson shows how empathetic learners connect more fully with each other and the world. This Gandhian pedagogy is based on the *transformative learning theory*, which promotes self-reflection to revise narrow worldviews. Narrating the steps of a reconciliatory-writing program that serves as an antidote to our culture's aggressive assertion and polarized argumentation, this chapter reveals how young learners are both inspired to use composition as a tool for social justice and to become change agents.

In Chapter 3, "From Self to Swaraj: A Learning Journey," Tazeen Rashid, a high school economics teacher in Florida, explores how Gandhi's *Hind Swaraj* led her to help students realize that the path to freedom from oppression starts with an understanding of the self. Connecting Gandhi's concept of *swaraj* to the ideas of Adam Smith and Socrates, she asserts that educators must do more than just inject content-based knowledge into students: they must also help them develop self-awareness. Rashid describes how her pedagogical transformation unfolded as she tweaked lesson plans and routines in her exam-based curriculum to integrate empowering skills for internal and external connection. Aiming to contribute to future shifts in teaching with the goal of creating more nonviolence and justice, this chapter reveals the broader benefit of such strategies for young learners to engage in self-reflection as it outlines the steps, significance, and benefits of this approach.

In Chapter 4, "Putting Sarvodaya into Practice: One Teacher's Journey to Create a Farm Program," Andrew Duden narrates his personal journey to create an organic farm program for secondary students, an enterprise that is now the state model for farm-based learning in Oregon. Describing his pedagogical application of *sarvodaya* and its outgrowth, he provides curricular insight for putting the principle of "uplift of all" into practice. Inspired by the Ahimsa Institute's lessons about Gandhi's use of constructive work to teach self-preservation, self-governance, and universal edification, Duden delineates the creation of a program that takes students from a suburban, competitive, traditional high school to a local farm. Relating how this idea evolved to include diverse stakeholders, he shows the involvement of community partnerships based on interdependence and mindfulness toward the land, offering a vibrant example for other educators who are interested in creating garden-based curriculum.

In Chapter 5, "How Teachings of Nonviolence Provide a Framework for Youth Engagement," Quixada Moore-Vissing, a civic educator in Maine, narrates how young people can mobilize nonviolent social change. Recognizing how educational contexts are often framed as one-way learning that posits youth as receptacles of knowledge rather than generators of it, she asserts that communities must be urged to cultivate civil, equitable, nonviolent, and participatory opportunities for youth leadership. Sharing examples of schools and communities that utilize youth engagement to develop a generation of nonviolent, collaborative, and unifying leaders, Dr. Moore-Vissing underscores approaches for building cultures that espouse ahimsa, increase youth representation on decision-making committees, and create community support outside of school for underrepresented youth and their parents. She reveals how dialogue is the foundation of an empowering framework for youth and community engagement.

Finally, in Chapter 6, "Journey to Action for Teacher Leaders," Danielle Mizuta, an educator in Hawaii, describes how she was inspired by the leadership characteristics of Mandela and Gandhi, prompting her to make crucial "breakthroughs" in her work. Narrating the trajectory of the steady evolution of her educational leadership, she credits the transformative lessons of the Ahimsa Institute as the foundation of her new role as a teacher-leadership trainer. At a time when schools and organizations are in dire need of transformational leaders, Mizuta shares the research she conducted so that she might apply the leadership lessons of Gandhi and Mandela—integrity, character, unconventional behaviors, and personal risks—to the classroom and the administrational realm. Charting her own personal internalization of those ahimsa-based ideals, she discusses her multifaceted creation of opportunities in leadership, including presentations to different groups of teacher leaders in Hawaii.

The following chapters point to ways that teachers can lead students beyond a restricted and basic understanding of nonviolence toward a more comprehensive discernment through the described pedagogies. By suspending a passive view and accepting a proactive one, and by moving from external to internal perspectives, young learners can more readily navigate the difficulties that they face outside the classroom. The contributors delineate specific pedagogical situations that enable these transformations, including strategies for engaging students' self-reflections, creating more empathetic relationships with others, becoming environmental stewards, and transforming classroom dynamics. As they reflect ethical visions and practices anchored in nonviolence, the authors all name their framework for a "culture of curriculum" (Joseph, Mikel, & Windschitl, 2011). This curricular culture is *ahimsa*.

References

American Psychological Association. (2018). Stress in America: Generation Z. Retrieved from https://www.apa.org/news/press/releases/stress/2018/stress-gen-z.pdf.

Joseph, P. B., Mikel, E. R., & Windschitl, M. A. (2011). Reculturing curriculum. In P. B. Bolotin (Ed.), *Cultures of curriculum* (pp. 55–77). New York: Routledge.

Sethia, T. (2015, July). Journeys of nonviolence: Gandhi and Mandela. Summer Institute for K-12 Teachers, Ahimsa Center at Cal Poly, Pomona, California.

Wang, H. (2018). Nonviolence as teacher education: A qualitative study in challenges and possibilities. *Journal of Peace Education, 15*(2), 216–237.

Chapter 1

Gandhi's Talisman

Inspiration for Cultivating Lessons in Empathy

By Danita Dodson

As an exemplar of nonviolence, Mahatma Gandhi bestowed compassion upon the poorest and the weakest, encouraging us to meditate upon suffering because the process can engender profound transformation. It is no secret: our world needs to be transformed. The daily news is engulfed with myriad visages that convey the agonizing truth about inhumanity, violence, and sorrow. While our recognition of suffering could mobilize us toward change, often it is easier to adopt a psychic numbing. This detachment from empathy is, in fact, the central transgression from which all other injustices stem. Though it is excruciating to absorb such pain, the awareness could alter our perspectives, inspire action, and help us improve others' lives and our own. Such cognizance is akin to the heart-opening practice of Tonglen, where one is guided to visualize pain on the in-breath and to imagine empathy on the outbreath. As a teacher, it has been my experience that educational practices that raise a similar mindfulness can indeed foster a kinder humanity and a more empowered youth.

My awareness of empathy-based instruction was palpably augmented by my experiential reading of Gandhi's most profound social concept. Recorded at the end of his life, these words counsel the reader to be observant of those who suffer:

> I will give you a talisman. Whenever you are in doubt, or when the self becomes too much with you, apply the following test. Recall the face of the poorest and the weakest... and ask yourself, if the step you contemplate is going to be of any use... (as cited in Pyarelal, 1958, p. 65)

C. A. Bracho and D. Dodson (eds.), *Teachers Teaching Nonviolence*, 27–37.

Introduced to this Talisman at the Ahimsa Center Institute for K-12 teachers, I now lead students to observe suffering as they connect to each other and the world, hastening their ability to put empathy into action. This pedagogy is an application of Jack Mezirow's "transformative learning theory" (2000), which maintains that a narrow worldview is altered when a person faces a "disorienting dilemma" and engages in a contextual dialogue about re-examined beliefs. By establishing a community of collective responsiveness, teachers urge students to share evolving views, making transformation possible. My own commitment to create such an organic, dialogic, compassionate classroom was inspired by one extraordinary idea: ahimsa, or nonviolence.

The following narrative is a roadmap of how my commitment to the principles of ahimsa has transformed the way that I teach. As a writing teacher, I feel compelled to help students attain the revitalizing skills of conscientious communication. By reconfiguring rhetorical argumentation through the lens of nonviolent exemplars like Gandhi and Mandela, whose most powerful discourses embodied civility and compassion, I have led young writers to accept the emboldening gift of writing with empathy as they examine society's most ponderous issues and humanity's most horrific situations. The ensuing agency laden in student voices—some of which appear in this chapter—affirms the merit of applying Gandhi's Talisman to the written word.

Using Exemplars of Nonviolence to Build a Pedagogy of Empathy

My motivation to create a transformational writing program began when I attended the Ahimsa Center's 2015 *Journeys of Nonviolence* Institute. Created and led by the inspiring Dr. Tara Sethia, this program assisted teachers in crafting innovative lesson plans aligned with the ethics of nonviolence. Because I have always valued opportunities that nurture positive change, I was deeply inspired when my friend Sam McHale shared his life-changing experience in the 2013 Ahisma Institute. While I am cheerful at heart, I cannot remember a time when I did not mourn the injustices and the disharmonies around me. Growing up and teaching in a rural community in East Tennessee, I have observed with sadness the colossal struggles of disadvantaged students who assiduously seek apertures in the rigid enclosures of cruelty, despondency, addiction, and poverty. Pointing to the guiding light of kindness, harmony, and respect for all life, the Ahimsa Institute affirmed just how vital it is that teachers connect pedagogy and nonviolence, especially given the current contexts of escalating aggressions, not only locally and nationally but also globally.

Focused upon such themes as forgiveness, freedom, and reconciliation, the Institute's expert scholars nurtured the Ahimsa Fellows' nascent understanding of how two significant nonviolent exemplars practiced the transformative lessons of ahimsa. By the end of our exploration of Gandhi, we jubilantly pronounced the vital applicability of *swaraj, swadeshi, satyagraha, sarvodaya* to our lives and to our classrooms. Amid the instruction of the rudiments of nonviolent social action, we engaged in a careful study of the Talisman, which became the most poignant institute experience for me. Pondering the benevolent wisdom that encouraged me to envisage "the face of the poorest and the weakest" whenever I act, I began to realize how my own service as a teacher could be a "talisman" of empathy. As I immersed myself in Gandhi's writings, I learned that he had suffered physical attacks, verbal abuse, and incarceration before he recalled the anguished faces of others. However, instead of personalizing his own plight, Gandhi cultivated transformative practices, such voluntary poverty, to relate more effectively to fellow sufferers. As he evolved, he found ways to creatively elicit empathy. Portraying suffering in fasts, and urging followers to conquer indifference through epic marches, Gandhi visually helped opponents recognize *satyagraha*, or truth force. Also, using the media as a vehicle of verity, he depicted violence as he promoted liberation.

Approaching Nelson Mandela's life through the lens of the Talisman, I witnessed his comparable responsiveness to the oppressed as he labored to diminish suffering and to facilitate freedom from apartheid. When the Nationalist Party reigned down terror in South Africa in 1948, Mandela was suddenly assaulted with harrowing images of people relocated to homelands, men carrying identification, children denied the right to an education, and protestors killed in peaceful opposition. His endeavors to eradicate such horrors led to his incarceration, which was rife with violence and indignity. However, after 10,000 days in prison, Mandela emerged to create a transformed nation anchored in restorative truth, dialogic process, and communal opportunities to break the long-imposed silence of suffering. The Truth and Reconciliation Commission's heroic courage to unearth disturbing stories of inhumanity was integral in making empathy a part of the new democracy.

Through the Ahimsa Institute's multifaceted framework, these exemplars of nonviolence transcended history and became a palpable part of the present moment, pointing the way toward a transformative pedagogy. Although we should not deify them since their lives, like those of all humans, are imbued with shortcomings, leaders like Gandhi and Mandela shaped the future precisely because the disorienting dilemmas they faced not only altered their worldviews but also impelled them to replace images of suffering with those of creative, empathetic response.

Establishing a Transformative Program of Reconciliatory Writing

As the lives of Gandhi and Mandela attest, images and imaginings of others' realities can prompt reconciliation and action. Similarly, by acting upon the Talisman's challenge, I now lead students to observe the faces of suffering, including visages in their community. My composition courses award dual high school *and* college credit to 12th-graders who live in one of the poorest towns in both Tennessee and in the nation. I have seen many of these first-generation college students "compose" their own personal stories of new beginnings. Celebrating the gift of writing with empathy while believing that I am obligated to help students escape the aggressive assertion of an "argument culture" (Tannen, 1998), I hasten conscientious communication and redefine rhetorical opposition through the lens of the exemplars of nonviolence. On social media and television, and in town meetings and grocery stories, people often compete for the most vitriolic refutations of another's stance, stripping logos of pathos. However, if we aspire to help young people attain a happy and sustainable future, we must teach them that the most powerful discourses are those that embody civility and compassion.

So how to begin such a transformative program where writing prompts empathetic thought and speech? In the years since the Ahimsa Institute, I have spent much time exploring this question as I create composition assignments that are anchored in the spirit of nonviolence. I have discovered that this attempt has been best initiated by exploring the depth of individual experiences that can bring an awareness of personal pain and triumph. I begin with a narrative essay about a life-changing event; using imagistic language, my students stir peer-readers by recording memories of transformative experiences, employing the idea of Mezirow's *disorienting dilemma*. For example, one student, Caleb Gunter (2015), wrote about the day that he, as a young child, first experienced the power of charity and empathy:

> I implore all people to empathize because the experience I have witnessed changed my life and showed me the power of giving and caring. The date was June 23, 2012, and my father was attending a community college in Virginia. As he went to school, I had the pleasure of going with him that day. Little did I know his professor was a prince of a small and poor village in Africa. Prince Chukks showed me pictures of the village and the orphanage that had recently

been assembled there. As I viewed the photos, I saw the children, and many looked so sad that it physically hurt. At that moment I realized that I needed to do something about this. I went home later that evening and went to the attic and pulled out all my old toys. Dad helped me put them into boxes, and we sealed them. The next day we went back to Prince Chukks and told him that we were giving this to the orphanage. I have never seen such gratitude or thankfulness in a man's eye before. As tears rolled down his face, he said, "Thank you so much!" and informed me that he would personally deliver the gifts. What happened next made me smile and my heart swell, and the feeling of joy was so powerful that it made tears cascade down my face. Prince Chukks came back from his village and displayed to me the pictures of the kids prancing and jumping with glee with their new toys...I had never witnessed such pure joy and blissful happiness on a child's face before that day. This personal experience shows that simple acts of kindness can impact another's life.

As Caleb's words reveal, we carry the lessons of empathy within us, but we often fail to narrate and share them. Doing so creates a dialogue about transforming the world around us.

After this assignment about life-changing experiences, my composition students advance to Socratic Seminars about "what unites humanity," deliberating how both an awareness of commonalities and an appreciation of diversities can enkindle positive change. One tool is to expose students to digital stories of others. For example, *Human* (2015), directed by Yann Arthus-Bertrand, is a powerful collection of video-stories. Based upon a two-year tour of sixty-five countries to record 2,000 people, these stories detach humans from their environments, focusing only on their faces and their words. The voices resonate with students as narratives that testify to universal topics like happiness, death, love, kindness, and pain. Such visuals have led my students to ponder how they relate to faces and voices in the videos. They subsequently produce their own video-stories based upon the prompt "What does being human mean to you?" Also, historical images related to the above-mentioned exemplars, like the stories in the *Human* documentary, can inspire empathy.

Following these visual lessons, I challenge students to "recall," as Gandhi advocated, faces of suffering and then to bring *satyagraha*, or "truth force," to their writing. After a detailed exercise with the Talisman, as well as Tonglen-inspired mindfulness activities, they evolve to writing research papers about social justice, weighing solutions to discern the most effective and compassionate path to *swaraj*, or freedom. Gandhi's "Letter to Lord

Irwin" serves as a model. Bailey Hopkins (2018) wrote this descriptive portrait to call others to action:

> Snowflakes begin to flurry from a gray sky and cover the sidewalk like a thin, white blanket. The crisp, cold air blows through the alleyway and sharply cuts through the thin jacket that is barely shielding a gray-haired, unshaven, middle-aged man's rumbling belly. His dark-green toboggan, covered in holes, barely sits atop his nippy ears, while a worn-out pair of blue jeans minimally keep his scrawny, sore-covered legs warm. While all of his belongings hang from his shoulder, the gentleman scavenges for a warm place to rest, as he has been walking from block to block all evening in hopes of finding shelter and—perhaps—a kind soul to offer him something to eat as well. This is not just for tonight, though; this is his life. This is the reality that hundreds of thousands of homeless people face every day in America, and the number of victims continue to multiply. So many individuals who are fortunate enough to have a warm home to rest in, clean food to eat, a stable source of income, and an opportunity for education fail to realize the extremity of this issue until they are living in it themselves. Mahatma Gandhi, a spokesperson against social injustice, preaches the idea of empathy towards individuals who are suffering in some way. He states, "Recall the face of the poorest and the weakest man whom you may have seen [....]" Imagine the faces of those such as the man described. Can the steps we take next aid them in any way?

Bailey evokes reconciliatory rhetoric as she advocates justice for the homeless in our area.

After my students establish expertise in writing about social justice, reflecting a deepened understanding about not only the similarities in human experience but also the differences, their composition abilities advance to extended-definitions of abstract concepts such as love, peace, happiness, justice, freedom, kindness, and tolerance. In this lesson, Gandhi's "Satyagraha" and "What Is True Civilisation?" are used as models. In response to this assignment, Josh Webb (2018) wrote an essay to redefine *empathy,* noting that empaths "are losing the will and motivation to convey empathy to others" because their actions are often considered weak or superficial:

> Showing empathy is not about the benefits or recognition an individual gets. It is about being a genuine person who tries to spread love throughout the world. The kindness shown to that stranger in public may potentially be the only love he or she gets. Awareness of another's mental states can be the key to human survival. Without empathy, there would be absolutely no point in communicating....Without it, the world will slowly deteriorate into a jungle of anger and bitterness.

Josh's essay advocates empathy as part of the "the radical hope" (Lear, 2008) that could keep our culture from collapsing. His insightfulness reflects the richness of thought that can materialize when young people are encouraged to contemplate their role as ethical beings. Another student, Jocelyn Ferguson (2019), similarly proclaims that "this empathy-based set of ethics greatly benefits society when it is present. In all things, empathy causes growth and enhanced perspective; it is the unifier of divides. Empathy closes the division among people; it fills the gap of misunderstanding that lies between." When such unity is the expressed vision and supplication of our youth, there is hope for a better future.

Following such training ground for visualizing suffering, understanding what it is to be human, and calling for ethical empathy-based action, students have a clear sense of how their words can mirror their own experiences and how they can be used to reflect upon the experiences of others. I next lead them to write literary analyses moored in the narrative empathy theory.

Imagining the Other as Self: Narrative Empathy as Ahimsa

Literature is a marvelous tool for imagining others. While some literary works can be negative—posturing the Other as different, demonic, dichotomous—others can help cultivate compassionate acts by exposing readers to diverse perspectives. The literary composition process is a humanitarian deed; it communicates an imaginative realm, inviting the reader to receive new realities and possibilities, to commune with all types of humanity. The best fiction writers endow us with the blessing of narrative empathy. Exposing us to unfathomable injustices and redemptions, they unseal our complacencies, uncap our insularities, and open us to caring. The act of reading fiction with full raptness, embracing myriad characters, allows suspension of accepted beliefs and, thus, opens the door to transformative learning.

The empathetic reader is an anthropologist of the text, asking, "Who is in conflict? Who is suffering?" In an experimental study with 1,000 participants, psychologists David Comer Kidd and Emanuele Castano (2013) proved that reading fiction improves empathy and enhances the ability to detect and understand other people's emotions, a process which "turns the mind to trying to understand the minds of others" because "the same psychological processes are used to navigate fiction and real relationships" (p. 377). Suzanne Keen (2010), the leading voice in literary empathy studies, refines the trajectories of literary theory, postulating the *narrative empathy theory*, which she defines as "the sharing of feeling and perspective-taking induced by reading, viewing, hearing, or imagining narratives of another's situation and condition" (p. 89). Azar Nafisi (2003), who once taught literature illegally in Tehran, confirms the transformative power of exposing students to literature that enlightens them about others' realities because great fiction places readers in "someone else's shoes and [helps them] understand the other's different and contradictory sides" (p. 132). Thus, literary imagination is "equated with empathy" (Nafisi, 2003, p. 132).

With Keen and Nafisi as my muses, and with ahimsa as my inspiration, I introduce my students to fiction that exposes the suffering caused by violence and that calls for nonviolence. For example, Shirley Jackson's "The Lottery" sparks a timely rumination about how society can become desensitized to suffering. We also read stories about war, exploring how violence destroys innocence in Tim O'Brien's *The Things They Carried*. In our related study of how empathy is possible even in the presence of the adversary in battle, we examine "Before the Firing Squad," a moving story by John Chioles that tells of a young Nazi soldier's surprising friendship with a Jewish boy in a small Greek town. In one of my composition assignments about this story, Amber Estes (2017) writes this about the empathy of the character Fritz:

> Fritz's heart behaves much differently than that of other soldiers; this young Nazi seems to only know goodness and cannot allow for the lives of honest souls to be destroyed. As a pawn in the game of genocide played by the evilest man in history, Fritz is expected to be as black-hearted as Hitler himself. He is supposed to be a villain, but...Fritz abandons his duties as a Nazi in order to spare the lives of the people whom he has grown to love, and he deceives the evil powers so that all of the villagers are *truly* safe. Though he directly disobeys his superiors, an unfathomably dangerous act for a German soldier in World War II, he does so bravely.

This Chioles story is one among many stories that can illustrate the power of moving beyond differences to tap into unfathomable compassion even in the worst of conditions. St. Luke's "Parable of the Prodigal Son" and Alice Walker's "Everyday Use" further explore forgiveness and reconciliation as vital to the act of recognizing another's suffering. Américo Paredes' "The Hammon and the Beans," Andre Dubus' "The Curse," and Z. Z. Packer's "Brownies" likewise steer readers toward the conscious choice to "recall the face of the poorest and the weakest," to transcend boundaries, to contemplate ethical action, and to consider in retrospect the choices that could have made a difference.

Toward a Pedagogy of Heroism

As a teacher dedicated to a pedagogy anchored in nonviolent social change, I recurrently renew and reexamine my commitment to make a difference in my Appalachian community and to ameliorate its struggles against opioid abuse, domestic violence, racism, poverty, and apathy. On one hand, Gandhi's Talisman has helped my students cultivate a capacity for writing with empathy—using composition as a tool for swaraj as we advocate social justice, create abstract definitions of ahimsa concepts, and construct literary analyses moored in the narrative empathy theory. On the other hand, the Talisman has propelled us to become change agents. As we write, we act—creating our own positive history together as we link compassion to vital choices. In icy temperatures and in heat waves, numerous times we have fed the homeless under the Interstate 40 Bridge in Knoxville. Brief physical discomfort dissipates as we serve. Action is tied to real faces, validating an everyday heroism: small self-sacrificing deeds that, when repeated, combine to create significant change. One can easily dismiss the impact of just one composition, call, protest, or donation, but history—as demonstrated by the exemplars—affirms the cumulative power of collective action. One single choice could create or extinguish thousands of possibilities—the lines of this butterfly effect radiate outward like winding roads across the planet, creating fences or building bridges. When classroom walls extend into the community, we can more ably consider if the step we contemplate will benefit anyone else. Since my time as an Ahimsa Fellow, I have gravitated increasingly toward this Gandhian concept of heroism because the negativity in society often eclipses the benevolence, so it becomes more urgent to identify nonviolent role models whose stories can positively guide us.

This contemplation of everyday heroism has inspired me to envision a project called *Hancock County Heroes* to represent positive deeds of ahimsa in my community in rural East Tennessee. Acting upon my desire to extend inspirational composition to a community writing project, in May 2019 I entered into partnership with Miranda Russell, a community builder and licensed professional counselor; Colby Collins, an innovative photographer and attorney; the Hancock County Government; the Hancock County School System; and the Tennessee Arts Commission. The purpose of this collaboration was to create a volume of written stories and photographic portraits of living local heroes. Many stories in our heritage testify to the positive strength of goodwill, self-sacrifice, and commitment to fellow humans, but they are lost because they are frequently overlooked and, consequently, unrecorded. The threads of these cultural narratives run through the fabric of our daily lives, and their preferment could be empowering and reconciliatory. The *Hancock County Heroes* project uses storytelling to remind us of our identity by inspiring youth and adults to use creative abilities to serve the community. Participating in an auxiliary seminar at the Ahimsa Center in June 2019, called *Leading Nonviolent Change Projects*, I was honored to use the dedicated space of my fellowship with ahimsa colleagues to refine the seeds of this project. It captures the heartening stories of community heroes who have struggled and persevered against challenging situations; they ultimately have been able to promote peace, selflessness, compassion, wholeness, forgiveness, and cultural awareness. Empathy is at the heart of such storytelling.

Giving, Forgiving, and Receptivity in Pedagogical Ahimsa

The community-based Hero Project is an example of how the lessons of the Ahimsa Institute have informed not only my pedagogy but also my communion with people around me. Through my dedication to helping others understand the power of empathy in their lives, I have learned that giving and forgiving are integrally linked to the educator's mission. This kinship can best be understood by the idea of *receptivity*. The reception central to the energy of benevolence is anchored in union and communion, unity and community, unification and communication. Efficacious and empathetic teachers, while giving and forgiving, simultaneously receive in multifaceted ways. They become not only communicators, but they also "tune in" mindfully to countless messages that their students relay, listening with their ears *and* their hearts. Over the past few years, I have found myself often uttering a morning prayer on my drive to work:

> Let me *receive* today. Let me receive the smiles of students and colleagues, their attention, their endeavors and offerings. Let me never grow too weary or busy to be blessed by these things. But also let me receive the pain, the frowns, the haphazard attempts, the inattention, the corrupt words, the conflicts.

Maybe this prayer has emerged from an increased understanding that teachers are vessels. Our minds collect data and knowledge, our hearts are conduits of emotions, and even our bodies are intermediaries of the subtle violence of stress, fluorescent lights, and fatigue. Or maybe this daily supplication derives from dealing with divisions. After all, the microcosm of the classroom mirrors society; young people carry with them the tensions of their homes, their communities, and their nation.

Though it often seems that educators are expected to use cookie cutters to shape students into perfect homogenies that fall within a statistical range, we dehumanize the learning process if we fail to emphasize the ways that redemptive pedagogy can transform humanity. To illustrate this, the scientific term *symbiosis* can be used in reference to conscientious teaching, which like conscious living must be concerned with kinship. Teachers who serve as givers *and* forgivers get into the habit of accepting, acknowledging, and assimilating not only all sorts of synchronicities but also disharmonies. Extraordinary things can happen in a classroom throughout the day, and we must not ignore them because they can lead to societal healing. The Ahimsa Institute has led me to believe that educators must create a transformative space for students to make all sorts of connections and explorations, even those that are unsettling and disorienting. In this way, an effective classroom becomes like a reception banquet—an inviting place to commune together and a welcome space to experience the authentic humanity of others. Such a learning community arises from an endeavor to make empathy a dynamic part of the curriculum.

References

Arthus-Bertrand, P. P. & D. D. (2015). *Human*. France: Kino Lorber.

Estes, A. (2017). *Heart vs. duty: A literary Venn diagram*. Unpublished student composition. Walters State Community College, Morristown, TN.

Ferguson, J. (2019). *Empathy: A virtue*. Unpublished student composition. Walters State Community College, Morristown, TN.

Gunter, C. (2015). *The power of charity*. Unpublished student composition. Walters State Community College, Morristown, TN.

Hopkins, B. (2018). *A home for everyone*. Unpublished student composition. Walters State Community College, Morristown, TN.

Keen, S. (2007). *Empathy and the novel*. Oxford, UK: Oxford University Press.

Kidd, D. C., & Castano, E. (2013, October). Reading literary fiction improves theory of mind. *Science, 342*(6156), 377–380.

Lear, J. (2008). *Radical hope*. Cambridge: Harvard University Press.

Mezirow, J. (2000). *Learning as transformation: Critical perspectives on a theory in progress*. San Francisco, CA: Jossey-Bass.

Nafisi, A. (2003). *Reading Lolita in Tehran*. New York: Random House.

Pyarelal, N. (1958). *Mahatma Gandhi: The last phase* (Vol. 2). Ahmedabad: Navjivan.

Tannen, D. (1998). *The argument culture: Moving from debate to dialogue*. New York, NY: Random House.

Webb, J. (2018). *Empathy: The art of showing care*. Unpublished student composition. Walters State Community College, Morristown, TN.

Chapter 2

From Self to Swaraj

A Learning Journey

By Tazeen Rashid

Whether it was Socrates who stated "know thyself" as a means to freedom from ignorance, Adam Smith who believed in rational self-interest as the key to freedom from the government, or Gandhi who believed in self-rule or swaraj as the means to freedom from the British for the Indians, each believed that the path to freedom from any oppression starts with an understanding and refinement of the self. I became aware of this connection as a Fellow at the Journeys of Nonviolence Institute at the Ahimsa Center in 2011. By understanding Gandhi's book *Hind Swaraj* at the Institute, and through an examination of his life and the lives of those he influenced, such as Martin Luther King, Jr., and César Chávez, I developed an important understanding of several ingredients needed to pave the path to nonviolence, peace, and freedom.

Of these, one ingredient that really captured my attention is the concept of *swaraj,* or self-examination and reflection. As a teacher of Economics and Theory of Knowledge, I was able to connect Gandhi's focus on the self to that of other philosophers such as Adam Smith and Socrates. It dawned on me that if all paths to freedom start with the sense of self, then we educators have an important role to play in promoting that sense of self in our students. But what are we doing to help our students develop this sense of self? We rush to inject content-based knowledge to get our students ready for college. This pattern continues in college, and then students become bound to earning, spending, and running a routine to sustain this cycle. When then do we educators systematically make time for knowing, hearing,

C. A. Bracho and D. Dodson (eds.), *Teachers Teaching Nonviolence, 39–48.*

and understanding the "self" and promoting "swaraj" for our students? With this awareness, I found myself taking miniscule steps within my vast exam-based IB and AP Economics curriculum towards integrating skills for developing the sense of self in my students.

With a series of shifts of my own perspective, and tweaks in lesson plans and class routines, I have sought to give my students opportunities to reflect on themselves. I have learned that any strategy that seeks to reach out to differentiated groups should first gear towards allowing learners to understand themselves and teachers to understand the unique sense of self with which learners present themselves. This effort has acted both as a small drop in the ocean and a spark capable of igniting a shift in my students. It has acted both as an opening to new horizons for some and a springboard to new levels for others. This chapter seeks to outline the steps I have taken since the fellowship to promote this effort, to explain how these steps have evolved organically, and to provide an anecdotal account of the meaning of these shifts. On a larger scale, it hopes to promote equity by bringing a more systemic focus on learners' personal journeys towards understanding themselves. This is the first step to freedom from learning barriers. In this way, this chapter aims to contribute to future shifts in teaching with the broader goal of creating more peace and justice.

Background

Teaching AP/IB Economics always brought me a high level of adrenaline. AP Macroeconomics and Microeconomics made me even more hyperactive as these are one-semester courses with vast and intense content. Each year, I was excited to teach the concepts and get the students ready to ace the skills needed to do well on the exam in May. The only time we moved more slowly was in the first unit, when we spent a lot of time getting to know each other and building our learning community through games and activities. After that, we were on a roll to complete the course. My teaching style consisted of mini lectures followed by group work and board work for formative assessments, and then we got ready for summative assessments. Desks were arranged in pods, and students sat in groups with differentiated skills, which allowed them to collaborate effectively. This is one way I tried to close learning gaps and helped create a flow. Normally circulating, I assisted those who struggled during class, and I encouraged tutoring at lunch or after school, as needed.

This system was quite engaging and worked well over the years in helping my classes move seamlessly from one unit to the other until we reached the end of the semester and, thus, the course. Throughout this process, I worked with two assumptions. My first assumption was that if I was totally focused on teaching the content skills needed to succeed in the exam, then I was doing a good job. My second assumption was that everyone who was in my class had the exact same goal, which was to succeed on the exam. Armed with these, I forged forward towards the finish line.

Seeking Change

The previous section describes my style eight years ago. While my system seemed to work well, I started to develop a sense of dissatisfaction. I had a nagging feeling that something was missing, and I could not quite identify it. Though every semester some students were struggling despite interventions, such as tutoring, peer help, and practice, these students did not really improve much by the end of the course. Before I knew it, the semester was over, and they were out of my room with no more connections. It was not so much tangible aspects like low grades that bothered me but the intangibles, such as students looking discouraged and giving up. I felt that the prescribed strategies were not making a difference. More importantly, I started feeling that I was not doing justice to these students. Thus, five years into my teaching career, I started seeking ways to improve in these areas.

In searching, I found a professional development opportunity for teachers at the Ahimsa Center in the form of a fellowship based on Gandhi's concept of nonviolence. This excited me: being a South Asian, this connection to Gandhi hit home right away. I grew up hearing about Gandhi and his role in liberating India from British Raj, but I did not know the details. I wanted to extend my knowledge and was curious to explore how the concept of nonviolence would enhance me as a teacher. I excitedly applied for the program with fingers crossed, hoping eagerly to get in. When I was accepted, I was thrilled! I arranged with my husband to take care of our two toddlers for the three weeks in July so that I could go to Pomona. The Institute mailed us the books that we needed to read before the fellowship started. One of them was Gandhi's *Hind Swaraj*. This book became the source of the shift in my teaching.

The Fellowship at Ahimsa Center

The fellowship was extremely enriching. We delved deeply into learning about Gandhi, César Chávez, and Martin Luther King, Jr. We dissected the assigned books and articles, had extremely engaging discussions, watched informative documentaries, and even had sessions on yoga and meditation.

We also touched on conflict resolution, forgiveness, and all the angles of violence generally. Tara Sethia, the Director of the Ahimsa Center, led this fellowship beautifully as she skillfully wove many aspects of learning into a personal journey of reflection and transformation. For our final projects, we each created a digital story, an essay, and a lesson plan. Though seemingly time-consuming, each task helped us synthesize what we learned and allowed us to create products that we could use in our own classrooms.

If I had to isolate one aspect that resonated most with me at this fellowship, it was Gandhi's concept of *swaraj*, or self-rule. I have always been a proponent of self-growth and of responsibility to developing the self. It started at home with my father, who was a self-made man, paving his path against all odds to be a successful surgeon and a well-known health official in Bangladesh. In addition to spending much time sharing his knowledge and experiences with us because he valued American education, he admitted us to the American School in New Delhi, India. This contrast to rote learning in an Indian/British system did wonders for me. Suddenly I was engaged, stimulated, and inspired to learn. This experience gave me a sense of who I was and what I could do through hard work and discipline.

The Gandhian focus on the "self" at the Institute really hit home. To understand the context better, through his book *Hind Swaraj*, Gandhi told Indians that they must first release themselves of their own oppressive ways before getting freedom from the British. This directive for Indians to rise, self-examine, self-discipline, and liberate themselves was very powerful because it presented a more sustainable route and guarded against the danger that the oppressed might become oppressors. To me this was extremely insightful and powerful advice, and I centered my digital board, my lesson plan, and my essay on the concept of swaraj.

The Teaching Shift: Focus on the Self

Because the Ahimsa Institute gave me a new dimension and an innovative pedagogical tool, I realized that most of us are teaching at a technical level (much like my teaching style used to be), without truly examining the sense of self that the learners own. In this way, we miss the opportunity to make the true human connection for helping learners, and for paving the path for their self-development. Therefore, students proceed through the education system and learn many skills and subjects, but are they really learning to self-examine and reflect? This training showed me that it is very important to teach about swaraj, self-assessment, and self-discipline so that students can start the process of self-examination early. I also realized that this focus on the self is the best way to engage students because it makes learning an individual experience. It dawned on me that students are sparked when the lesson hits home at a personal level, either in terms of content or study skills. In this way differentiation and engagement may remain elusive despite the use of various strategies. In my class, the perfect place to weave in a discussion on the self is when I teach about Adam Smith's concept of self-interest and rational decision-making. This is an opportunity to teach economics at a deeper level, bringing the attention of the students to themselves. After all, how can students weigh their costs and benefits and make rational decisions and choices if they do not have a deeper understanding of who they are? No wonder Socrates said, "Know thyself."

Realizing that this is exactly the shift I was seeking, I also finally understood why I was dissatisfied. This fellowship allowed me to reflect further on myself as teacher, and I became aware of two of my fallacies. One was the first assumption that I listed previously. Instead of having the intensity of passion that I assumed they did, students are, in fact, at different levels in terms of how they view themselves and their successes. The other fallacy was the second assumption I listed earlier. Instead of feeding into the supposed passion for success, I realized that I needed to identify the differences in how they viewed themselves and to take them to a higher level from where they were individually. Through further self-examination, I realized that, due to my assumptions, I was not really making a deeper connection with my students. In fact, I even asked myself if I was violating their sense of self by being totally unaware of where they placed themselves in the learning journey and what they really needed to enhance. Was I in some ways violating them by promoting a system and a goal that did not take care of their inner journeys? This hit me hard!

Eventually, I started to rearrange my lessons. I took the lesson I created at the Institute and used it to discuss Gandhi and swaraj and then connected it to Adam Smith's "self-interest" and Socrates' "know thyself." This lesson ended with a lot more discussion and reflective writing, and I realized its beauty pivoted upon the focus upon self-examination, which also served the purpose of allowing students to examine their learning habits, study skills, and attitudes and to identify their own struggles and goals. Additionally, because they were given a voice, they learned to be proactive in aligning their goals or, in some cases, setting new academic directions. I realized that first hints of their sense of self arise from their study habits and study patterns, which signal the level of self-awareness of their goals, self-evaluation, confidence level, and attitudes. Furthermore, I became aware of another assumption that needed to be changed: I assumed that students have a such a sense of good study skills by 11th grade that I can move forward with teaching the content. However, in fact, poor study habits are often overlooked in lower grades, so over time these become the debilitating patterns that build negative attitudes. The focus in higher grades is more on mastering content skills, so these habits and attitudes may remain unaddressed. In fact, I had done the same: I had taught and retaught the skills, even tutored struggling students on content, and most times it made little difference.

With my new realization, I started to teach about study skills, organization skills, listening skills, and self-management skills in the first few weeks of the course. After I had my students identify their strengths and weaknesses, they collaborated to see how they could grow by learning from each other too. I created time in class for them to discuss their learning struggles with partners. Many times, they reported that it felt good to know that others were in the same boat, or they found mentors in their partners for collaboration outside of class. This brought a relief to the students, and they felt validated. Clearly, all these meta aspects of learning must be addressed before we can move forward with engaging them more deeply in the subject area. Now I could see my students reflecting, thinking, and connecting. My perspective changed too: I began to feel that even if they forget everything else after the exam but remember this connection to themselves through self-reflections, it is all worth it. Moreover, the concept of swaraj revealed a new goal for me: I tell my students that I aspire, in addition to teaching Economics, to teach them about themselves so that they can reach their full potential. My hope is that by knowing themselves better they will make more rational decisions and better choices, thus applying economics in a true sense in their own lives. In this way I feel that I am helping not only to make them stronger in the subject area but also that I am sowing the seeds for swaraj and freedom from learning barriers.

Additionally, I have realized that violence can exist at various levels. One such level is the action of rushing, and getting too controlled, as I used to be initially. By being constantly in a hurry and confined to expectations, we end up disregarding the human angles and individual experiences. I used this realization to tweak my own approach, making it less structured and more flexible. By getting rid of my assumptions, I was now able to take various human shades of learning into account. This also made me slow down enough to stop, observe, and reflect more as a teacher.

My awareness and connection with my students also enhanced my empathy for them. For example, when I realized just how overloaded they are with work from all subjects, I started to dedicate a few minutes of silence in the beginning of class, which I call decluttering time. This allows them to leave all thoughts, work, and worries behind and focus only on the moment. My students love and seek it as soon as they enter the room. More focused in their own wellbeing now, they have added stretch time to the schedule too. I love it that they are being proactive and more aware of their own holistic needs before they can start to study. How did I not notice these needs before? I guess we tend to get oblivious to the intangible aspects of learning and teaching when we are too focused on tangible goals as I used to be. I realized that these intangible aspects enrich learning experiences and that it was exactly these opportunities that were missing prior to my time at the Ahimsa Center Institute. A happier teacher now that my classes have evolved organically with a more holistic angle to teaching, I have more authentic relationships with my students.

In this way, the Ahimsa Center Institute has helped me to make both a deeper impact on my students and lasting connections with them. I even started to include the book *Gandhi as a CEO* for summer reading. Students who were most keen on climbing the ladder of success picked up this book and noted a few salient points that will stay with them as they become leaders in their chosen fields. To me this is impactful. Now seeing the subject differently and teaching it differently too, I understand that it no longer just a set of skills of graphing and analyzing but quite the bridge to self-exploration and self-enhancement, thus making it more human-centered. Therefore, clearly this fellowship at the Ahimsa Center marked a turning point for me as a teacher, and I have been committed since then to allow time in my lesson plan for students to reflect, connect, and develop their own inner selves. Since the fellowship, I have taken the opportunity to present at the Ahimsa Center conferences in 2012 and in 2017. Both presentations helped me dig deeper and reflect further upon my teaching, and I am thankful I was able to share these gems with other participants.

Extension of the Shift: Teachers for Equity

It has been eight years since the Fellowship at Ahimsa Center, and things have developed organically, creating new paths and by-lanes for me. This journey has led me to new avenues to which I probably would not have access had I not started to focus on swaraj. However, along the way in my teaching journey, there still seemed to be a missing piece somewhere. While I had a more student-centered classroom with more engagement and ownership of learning, there was still a nail that was not hammered or a screw that was not tightened. I felt that some students were just not making the shift from habits that did not work to develop new ones for success. Thus, I started to search again, and this is when the Teachers for Equity Fellowship came to me.

Teachers for Equity (T4E) Fellowship was conducted by Business Innovative Factory (BIF) in Providence, Rhode Island. In a nutshell, we were trained for a year in a very engaging manner to use the tools of Courageous Conversations by Glenn Singleton. This training added more dimensions to helping me understand the sense of self in my racially marginalized students. Again, an assumption had to be tweaked: given the various tools for self-reflection and self-growth, students would be able to make the transition to proactive learners. What I did not realize until this second fellowship is that the experiences of some students are different due to race and that this, in turn, feeds their own narratives when defining themselves. Having had a multicultural experience since childhood and never being truly socialized in any one culture, this was new to me. I realized with much sadness that the inner narrative of success can be shaped by society; if it is a negative narrative, then it is one of the biggest barriers to success. Many struggling students are going through this negative self-talk about their own skills without seeking help, and thus eventually giving up. As a result, they are caught in a vicious cycle of low grades, lack of belief in self, failure to seek help, the system's tendency to overlook this, lack of trust in the system, and, thus, low grades again. While there may be variations of this, generally, this is the pattern I started noticing once I delved deeper in my interaction with some of my black and Hispanic students.

Reaching Swaraj

My enriched experience with the Teachers for Equity training helped me to understand even more the difference between technical support and support given at a human level through conversations. Conversations often reveal the social and emotional aspects of learning that are bottled up probably for years. However, these conversations can lead to validation of the self in the student and, thus, a sense of liberation. This then becomes the catalyst for change and growth, breaking the vicious cycle of low grades, paving the path for self-realization, liberation, success and swaraj. Using the various tools of Courageous Conversation, my conversations with students about sense of self allowed me as a teacher to truly differentiate their learning needs and then to tweak interventions accordingly. These conversations and reflections may reveal personal blockages and struggles, but without knowing these we cannot just hope that our technical strategies are going to be effective in improving grades. In fact, they do worse: they act as bandage without curing the symptoms. I realized that these strategies will only be effective once the conversations happened and the students have been given the opportunity for reflection and connection to self and others in the learning arena. There is an inner invisible meta-level shift that is needed for students to really be authentically involved in their own growth and learning. For this to happen in my classroom, I use the tools I learned at T4E to allow students to share and learn more from each other. I never realized how liberated and validated students feel when they share their worries, anxieties, stress, and personal stories with others, especially their peers. Nothing adds more to their sense of validation than someone listening to their stories.

One of the tools I use often is mindful inquiry, which allows students to talk and listen in pairs. Person A talks for two minutes about a personal topic, and person B just listens mindfully in silence. Then after two minutes, Person B will get the chance to verify what he or she heard by saying "I heard you say..." and asking questions for clarification if needed. Then this is repeated with Person B talking and Person A listening. I usually end this with a reflective-writing session so that they can process and acknowledge the impacts of this. The first time I did this I could feel a sense of joy in class. The students literally told me, "I feel a burden is off my shoulders!" Through this process, they feel validated as they are being heard by peers. They also get to know more about their own inner journeys, and they find how they are different and yet similar. Many students have said, "It was good to know that my partner too had similar experiences." At other times, I have heard them say in their pairs, "Wow, I never knew this about you." This has been a very important community-building exercise—a community of various races and cultures. It helps to validate the diverse races, experiences, backgrounds and, thus, feeds into the social and emotional aspects of learning. When students are emotionally engaged, validated, and in touch with their core selves, they can be better engaged intellectually and academically too.

It is also important for teachers to state and validate our own feelings explicitly. Too often, we move from one task to another and do not really create time to explore the emotional sphere of learning and monitor how we are doing. The compass I use is the tool of Courageous Conversation. It is a circle with four quadrants: Feeling, Action, Thinking, and Believing. It is a great one to get students to talk about their emotional states as they settle in. Sometimes, we declutter by sharing our feelings. I will normally pull out the compass on the projector and have them to identify (in pairs, as a class or in written reflections) where they are on the quadrants. This is powerful because it considers their feelings or beliefs. It also allows them to see how being in different quadrants can create differences in opinions. These tools for self-validation have helped my students by promoting self-examination through reflections and, thus, promoting swaraj. Some students have been able to free themselves of years of negative self-talk (due to racial experiences) and have learned to believe and rely on themselves as they truly are. This is a breakthrough in the learning curve, and in life, when you have always felt less than the others. In my experience, it is what helps them climb higher sooner than any other strategy. In this way, I have students center themselves; once they are centered, they are better able to acknowledge their learning needs, to self-advocate, to seek help, to collaborate, and even to lead others. I have had several students tell me, "Thanks for not giving up on me." This is very satisfying, as these students are the very ones who would have remained in the shadows of low grades and poor performances had it not been for the empowerment they felt through this journey to self-realization. This to me is the greatest impact of learning and schooling.

Reference

Gandhi, M. K. (1997). *Hind Swaraj and other writings* (A. J. Parel, Ed.). London: Cambridge University Press.

Chapter 3

Putting Sarvodaya Into Practice

One Teacher's Journey to Create a Farm Program

By Andrew Duden

A couple weeks before the start of school, I drive onto the farm and park by the old milking barn across from the plum tree and blooming clematis; the chicken coop with pigeons and chickens cooing and clucking; the orchard of apples, plums, figs, and pears; Laura's fields of corn and winter squash, next to the parked cars of community gardeners who tend their roses, California poppies, marigolds, black-eyed susans, nasturtiums, sunflowers, and calendula; their cucumbers, lettuce, kale, carrots, and tomatoes. I walk over to an old, corrugated tin shed with a sign on the door that reads "Luscher School to Farm Internship Shed." Note to self: *The lock on the shed is broken and needs replacement.* Garlic cures in crates stacked halfway to the ceiling. Onions cure everywhere: hanging from the ceiling, on shelves, and in crates stacked carefully on the floor. Note to self: *Thunderstorms. Might want to take those to your basement at home so the onions don't rot.* I walk out to the Children's Garden along the newly mulched pathway towards the greenhouse, the three-bin composter, and our small farm plot. School starts in two weeks. I stand in that small field and think, plan, worry, and hope. "I don't know," I say to myself out loud as an exhale. I say that a lot when I stand in the middle of this place.

Sometimes, on days like these, I stop to think about how I got here. I'm twenty-three years into my career. I mostly teach social studies at a suburban high school in Portland, Oregon. Most of my students are surrounded by consumer comfort and advanced technology, and they strategize to become competitive professionals and entrepreneurs in the

C. A. Bracho and D. Dodson (eds.), *Teachers Teaching Nonviolence, 49–58.*

global marketplace. They consume mass-produced, commercial goods and services. A surplus of everything is omnipresent. Also, because technology often impedes face-to-face interaction, students may see the relationship between each other and their relationship to the world around them increasingly as an abstraction. I worry that my students may not be provided enough opportunity in the classroom to critically examine their own habits in this market-driven, technologically advanced, consumer culture. I don't judge them for this shortcoming. They are wonderful, inquisitive, creative, and hardworking people. I do worry that systemic economics, politics, and education sometimes compel students to wind up self-interested, competitive, profit-driven, and cynical.

As a result of my concern, over the years I've pondered many questions. What if I take kids out of this context? What if we go outside and work together collaboratively in order to create something organic? What if I allow students to interact with nature, to study its systems, and to develop a relationship to nature where, in order to grow and thrive, they learn to partner with it? What if I compel kids to solve problems rather than passively wait for problems to be solved? What if I provide students tools to solve these problems, tools to create things essential to their health and well-being, and compel them to work with their brains and their hands simultaneously? What if I compel kids to do this even though they will not profit by it in any material way? Why not compel them to work all year on being healthy, peaceful, and content in a self-sufficient, self-sustaining, local agricultural community? What if they continued to come back, again and again, over the course of their high school career to develop these skills and knowledge and to experience this as they grow and develop into adulthood?

Inspirational answers to these questions surfaced when I participated in the 2011 Ahimsa Summer Institute at Cal Poly Pomona. I studied Mohandas Gandhi and César Chávez's philosophies of nonviolence. I learned that Gandhi's vision for India was a self-sufficient, self-sustaining, localized network of over 700,000 agricultural villages whose primary unification was based upon a common commitment to nonviolence, religious devotion, trusteeship, and local artisan production. Gandhi (1939) advocated self-rule that also takes into consideration the "well-being" of others (p. 79). In 1917 he created the Satyagraha Ashram (now known as the Sarbarmati Ashram), where people from all walks of life, all classes, all castes, all religions, regardless of sex, could participate actively in this constructive work program (Sethia, 2012, p. 77). It was inspired by his reading of John Ruskin's 1860 essay *Unto This Last*. Gandhi wrote that this book was both "practical" and "transformative" for him. He concluded from Ruskin, "That a life of labour, i.e., the life of the tiller of the soil and the handicraftsman is the life worth living" (Gandhi, 1929, p. 299). Gandhi went on to translate *Unto This Last* into Gujarati with the title *Sarvodaya*. This was it. Gandhi offered the guidance I needed to get kids outside the box, working together for the community at large, in a way that was different, exciting, new, unfamiliar, and potentially transformative.

At the Ahimsa Institute, inspired by these ideas, I wrote a lesson plan that would require students to collect food waste in the cafeteria for compost as an entry point into constructive work based upon the principles of *sarvodaya*, the universal uplift of all. I decided to use my Political Action Seminar (PAS) students as compost collectors. PAS is a unique elective that offers students the opportunity to work collaboratively to design and execute campaigns about issues relevant to their lives. In order to get this program started with my PAS students, I had to be creative. Ultimately, my plan for an ambitious school-wide composting program and food garden was not in the course description, and I doubted that many students signed up for the class expecting to be garbage collectors or gardeners. Students did not democratically decide that a composting program at Lake Oswego High School would be good for the community. I did. Admittedly, this mandate by the teacher is not democratic, and it may be the least desirable method for introducing a constructive work program. I had to move carefully and transparently, being mindful that what I was doing might cause consternation among my students, my colleagues, and my community. I looked to the tactics of political organization used by César Chávez (1969): "Nonviolence forces one to be creative; it forces any leader to go to the people and get them involved so that they can come forth with new ideas" (p. 64). Emulating Chávez, who asked farm workers to join in the coordination of La Causa, I asked PAS students to get involved, and I looked to their collective imagination for ideas about how to make this a sustainable project.

Together we developed new ideas to build momentum for the program, collaboratively using our collective imagination, creativity, and skills. I got a positive response from students. They offered to bring in recycled buckets, gold and silver spray paint to decorate them, and old community workday t-shirts from the main office to use as our uniforms. They brought gummy worms that we handed out to students in the first two weeks of the project, both to get the attention of kids in the cafeteria and to reward them for composting. Some students wore goofy costumes voluntarily to bring attention to their work. Many of them paired up to collect compost in integrated groups of juniors and seniors. All these brilliant ideas came from the kids.

By engaging in the work of collecting food waste, walking from one student to the next, and asking for their food scraps with a bucket, my students had to confront their own sense of entitlement as well as to confront their peers. They faced this struggle daily. When collecting compost, they needed to overcome a sometimes hostile environment in the cafeteria. Their peers refused to cooperate. Some students defiantly chose to throw away their food waste. PAS students received rude comments and, in some instances, had food thrown at them. My students began to get frustrated. Some wanted to retaliate. Some wanted to quit. Some simply stopped collecting compost on their assigned days.

These challenges provided a great opportunity to ask questions about our own limitations. Why is work like this hardship or demeaning? What does our negative attitude say about us as individuals? If we could recognize our frustrations about this program, forgive others, and move forward in a cooperative way, we would be faithful practitioners of universal uplift in our school community. We discussed how to respond when we became frustrated with students in the cafeteria. We determined that it would be best to invite these aggressors to join us and to make them feel welcome. Even with the careful language of a letter to the editor in the school newspaper, and the encouraging discussions we had together, many PAS students demanded that they get some form of grade credit for their work, some compensation for having to demean themselves in this way. I felt frustrated. The program drifted towards a coercive act by me, another traditional market-driven, "I'll-do-it-for-points" homework assignment under the cloak of goodness, the uplift of all, and positive interdependence.

Yet I persisted. After we started composting, I realized we needed to build a better system of composting on the school campus. A better system of composting bins led to the construction of a small food garden on campus. The progression of the program sounds logical. However, over the course of three years, the whole project became fraught with problems. The only site acceptable for the garden by our principal had no water access. Dirt on the tennis courts angered the coaches. Food services, worried that the composters would attract wild animals, contacted the Department of Health. Resistance and antagonism from other teachers and administrators seemed constant. I did not foresee that a food-producing garden on campus would invite so much conflict. There was a lot of apologies, re-examination, and revision at every step. And I got more frustrated, was quickly burning out, and even sought jobs at schools elsewhere. Gandhi's famous quote "first they ignore you, then they laugh at you, then they fight you..." never seemed to reach the ultimate conclusion: "then you win."

On the other hand, students who participated in the program demonstrated some measurable change in their thinking and investment in the program's sustainability. They arrived regularly and watered, weeded, and observed. Their field observations, recorded in a daily log that we used to keep track of our progress, highlighted a burgeoning awareness of their role as caretakers. Much of their early data was helpful, repetitive, quantitative observations: soil temperature, air temperature, wind direction, weather patterns, and plant growth. Students also were encouraged to make field notes about their observations related to the progress of the garden. They tended to note negative human impacts early on: "trash on the ground around the garden," "loud music is playing over a loudspeaker," "lots of people and cars passing by," and "traffic noises." However, as time continued, their observations became less critical and more attuned to how to nurture our garden. One student noted that we should plant perennials along the fence to create a barrier from traffic and left a website link via email for us to research suitable plants. Another student wrote an email to me that he and his father were talking about organic gardening, and he shared a link with the group about the film *Food, Inc.* Another sent me pictures of the chicken parmesan that his family made with the tomato sauce we canned.

Addressing all these setbacks, in 2012 I wrote an article in the *Oregon Journal of the Social Studies*. In the article, I blamed myself for the problems our garden faced:

> One of my greatest shortcomings as a practitioner of ahimsa [in our school garden program] was my failure to take into account the impact of my actions on everyone. To practice ahimsa, one needs to also seek out and nurture potential community relationships that may have gone derelict due to personal neglect. An ahimsaka (practitioner of nonviolence) must take an active interest in, care about and labor selflessly for their community's benefit.

In the article, I also blamed myself as the perpetrator of harm. Among my colleagues, I stated that I overlooked their opinions and concerns rather than seeking advice and input before making a decision. In hindsight, this self-blaming missed the point. In fact, there was no capacity for shared uplift when all the stakeholders who should be invested in the success of the project were not willing to be *partners* in the project. This was a great object lesson in my nonviolence journey. All these people were good people, and all of them worked hard to provide the best education possible for kids at our school. They all cared deeply about kids and achieved wonderful things for our students. The problem was that they could not see beyond the status quo. Burdensome cultural forces of high achievement, competition, and market-driven outcomes clouded their capacity to see the potential of this project. Whenever people want to do something new and unorthodox at school, it seems that they face institutional bureaucracies with large scale administrative systems and a lot of stakeholders who often operate in a competitive battle for scarce resources.

I learned the hard way that, in this competitive cultural context, a Gandhian constructive work program which embraces the ethic of universal uplift cannot sustain itself through martyrdom by a few good natured, generous, well-informed actors. To be sustainable, sarvodaya requires a positive interdependence among every stakeholder in the program, such that everyone involved can see in a simple, fundamental way that the beneficial actions of one actor is essential to the well-being of the entire system. All participants in the system are dependent on each other, must hold each other accountable, and must take responsibility for each other for sarvodaya to be actualized. Creative nonviolence seeks to include as many possible actors working collaboratively together in that ecosystem of positive change.

I also learned that there is an element of intersectionality between sarvodaya and nonviolent civil resistance, or *satyagraha*, that I did not expect. Sarvodaya works two ways. All means all—in other words, no one is excluded or denied social, political or economic participation and benefit. And sarvodaya also means uplift; in other words, everyone moves from a lower station in life to an improved station through the execution of interdependent, beneficial constructive work. What happens when we don't make progress because systemic forces disrupt this beneficial, productive work? The answer becomes simple. You do it anyway, and you persist in the face of those oppressive headwinds. Persistence is the primary force of satyagraha.

I didn't expect satyagraha to be part of my journey. However, I came to understand that satyagraha is any pursuit of universal uplift where you ask permission, permission is not granted, and you persist. This sounds subversive, but it is not. The reason it lacks the element of subversion is because the act of persistence comes from the appropriate, well-conceived, positive position of universal uplift. My experience has been that the risk almost always pays off eventually. As a result, when you have an orchestra of people working in concert nonviolently to achieve sarvodaya, and you employ the satyagraha of persistence, the outcome is often successful. Those who view the world fearfully through a lens of scarcity and competition are forced to see the interdependent benefits that arise from community uplift. The act of disobedience often compels the stubborn power broker the opportunity for moral self-examination. It also nurtures the whole community by empowering those nonviolent actors organized within it to learn, grow, and thrive. These two truth forces are a double helix. They work together.

In my flagging search for partners, rather than competitors, I met and became fast friends with a parent at one of our district's elementary schools. She and I hoped that we could get high school students mentoring elementary students in her elementary school garden program. As we began talking and developing a friendship, we both recognized the kinship of our experience. We both had built gardens at our respective schools. We both struggled and shared a lack of partners. One day she wrote to me, offering me an opportunity to attend a meeting with a non-profit called Friends of Luscher Farm. She served on the board of this group. Luscher Farm was a dairy farm in our community that had been purchased by the city in 1990. The city transformed the farm into a city park with an outdoor classroom for garden-based education and community garden spaces, and it also leased some of its land to a commercial farmer.

I arrived at the Friends of Luscher Farm meeting a little late from school. I thought my role would be to sit off to the side and listen to the discussion. When I walked in, I quickly realized that everyone had been waiting for me. Heidi, my new friend and partner, introduced me and asked me to share what I did. At the end of my impromptu description, another board member of the group asked, "Can we do that here?"

The Luscher School to Farm Internship Program began in 2016 and provides students a hands-on, farm-based curriculum where students learn the skills and knowledge necessary to produce year-round food at Luscher Farm that is free from pesticides, herbicides, and chemical fertilizers. Our campus includes a shed, a small greenhouse, composting and vermiculture space, approximately 2,000 square feet of cultivated land, and a small fruit orchard. Students earn .5 elective credit per semester in the program and can take the course for successive semesters during their high school career. The program also includes a summer internship in which students receive elective credit and a stipend. Some students are now two- or three-year veterans of the program, and they have had the experience to see a four-season growth cycle on the farm.

Admittedly, in 2016, I had no idea what I was doing. I had stuck my toe into developing the knowledge and the skills necessary to teach kids out at our faltering little on-campus school garden. Mostly, up to that point, we were using trial and error as our model in a state of triage, trying to get the basics off the ground. Luckily, in Oregon, there is an abundance of professional development opportunities for teachers related to garden-based education through Lewis and Clark's Teacher Education Program, Portland State University's Educational Leadership Program, and the School

Garden Coordinator Certificate Training Program offered by Growing Gardens, a nonprofit in Portland. Also, I read the best educational resource for garden-based education by Dilafruz R. Williams and Jonathan D. Brown (2012), *Learning Gardens and Sustainability Education*.

Since 2016, the program has expanded exponentially in its capacity to partner with numerous other educational, professional, and community-based organizations. In order to gain professional expertise at large scale organic farming, students work in the field with 47th Avenue Farm, a community supported agriculture (CSA) commercial farm founded by Laura Masterson at Luscher Farm. We also take field trips to other organic farms and farm-based education programs. Oregon is blessed with over 500 school garden and farm-based education programs, making it one of the best places for our kids to get out, get involved, and see what is going on in our state. Primarily through the Oregon Farm to School/School Garden Network (OFSSGN), our program connects us with our colleagues on other farms, schedules times to visit, tours their facilities, helps with work on their farms, and heads back to our farm to make improvements. The knowledge and skills students develop from their field work with 47th Avenue helps them improve our own operations. This field work has been transformative for the school farm: our yields continue to improve, our soil quality continues to improve, our use of space continues to improve, and our technical skills continue to improve. All these opportunities to collaborate with other students at other farms in an ever-widening circle of kinship brings the program closer to sarvodaya and purna swaraj.

The program also has expanded in terms of the different types of entrepreneurial work that our students can do. The food produced by students primarily is used by food services in Lake Oswego High School's cafeteria to promote healthy eating habits. Again, OFSSGN has provided a host of great resources that helps us tremendously with food handling, food prep, and the movement of farm-direct produce into cafeterias. We also have researched and worked collaboratively with Oregon's Department of Agriculture and Department of Education to be able to produce and to sell acidified food products, like pickled jalapeños and green tomato relish. Now our products are sold both at the Lake Oswego Farmers Market and at a farm stand on back-to-school night and during fall football games. We even sell some of our produce to local restaurants, and we vend surplus greenhouse starts to faculty at our high school for their home gardens. All these ideas have arisen through the process of trying to solve problems cooperatively with students.

Two important features of nonviolence are critical in this program. First, our students become better self-governing entrepreneurs who contribute to the fiscal sustainability of the program. Second, by using their creative and entrepreneurial energies, they engage themselves in the community in a positive way for the wellbeing of everyone. In keeping with the goal to promote sarvodaya, students also work to nurture partnerships with community-based non-profit groups working to assure food security. Surplus produce is donated to Hunger Fighters—a local non-profit organization that operates as a food bank. Hunger Fighters sponsors a Saturday afternoon free-food pantry for food-insecure families in our local community. Such local food banks are in desperate need for fresh produce. This whole strand of the program has opened doors to food justice, which has become a facet of the curriculum for our interns.

My work with students on the farm continues to echo the transformative ideas of Gandhi and the spirit of ahimsa. On July 28, 1946, shortly before his death, he granted an interview in which he articulated a political vision of what he described as the "oceanic circle." The oceanic circle began with the individual and extended to neighbors, to the village, and out into a structure composed of innumerable villages (Gandhi, 1946). In keeping with Gandhi's idea, the farm program provides for an individual student the opportunity to find meaningful, constructive work outside, in the fresh air, among friends, for the well-being of all in our village. In a field full of life among the long shadows of a late-afternoon summer sun—with cauliflower and beans that need water, crabgrass nagging me, a composter in need of repair, and cucumbers ripe for the picking—I think, plan, worry, and hope. I inhale some wind from the southwest as it brushes across my face, and I detect a trace of the briny Pacific Ocean in the wet straw grass and Douglas fir. Note to self: *Cooler, wetter air. Take care of the onions.* I remind myself that the resonance of the oceanic circles takes a long time to develop and evolve. Patience is essential to teaching nonviolence. According to Chávez (1969), "Nonviolence forces you to abandon the shortcut, in trying to make a change in the social order" (p. 64). I try my best to be patient, and I persist in my effort to seek out ways to connect my students to each other, to connect my students to the land, to connect the farm in positive ways to our school, to connect this program to our community, to breathe in this air, and to note mindfully the expansion of our oceanic circle.

References

Chávez, C. (1969). Creative nonviolence. In I. Stavens (Ed.), *An organizer's tale: Speeches* (p. 64). New York, NY: Penguin.

Duden. A. (2014). Educating for ahimsa: One teacher's journey towards nonviolence. *Oregon Journal of the Social Studies, 2*(2). 19–28.

Gandhi, M. (1929). *Autobiography: The story of my experiments with truth.* Boston, MA: Beacon Press.

Gandhi, M. (1939). Enlightened anarchy. In R. Mukherjee (Ed.), *The Penguin Gandhi reader* (p. 79). New York, NY: Penguin Books.

Gandhi, M. (1946). Gandhi's political vision: The pyramid vs. the ocean circle. In A. Parel (Ed.), *Gandhi: 'Hind Swaraj' and Other Writings*, Centenary Edition (pp. 181-183). London, UK: Cambridge University Press.

Sethia, T. (2012). *Gandhi: Pioneer of nonviolent social change*. Boston, MA: Pearson.

Williams, D. and Brown, J. (2012). *Learning gardens and sustainability education: Bringing life to schools and school to life*. New York, NY: Routledge, Taylor & Francis Group.

Chapter 4

How Teachings of Nonviolence Provide a Framework for Youth Engagement

By Quixada Moore-Vissing

As political polarization escalates, racism and discrimination grow, and a rhetoric of incivility thrives, scholars posit that the United States is more divided than in any other era save the Civil War. Further, national and global social and political trends are laying foundations for tyranny and discrimination to gain momentum. We are in dire need of leaders who can work across difference and bring people together, rather than further divide them. How do we cultivate this next generation of leaders who are prepared to peacefully navigate an increasingly volatile, divided future? We often just expect that leaders have the capacities to listen to others, collaborate, manage conflict productively, and act as true public servants. We also think that they make decisions based not on their own needs but the needs of those they serve. However, we do not often consider what foundations future leaders need to establish in order to effectively cultivate these capacities. Teachings from nonviolence offer us an opportunity to develop such foundations—including an ability to be compassionate and loving to ourselves, to understand ourselves in relation to others, to listen to another's point of view and feel compassion, and to navigate difference. In this essay I will share examples of how laying these foundations has resulted in meaningful youth engagement and leadership.

For over a decade, I have returned often to three key learnings that I first discovered as an Ahimsa Center Fellow in 2007:
- Truth is not static; rather, every individual has a truth that governs how they make decisions and live their life. Moving forward productively when we differ requires acknowledging and trying to understand the truths of others.

C. A. Bracho and D. Dodson (eds.), Teachers Teaching Nonviolence, 59–69.

- The act of listening and sharing with those different from oneself, including those who might be considered enemies, can have transformative results for both parties.
- Nonviolence is broader than simply opting out of physical conflict—it spans the way we talk with each other, talk to ourselves, consume goods, and live our daily lives.

Although I entered the Ahimsa fellowship as a high school American Studies and Literature teacher, shortly after the fellowship I left K-12 teaching to pursue my doctorate in Education. In graduate school, I focused on the field of civic engagement, particularly the study of how bringing communities and schools together to engage in dialogue and deliberation can facilitate lasting school improvement through more collaborative, equitable, participatory policy and action. As I have grown as a scholar, I have been inspired by the teachings of my mother, Dr. Yvonne Vissing, who currently serves as the United States Policy Chair on Child Rights to the United Nations. My mother is one of my greatest teachers. We have spent numerous dinner hours discussing the exciting shift we are seeing globally to recognize young people as valuable resources of wisdom in their communities; rather than thinking of young people as minds that need molding, we understand that they have much to teach both each other and adults. Out of the senseless violence in Parkland, Florida, my mother and I found ourselves hopeful, inspired by how Parkland students showed America that violence cannot destroy a community and that youth can lead with grace and strength while adults stand paralyzed by politics and fear.

If we look at history, there are numerous examples of how young people have led nonviolent social change. The 1960s and 1970s counterculture movement protesting the Vietnam War was mostly composed of young people. Students and youth were pivotal in the Civil Rights Movement, including the 1963 Children's March in Alabama, where school age children walked out of their schools in protest of segregation. Media coverage of the Children's March exposed Americans to the brutal treatment and arrests of these children, some of whom were not even yet teenagers, and only a month later President Kennedy passed Civil Rights Legislation to end school segregation. Dr. Martin Luther King, Jr. himself was only twenty-five when he started the Civil Rights Movement.

Understanding the impact of youth action, I recall how one of my biggest learning moments as a teacher came from my students. One morning I came to school to learn that one of my students, Efren Najera, had been tragically killed in a car accident. Efren's laid-back attitude and easy smile made him popular among the students, and even though I could never get him to do his homework, I enjoyed Efren immensely. A few months prior to his death, when Efren became the legal age, he left high school. When he died, my students were upset that the administration made no formal announcement on the intercom—no moment of silence for our student, friend, and peer, no acknowledgement that he had even been a part of our school community. Many students felt that because Efren had not had high grades and frequently spent time in the discipline office, he was overlooked in a way that an honors student wouldn't have been. Efren was also one of the few Latino students in a predominantly white, affluent school district. In reaction, students photocopied Efren's photo and papered the hallways with it, protested their classes, and raised disruptions until the administration finally acknowledged Efren's death. After weeks of teaching Thoreau and King's notions of civil disobedience, I secretly felt proud of the students for exercising their rights to be heard and for Efren to be seen for all he was, not just a score on a test but as a human being. The students showed the adults that we *all* matter and have value, and that we have much to share in this world, regardless of our credentials and background. The students taught the adults to do the right thing when the adults were mired in the insensitivity and bureaucracy of "Well, he's not technically a student here."

And yet, the ways that we have structured our educational systems historically give students little opportunity for voice and leadership, and when we do give these opportunities, they are often reserved for the highest achievers and "model students." We have made the grave mistake of treating our youth as if they are receptacles for information, rather than creators of knowledge; as if they are there to learn from adults and to behave, rather than sharing their wisdom and finding their power. What gives me true hope is that there are schools and communities that are reversing this trend—and recognizing that youth voice and youth leadership are beautiful resources to be cultivated and valued. However, for youth to be able to express their voices and effectively lead, they need to cultivate three key foundations in themselves:

— Self-love, and a belief that one's own experience and perspective is valid and important
— An ability to understand oneself in relation to others and to recognize that multiple opinions can exist and be valid at the same time
— The capacity to listen to and share with others in civil, honest ways and to collaboratively shape decisions

Nonviolence as the Foundation for Youth Leadership and Engagement

A critical aspect of supporting youth in developing their voice and power is to encourage them to reflect on how they decide to interact with themselves and the world. Although Gandhi is often praised for his ability to mobilize thousands to nonviolently resist British colonization, it is important to remember that all these actions stemmed from the way he interacted with himself and with others daily. His words "my life is my message" are particularly apt here. Gandhi showed Indians how to take back their country by ceasing their reliance on the British economy and by creating their own, self-sustaining communities through home rule, including procuring salt from the earth and weaving their own clothing. Part of this process was to help Indians build self-reliance so that they did not need the British in order to survive—underlining the truth that all they needed was already within themselves.

Similarly, young people need our support to uncover the gifts inherent within themselves. I have talked with my friend and thought partner Poonam Singh, whom I met at an Ahimsa Center conference, about how we often push young people to take on leadership roles and engage in conversations across difference when we have not even provided them an opportunity to learn to love and respect their own thoughts. How can we expect people to be civil and respectful of the thoughts of others when they are not even doing this for themselves? In schools we often assume that developing self-love, confidence, and resilience are aspects that students will develop elsewhere—with their families, at religious institutions, through therapy—but not at school.

The Youth Risk Behavior Survey once measured whether students felt that they matter to their communities, but this question was recently from the survey. Interestingly, the survey is mostly focused on safety concerns such as "risky" behavior—texting while driving, sexual activity, and drug use. But measuring whether students feel valued in their community is also important, since lacking this is a risk factor. Feeling disconnected and as though we don't belong is so powerful of a force that it is now predicted to be as deadly to our physical health as cancer. The rate of people who feel lonely has doubled since the 1980s, and 40% of adults feel alone. Mental health is becoming our new health epidemic, particularly among youth. If we want to support young people in finding their voice and becoming leaders, it is vital we demonstrate to them how much they matter to us. Some of the key ways we can show people they matter is by acknowledging what they have to offer, respecting their opinions, and allowing them opportunities to contribute and lead. These ways cultivate kindness, both toward others and ourselves. It is our obligation to take on this challenge in our schools and communities, rather than assuming "someone else" will help young people achieve these skills.

The Importance of Accepting Multiple Truths

Part of where we seem to be getting stuck in recent times is in the notion of one truth—that if I believe what I think to be true, what you are saying cannot possibly also be true. This becomes particularly challenging when one person's truth seems to infringe on another's safety. For instance, when public leaders use language that some individuals interpret as racist, but that the leaders insist is not racist, it begs the question whether there are some personal beliefs that are so harmful to others that they need be censured. However, until we start acknowledging that we will only make progress when we listen to others' different viewpoints and seek to understand why they hold these perspectives, we will remain in a dichotomy of right vs. wrong that can feel like we are spinning our wheels in the mud as both camps refuse to authentically explore the other's feelings. At the root of some of these challenges is that we are ill-equipped to explore the feelings of others when those feelings are uncomfortable to us—gravitating toward conflict or shutting down rather than participating in processes that allow us to seek understanding, identify common ground, or simply express compassion for another being's reality. Gandhi understood the value of engaging with and listening to those who disagreed with his perspectives, as demonstrated by his frequent interactions with British leaders, such as his letter to Viceroy Lord Irwin notifying him that he would be breaking the Salt Laws.

In recent years, schools have begun to acknowledge the need for unpacking equity and cultural competence so that students can more effectively understand themselves in relation to others. Such work requires that students and their teachers and administrators all commit to deepening their understanding of the ways that their own social identity and experiences have impacted how they come to interpret the world. It is only when we are reflective about ourselves that we can begin to understand the realities of others. Part of this is accepting that our truth is not the only reality but rather one version of a bigger picture. For example, a tax increase may indeed help Anna to feed her family because she receives more social benefits; however, at the same time, it strains David to feed his because he has less money in his pocket. Both experiences can be true simultaneously. The question then becomes, How do we lead across those experiences so that we acknowledge both Anna's and David's truths and many, many others' experiences? How do we create policy and practice that are fair to both Anna and David? When we prioritize one person's needs over the other, how do we still explain and value the other's experiences? When we learn that there are many experiences that compromise reality, it encourages us to think about the decisions we make in more inclusive, nuanced ways. Even more importantly, it helps us to lead with compassion so that any time we make a choice, it closes options and opportunities for some while it creates them for others.

However, we often teach with "right" or "wrong" answers in mind—we look to see if students remember a certain fact or not, rather than ask them to consider multiple interpretations or realities and then identify what resonates with them.

Dialogue as a Means for Personal and Community Transformation

A unifying feature of many leaders of nonviolence is that they listened to and engaged with those who disagreed with their perspectives. Perhaps the most extreme example of this is Gandhi's letter to Hitler, which asked him to engage in conversation and addressed him as "Dear friend." Gandhi regularly talked with British leaders in order to build mutual understanding and to forge a path forward toward India's independence.

Many leaders throughout history have not had the ability or willingness to listen, share, and deliberate with others about decisions. However, as evidenced by the longest government shutdown in U.S. history, it is critical to our functioning as a nation and world to be able to work across differences to make decisions. Further, when we engage in dialogue and deliberation with others, it allows for us to better understand our own perspectives.

An example of how youth-focused dialogue can make lasting social change is evident in a story of school change. In 2011, Pittsfield, New Hampshire, was a small, rural community with beautiful woods and lakes and an economically depressed downtown, complete with empty storefronts and homes that needed repair. The New Hampshire Department of Education had rated Pittsfield's middle and high schools as some of the lowest performing school districts in the state, and the superintendent, John Freeman, knew that the schools' survival depended on positive change. John decided that it was imperative to listen to the community to envision a path forward, and he collaborated with a University of New Hampshire program called New Hampshire Listens. New Hampshire Listens works with communities to design and engage in conversations across difference by training local people with the skills to facilitate dialogue. NH Listens and the Pittsfield community collaborated to create a series of local dialogues focused on how to strengthen education and support for youth in the community. Youth, parents, community members, school staff, and local business leaders all participated in these conversations.

One of the themes that emerged from the initial dialogues is that Pittsfield wanted the schools to be student-centered. With this aim, the school district implemented many new structures, including a site council, which was a collaborative governance structure in the middle and high school composed of students, teachers, administrators, and community members (both parents and non-parents). The site council works alongside the school board to make decisions about the school district, and students' voices hold equal weight to adults in the room. Students learned to exercise this right through a dress code policy proposing no hats in school. Student site council representatives learned that this was an unpopular proposal in the eyes of students for various reasons, and a large group of students assembled at a school board meeting in protest of the policy moving forward. A school board member who supported the "no hats" policy listened attentively to testimonies of students and ultimately concluded that although as a veteran he felt that removing hats was an issue of respect, after listening to the students, he understood and supported their point of view. The "no hats" policy did not pass. Although this may seem small in the face of the pressing social issues that we are experiencing both in society and in our schools, students learned through this experience how to exercise their right to have a voice, how to oppose policy, how to make respectful arguments when they disagreed, and that when they did these things it made a difference.

The power of youth engagement in Pittsfield spilled beyond school walls into the community. Molly Messenger, a fellow with New Hampshire Listens and a professional trained in youth activism, developed a program called Pittsfield Listens. Like New Hampshire Listens, Pittsfield Listens places value on equitable and participatory community engagement. This means that Molly works daily to ensure that the voices of all people in the Pittsfield community are heard and represented in town and education policy, particularly the voices of those who have been historically left out from the decision-making table. A key component of Pittsfield Listens is a youth development program for marginalized youth in the community to develop self-confidence and self-advocacy and to learn about how structural inequalities like racism and classism may affect their experiences to lead and to be heard.

Pittsfield Listens used a New Hampshire Listens design called "Meet the Candidates Nights" to ask people running for local public offices to participate in small group dialogues rather than to stand up at a podium talking at the audience. Local people who have been trained as facilitators by NH Listens or Pittsfield Listens manage conversation in each small group of about 10 local Pittsfield residents. Often these facilitators are youth who are involved with Pittsfield Listens. The candidates briefly share a few facts about themselves, but most of the conversation is focused on local people asking candidates for public office questions through facilitated conversation. Each group member gets a chance to ask questions or respond to the public official, and the facilitator ensures that no one person in the group including the candidate is dominating the conversation. After a given period, candidates are asked to rotate groups so that people at the event have an opportunity to talk with all candidates on a personal level.

Several stories of how youth have impacted community emerged from Candidates Nights. One candidate running for office initially scoffed at having to sit in a group with young people, feeling that the exercise was a waste of his time if these youth couldn't vote. After the conversation, the candidate shared that the questions the youth group had asked him were the most insightful and deep questions he had gotten at the event, and he stood corrected by his original bias. A young man involved with Pittsfield Listens encouraged his mother to come with him to a Candidates Night. After participating in the evening's events, his mother voted for the first time.

The Pittsfield schools also decided to bring restorative justice into the classroom—an approach rooted in Nelson Mandela's work in South Africa, which emphasizes that to heal from harm it is important for those in conflict to share their experiences and forgive each other. A Pittsfield student had jokingly taken a peer's phone and texted her mother a bunch of mean-spirited messages, and shortly after doing so, the phone's battery died. What the student who took the phone did not know is that his peer had a strained relationship with her mother, and that sending those text messages, plus the time lapse where the young woman was not able to clarify that she did not send these messages, created a significant family conflict. Later through restorative justice, the texting student learned the harm he had done to his peer's family. When he asked how she could make amends, the young woman responded that she accepted his apology, but that what she really needed was for him to talk with her father. The young woman's father came to school and explained how much damage this act had done to his family and how angry he was at the student. The young man was able to apologize and take ownership for his actions. Ultimately, the conversation ended in the young man and father talking about the Red Sox and the local sports team, and everyone was able to move forward past the incident.

What these stories represent is that when we communicate to youth that their voices matter and support them in developing the skills to navigate difference and conflict, we all learn from the experience. Yes, these experiences can provoke personal reflection, growth, and change for youth in themselves. But youth can also bring about change in adults. Youth can impact policy. The power of youth is infinite, as is the power in all of us, when we can learn to love ourselves and feel grounded enough in our own value that we are able to openly listen to others. And when we can openly listen to others, we are more likely to be able to make collaborative decisions that are in the best interest of all our community members, rather than a select few.

Participatory Budgeting – Putting Money in Students' Hands

Pittsfield's story demonstrates the impact that youth engagement can have at the personal level. The Center for the Future of Arizona's participatory budgeting work demonstrates how youth engagement can impact thousands of students as well as their schools. Participatory budgeting (PB) is a process rooted in democratic values where community members, rather than public officials, have an opportunity to decide how to spend a portion of a public budget. PB has been practiced at the large scale around the world, particularly in Brazil, where Porto Alegre residents engaged in dialogue and deliberation to allocate 20% of the city's budget. Phoenix Union High School District in Arizona worked with the Center for the Future of Arizona to engage over 3,800 students in a participatory budgeting process in 2016 to 2017. Students have been presented over the past few years with a total of $55,000 intended to benefit them as students as well as the schools. Each grade level cultivates about 50 ideas, and then a student committee works to narrow down the ideas and presents them to the student body. From there, a range of proposals were developed. Students (not teachers or administration) vote on which proposal they would like to fund, and then the leading proposals were implemented.

As a result of this process, students have learned how to work with others who have different opinions than themselves to generate proposals to make change and to make decisions. One student, who was a budget delegate, shared that the process made her think about being a citizen because working with other people and their ideas expanded her mindset.

The Center for the Future of Arizona (2019) claims that this process made had several impacts, including that it
— Empowers students to discover their collective voice
— Emboldens students in decision-making processes
— Fortifies youth-adult partnerships
— Builds critical thinking and communication skills
— Creates meaningful solutions to everyday problems
— Mirrors actual voting processes

In the participating schools, 84% of students voted, compared with a 31% voter turnout for ages 18–29 in the 2018 election (McAndrew, 2018). This statistic is compelling, and it may indicate that when young people believe that their votes will make a difference and that their voices are valued, they are more likely to participate in voting.

The story of Pittsfield demonstrates that when youth engage, they can make significant, lasting change in their schools and community. The story of Arizona demonstrates that when youth believe their engagement matters, they will show up in record numbers.

Closing

Several forces will affect the realities of our young people in their future— including an increasingly diverse society, and, if trends continue, escalating levels of social isolation, record political polarization, and a dark age of resurging racism and extremism. We are at a critical juncture where we can build community, embrace our differences, lean into the discomfort and rewards of talking with those different from ourselves, and collaboratively vision a collective future. Or we can continue to shut each other out, turn away from those who are different, and disconnect, which will likely breed further conflict, hatred, polarization, and violence. If we want a connected, peaceful future, we must start with showing young people that they matter, in their schools and in their communities. This means creating authentic opportunities for youth's voice to be heard and to practice real leadership rather than tokenistic acts. We need to create safe spaces for youth to learn how to navigate difference, to understand the reality of multiple truths, and, considering these varying perspectives, to find ways to make effective, respectful, civil decisions.

The stories I have shared suggest that when we provide youth with these opportunities—or when youth ask for these opportunities themselves—it yields more connectedness, stronger communities, greater understanding of each other, and more peaceful interactions. Further, when youth feel their voices matter and their leadership has impact, they are more likely to be civically engaged, contributing to their communities and to our democracy. If you believe any part of this, think back to Gandhi's words of "my life is my message" and simply try treating a young person in your life as a peer instead of a mind to be molded. You might be surprised how much you will learn.

References

Center for the Future of Arizona. (2019). Participatory Budgeting in AZ. Retrieved from https://www.arizonafuture.org/participatory-budgeting/overview/

McAndrew, J. (November 7, 2018). Exclusive analysis: Youth turnout rate way up in 2018. Tufts Now. Retrieved from https://now.tufts.edu/news-releases/exclusive-analysis-youth-turnout -rate- way-2018

Chapter 5

Journey to Action for Teacher Leaders

By Danielle Mizuta

As a 1996 Cal Poly Pomona alum, returning to my undergraduate home almost twenty years later was nostalgic and filled with wonderful memories. When the opportunity to apply for the Ahimsa Institute came my way, I really did not feel the relevance to return to this path, as I have always been a Special Education Teacher in the classroom and did not see a connection. The application stated,

> This institute provides an extraordinary opportunity to a select group of teachers for educational leadership and facilitates the development of innovative lessons based on a balanced understanding of Gandhi and Mandela, their respective journeys in seeking freedom and social justice.

I had just completed a grant-funded position to support teachers at the state level in a leadership position of mentoring and coaching three complex areas (commonly understood as a school district). I had also recently begun a stint as an Autism Consulting Teacher, where I supported other special education teachers by leading and teaching students in a model classroom. Being back in a classroom setting, teaching students with various degrees of disabilities, reminded me of the lack of justice for these students to access their education. I was feeling so much change as a result of moving positions, had my eyes open wide from the state-level perspective, and wondered what my future in education held, especially in leadership, so I took a leap of faith and applied for the Ahimsa Institute.

This institute taught me about *ahimsa* as the principle and practice of nonviolence; Gandhi's value-based leadership; his vision of *swaraj*, or self-rule; acceptance; and personal inner peace. The experience really opened my eyes to a new "set" of teachers. I gained a fresh vision and perspective of teacher leaders, and I witnessed how teachers can take their practice further (and without going into administration, which is the only path many

C. A. Bracho and D. Dodson (eds.), *Teachers Teaching Nonviolence*, 71–81.

feel advances their careers). Teachers have the potential to advance beyond their classrooms, districts, states, or even countries! My role in education at the time was a resource teacher/mentor/coach, and "teacher leadership" was a hot new term in my state of Hawaii. Immersing myself in a two-week intensive fellowship to learn about how two leaders of nonviolence were fearless, ethical, and highly influential materialized into somewhat of a *breakthrough* in my personal and professional self.

Institute requirements included developing a lesson plan to bring back to our schools. I created a professional development piece because my focus was more on teacher leaders at the time. Both Gandhi and Mandela attributed significant life events for moving into their leadership roles. Gandhi's unwavering reverence for his father's qualities of truth, generosity, integrity, and unconditional forgiveness made an impact on him. Amid financial obstacles, family commitments, and life in a caste system that viewed overseas travel as taboo, Gandhi was not deterred from his dreams of continuing his education in England. After receiving his law degree, he was met with extreme racism; instead of leaving, he faced it, looked for the root issues, and began to formulate his vision on rights, justice, and courage in his approaches to enduring transformation and change. He was driven to conflict resolution, engaged in non-cooperation like his resistance against the Black Act in 1919 and his famous Salt March in 1930, and launched a global recognition of nonviolence and the true spirit of civil disobedience.

Nelson Mandela also attributed significant life events to his success as an effective leader. He was influenced by his father and by a regent who provided him the opportunity to observe him conducting affairs in democracy and leadership. Mandela was especially impressed when the regent shared his view that a leader is like a shepherd, staying behind his flock while letting the nimblest members go forward, ahead of the rest. When he began his law studies at Fort Hare University, Mandela experienced social injustice between upper and lower classmen and refused to serve on the student council, resulting in his suspension. He fled from an arranged marriage, was ordered arrested, but used his skills to talk his way out of his arrest! His political involvement began as a member of the African National Congress. And after over 25 years of imprisonment, he emerged as the first Black president to lead a Democratic South Africa.

My final product for the institute was a presentation to share what made Nelson Mandela and Gandhi such effective leaders, but it turned into so much more. I learned how to take action with my leadership role and also how important it is to *work to change the status quo* when necessary. Furthermore, I felt compelled to continue the work of Gandhi as I continued my own journey as a result of the feedback I received when I shared my experience with other teacher leaders. It resulted in my taking action as a result of a series of *breakthroughs* that I have continued to experience and cultivate in education over the past four years. What I have accomplished professionally as a result of this Institute is nothing that I could have ever imagined, and I am honored to share my journey with you.

Breakthrough #1: September 2015 Presentation

Through the previous training that I received to become a mentor teacher, I learned how to present with engaging materials, create a guided script to use, and interact with participants to encourage a meaningful professional development day. I developed a dozen PowerPoint slides, entitling my presentation "Lessons from Gandhi and Mandela for Teacher-Leaders." I reviewed my experience at the Ahimsa Institute, included alignment with the Hawaii State Leadership Competencies, and provided a brief overview of the lives of Gandhi and Mandela. Through the research I had completed during the Institute, I learned that neither leader was simply born into effective leadership. They both had significant events in their lives, *breakthroughs* that led them to their roles.

Sharing what I learned about transformational leadership, I encouraged the participants in my leadership-training presentation to consider a moment of reflection to identify both the *breakthroughs* that have led them towards their leadership roles and the people in their lives who could be considered charismatic leaders of positive change. I created an accompanying workbook for the participants to use during my 45-minute presentation. Maybe I was even trying to encourage them to move to a little action for themselves too? Also, I told them about the term "values-based leadership," used by James O'Toole (2013) to define the philosophy of the few leaders in politics and business "whose behavior was equally and unequivocally both effective and ethical" (p. 141). Furthermore, I emphasized the three stages of charismatic leadership identified by Conger and Kanungo (1994), which truly impacted me as I began my journey as a teacher leader: Stage 1 (Environmental Assessment), the awareness of the need for change; Stage 2 (Vision Formulation), the communication of an "inspirational vision" to followers; and Stage 3 (Implementation), the establishment of "trust" and empowerment of followers (pp. 439–452).

I had never done a presentation of my own work before. This was a big step for me, and I was extremely nervous. What I felt during that presentation was authentic care and passion for the message I was sharing, which focused on how learning about Gandhi and Mandela's leadership caused a *breakthrough* for me and my teaching, how supporting students was critical, and how change could occur with charisma and value-based leadership. The feedback was overwhelming.

Breakthrough #2: Continue to Share the Message With Teacher Leaders

A colleague and thought partner invited me to share my presentation with her group of a Teacher Leader Academy teachers' cohort. These were 50 selected teacher leaders from the state who were participating in a year-long leadership practice. I focused on the leadership aspects of Gandhi and Mandela, and I discussed what separated them from others and allowed them to emerge as *great* leaders. Because I am interested in teacher leadership and have seen a divide between classroom teachers and administration, it was of interest to me. I wondered how school leaders might be able to reflect on their own practice and compare what they are or are not doing, along the lines of the trends and observations of Gandhi and Mandela's unique leadership qualities.

I used readings provided from the Ahimsa Institute and then did more research focusing on Gandhi and Mandela's leadership qualities, specifically charisma, and their ability to relate to their followers at EVERY level. Instead of just taking that "top down" approach that we are so used to (that has been shown to be ineffective), both leaders were able to get to everyone's level. They didn't have people go to prison for their cause; THEY went to prison. They also were humble and creative in how they worked with other leaders in a peaceful, honest, and nonviolent way. Encouraging participants to consider who in their lives might they identify as charismatic and transformational, I reminded them of what I learned from Gandhi and Mandela about charisma. Both focused on human relationships and sensitivity to others, were inspirational, and saw the goal as more central than their role.

My presentation concentrated on Gandhi's characteristics and included activities for teacher leaders to consider how their practice was helping the relationships and moving their schools forward, or to identify areas where they might consider different approaches that focus more on collaboration and less on punitive/evaluative measures. I intended for participants to consider how they were going to present themselves as teacher leaders so that the conversations they have with others and even their self-reflections could provide insight on how to move both self and school teams forward. I liked the self-assessment that the leadership cohort incorporated. For example, under "Cultural Competence," I created an activity based on the "groundwork" that teacher leaders will need to create/establish an environment where their teachers truly feel they are able to share diverse opinions safely without worrying about disciplinary actions, etc. HOW will a teacher leader create that safe environment for teachers to take responsible risks, learn, and share? WHAT are they planning to do (or are currently doing) to build trust among colleagues? The following is the worksheet that I created and included in the participant packet:

Consider your project plan – Can you see these 3 stages in your plan?

2015-2016 Preliminary Project Plan

Conger – Kanungo Scale – 3 stages of charismatic leadership
Briefly describe a project idea: (What do you want to implement/improve/change?) Stage 1 (Environmental Assessment stage) – Sensitivity to the environment and member's needs. A charismatic leader in this stage is aware that the status quo is in need of change and also considers the challenges and needs of the whole group
Compose a brief rationale for this project: (How will it make a difference for colleagues/school/program?) Stage 2 (Vision Formulation Stage) – The charismatic leader shares an inspirational vision to his or her followers as idealized and shared. This vision is usually unconventional and innovative.
How does this align to your school, district, or state goals? (What structure/format will be followed?) Stage 3 (Implementation Stage) – Charismatic leaders are able to build trust and empower their followers because they are willing to take personal risks and/or sacrifices for the greater good (Rowald et al., 2009).
How will you collaborate with colleagues to improve professional learning? (How will your leadership skills-set be utilized/highlighted through this project?) Reflection and Integrity: An educational leader promotes the success and well-being of every student by regularly examining decisions and actions to continuously improve while maintaining high ethical standards. Change Leadership: An educational leader promotes the success and well-being of every student by strategically and systemically adapting to, and shaping, change.

I was met with a great reception by those who attended. Several teachers approached me after the presentation and shared connections they immediately made with their roles at school and what they just learned about Gandhi's and Mandela's journeys towards action. Administrators who watched from the back of the room complimented me on the connections I made with my Ahimsa experience and classroom practice.

My colleague was able to share a few reflections by the teachers later who found my work impactful. When the feedback for the intense two-day training contained specific highlights referring to *my* presentation, I felt extremely validated. Comments included its relevance and meaning for teacher leadership, its connection to the human spirit, and reminders to consider its environmental implications at schools. The administrators approached me immediately afterward and encouraged me to continue to share my message, which I did. They complimented me on my presentation skills and my ability to engage the audience. Was I developing my own sense of charisma? Was this a significant event shaping my professional journey? Had I been positively influenced to adjust my own approach as a leader and create a safe space within the hour I had? This was another profound *breakthrough* for me. Being in the presence of decision-makers in this specific audience allowed me access to continue to share my message from Gandhi. I submitted a proposal to present at the Hawaii State Department of Education's Leadership Symposium. I was accepted, and my session was "sold out" before the date. Once again, I was validated with positive participant feedback: "It was awesome...and I really learned a lot!!! Also shared quite a few inspirations with my Principal at our school debrief. I bet that fellowship was amazing!! So happy I attended!!"

Breakthrough #3: Hope Street Group 2016

My confidence was building. I had applied to Ahimsa on a whim, as I was in a "rut" at the time. I wondered where my career was going and how I was going to have an impact when I didn't want to become a principal anymore, but I wanted to continue developing professionally and moving within and beyond the classroom. After reflecting on how my Ahimsa experience took me so far personally and professionally, I applied to Hope Street Group (HSG), a nonprofit organization dedicated to educators trained in community engagement, education policy, and empowerment to use their voices to affect change. I acted, applied, and was accepted. There I met MORE teacher leaders, this time in my own backyard. This opportunity developed in a new sense of responsibility to take ownership of reforming education to encourage more teacher engagement and to elevate the profession. It was another view for me of how teachers were taking their practice further, this time with their voices, which are so underrepresented in education.

Furthermore, I felt the lessons from Gandhi emerging again. This, perhaps, was a significant event in *my* life that was shaping me into a charismatic and effective teacher leader. My colleagues were making visits to their legislators, creating focus groups with teachers at their schools, and meeting with their superintendents to begin discussions about elevating the teaching profession. Part of the commitment for Hope Street Group (HSG) was to use our voices to publish relevant and meaningful pieces of written work on public education in Hawaii. As a SPED teacher, I was familiar not only with the overall teacher-shortage crisis in Hawaii but also the SPED teacher shortage-crisis. I was living it. As a fellow, I was immersed in a new professional learning community of like minds who were passionate about finding solutions-oriented approaches and using our teacher voices, like Gandhi and Mandela.

Breakthrough #4: The Troublesome Transportation Trap

An event at school put my transformational leadership teachings learned from Gandhi into practice. Students in my model classroom received special transportation services, and a new bus company contract provided many challenges, not only for my students but also for youth throughout the elementary, middle, and high schools in the area. Because many of the students I worked with were medically impacted and non-verbal, their ability to communicate and advocate for themselves was limited. The bus company (which I assume had good intentions) was contracted to provide my students with their mandated, legally binding services, but to minimal avail. The bus would do all the other transportation runs and arrive to pick up my students up to an hour after their designated time to and from school. These students missed valuable instructional time and services at the beginning of the day and were dismissed as insignificant at the end of the day. I approached the administrators several times via email, in person, and through my supervisor. I also made several attempts to communicate to the transportation company the need for my students' transportation to be a bigger priority due to their medical conditions, which required scheduled medication management for seizures, physical movement, and one-to-one supervision by my staff, who were not paid overtime to stay for a late bus. None of these avenues provided any changes.

However, this would become another *breakthrough* moment. I reflected on what I learned from the institute and acted. I continued to tell all the key stakeholders about the importance of my student's needs, their limitations with self-advocacy, and their rights. I shared with stakeholders appropriate, nonviolent, and effective options; and I presented a timeline in hopes of a positive outcome. Reflecting on what I learned about transformational and value-based leadership, I worked with my team to formulate an action plan to convince the stakeholders that something must be done, even providing appropriate dates and timelines for changes. I communicated on a regular basis, choosing my words carefully. The "deadline" was fair, and I articulated the outcome repeatedly. I set expectations, empowered my team, and modeled consistency, patience, and persistence. A few days before my team, students, and I were set to implement our plan, I sent a final email to all the stakeholders. Before our deadline, the issue was resolved. This specific journey through nonviolence worked! The triumph, relief, and gratitude that I felt were immense.

Breakthrough #5: Getting Published

Following this success, I was deep into my Hope Street fellowship, feeling that it was time to work on an article to share teacher voices to a larger audience. I was reminded of when Gandhi took to the local newspaper in South Africa calling for ethics and morality in the issues facing the Indian community. Choosing to communicate what I was experiencing, and focusing on a solutions-based approach as a Special Education teacher, I wrote about the SPED teacher shortage and ways that the Department of Education might spend less money recruiting teachers from out of state and, instead, focus upon growing our own SPED teachers from a very qualified pool of Education Assistants, Paraprofessionals, etc. My op-ed, which I titled "Address Teacher Shortage by Developing Educational Assistants," was published in *Civil Beat* in January 2017. Drawing upon the intensive support from HSG and my colleagues, the confidence and perspective gained through the Ahimsa Institute, and my triumph with the bus company, I voiced how my call to action led to new connections. I was thrilled to be recognized and motivated even more to know that there were other like minds out there who felt the same call to action I did. If I had not written that piece, which was a result of becoming a Hope Street fellow, which was a result of presenting my Ahimsa product, which was a result of attending the Ahimsa Institute, none of this action would have happened.

This call to action became more and more comfortable to me. Learning that action can be peaceful—and understanding the importance of communication, bravery, and focus on the goal instead of my role—I started taking other opportunities that came my way. I continued to present to educators at local and national conferences. I wrote another piece, published by the Association for Middle Level Education, which advocated parent and teacher collaboration. Also, I was offered two new jobs and invited to attend the East Asia Regional Council of Schools Conference in Bangkok, Thailand.

Breakthrough #6: Continued Opportunities for More Action

Leeward Community College, part of the University of Hawaii system, reached out to offer me a position as an instructor in their program for pre-service and emergency-hire teachers I had cited in my op-ed. A faculty member had read my article and contacted me to share gratitude for mentioning their teacher preparation program in it. I took action! I revised and rewrote my curriculum and started teaching those very teachers about whom I spoke about in my op-ed. I was then asked to present at a teacher-recruitment fair on Universal Design for Learning. This inspired me to write a proposal to present at the national Schools of the Future Conference in the fall of 2019, and the paper was accepted for presentation.

Breakthrough #7: Keep Learning, Moving, Reflecting, and Growing

I never imagined that I would leave the public education system, specifically the Title I schools where I chose to work. Offered a job at an independent private school in Honolulu as a Learning Support Specialist, I quickly and humbly realized that students benefit from support no matter what educational institution they attend. I consult with teachers, students, families, and leadership on learning differences, exceptionalities, and more. In my new role, I support teachers by focusing on best practices and different ways to provide instruction for students to gain access to the curriculum. The past two years have been an extreme time for reflection as I try to imagine the challenges that Gandhi faced when working with others to build bridges, encourage understanding, and invite new perspectives. Though I have been met with some adoration, I am more often met with distaste, judgement, and disapproval about why I am at this elite school of master teachers who happily maintain the status quo. Recently I returned from a two-week visit of public, private, charter, and international schools in Denmark, Sweden, and Finland. My group and I met with school personnel to learn more about the similarities and differences, to build an understanding of effective teaching practices, and to spend time with students and teachers in similar roles as ours.

This new position at an affluent private school affords me opportunities I never imagined possible. I have ever before seen such resources available to the faculty, staff, and students, and yet the resistance to change for the under-served population mirrors what I believe Gandhi and Mandela addressed in their lives. Challenging the status quo daily now, I struggle to make connections and act with a group of colleagues who would like to keep things as they are. For example, a colleague of mine sees a child who struggles with dyslexia not as a gift but a burden; even though she has an IQ in the gifted range and incredible insights to share, this student is ostracized because she cannot read aloud as fast as her peers. The teacher does not want to provide text-to-speech options, audiobooks, or verbal directions because this provision is viewed as a crutch. My attempts to bring to light the social emotional toll on this child and the resulting impact on her behavior seem futile. However, my experience as an Ahimsa Fellow and all the other ensuing experiences have changed me. I no longer can sit back and be a part of the status quo.

Toward a New Breakthrough

In my current role, the need to act is apparent, but how do I begin? Through the principal? Parents? I have been struggling. It is new territory for me, and I was not expecting these barriers. I cannot go back to the simple life of wanting and hoping for change in secret. What's next? What call to action can I take to support students in their current environment? How can I use what I've learned from Ahimsa to take positive and necessary action to support the students and teachers at my current school? Perhaps I will go back and refer to Gandhi's Oceanic Circle: "Life will not be a pyramid with the apex sustained at the bottom, but an oceanic circle whose center will be the individual." I am moved by the need to turn inward and reflect. I am reminded of another Teacher Leader Academy's feedback on charisma and transformational leadership: "Something Danielle said when talking about these two characteristics was, if they are lacking in us, we may just be sitting back and *being a part of the status quo*. There are so many obstacles I face in my position and I really must consider—is it worth the time and effort it will take to make the change? I need to do some deep reflecting to decide how I will act to get us there." I, too, am wondering how to address these unexpected challenges. I know that the answer and the breakthrough will come from within as I continue the work. As a guide, I will look to Gandhi's behaviors, which illustrate humility, patience, and persistence as he engaged in honest self-examination and displayed moral courage, reflecting on his experiences and learning from his failures and mistakes (O'Toole, 2013, p. 161). I look with anticipation and energy toward the next breakthrough in my story.

References

Conger, J. A., & Kanungo, R. (1994). Charismatic leadership in organizations: Perceived behavioral attributes and their measurement. *Journal of Organizational Behavior, 15*, 439–452.

O'Toole, J. (2013). The practical idealist: Gandhi's leadership lessons. In T. Sethia & A. Narayan (Eds.), *The living Gandhi: Lessons for our time* (pp. 141–162). London: Penguin Books.

SECTION 2

Integrating Mindfulness and Compassion

Section Overview

Integrating Mindfulness and Compassion

By Danita Dodson

There is an established and substantial body of scientific evidence that quantifies the importance of mindfulness. Forty years ago, the Stress Reduction Clinic at the University of Massachusetts Medical School pioneered the introduction of mindfulness into mainstream health care when Jon Kabat-Zinn (1990) first offered an eight-session, group-based Mindfulness-Based Stress Reduction (MBSR) program to help reduce suffering of chronic pain. Since the first research decades ago, studies of mindful practices have increased dramatically (Funderbark, 1977; Brown, Forte, & Bysart, 1984; Hayes, Strosahl, & Wilson, 1999; Canter & Ernst, 2003). In particular, the findings about neuroplasticity have revealed that repetitive mental training can rewire the brain with new neural pathways that allow practitioners to respond to situations in healthier, more positive ways (Treadway & Lazar, 2010). Also, researchers have discovered that mindfulness improves attention, memory, immune response, emotional regulation, calmness, and self-awareness (Hanley, Mehling, & Garland, 2017). Facilitating the reconfiguration of the neurobiology behind the "fight-flight-freeze" response, mindfulness practices create new apertures for attaining balance, nonjudgment, positivity, friendliness, and encouragement.

Due to this growing scientific research, it is no wonder that mindfulness has recently gained traction as a meaningful pedagogical innovation, and such practices in the school setting seem to arise at a time when students are increasingly bombarded with tension, violence, and stress. According to the American Psychological Association (2018) in the Stress in America survey, young people—particularly teens—are the most stressed demographic in the United States. However, Michael Mrazek, the director of research at the Center for Mindfulness and Human Potential at the University of California Santa Barbara, maintains that young minds are also well-suited to

C. A. Bracho and D. Dodson (eds.), Teachers Teaching Nonviolence, 85–89.

comprehend mindfulness and reap its benefits (Mrazek, Mrazek, & Mrazek, 2017). The value of exposing youth to integrated wellness is also echoed by Stacy Sims (2019), a mind-body educator who addresses the subject of trauma in *True Body Project* and *City Silence*. Asserting that mindfulness practices can enhance young people's lives, in a lecture at the Ahimsa Center, she encouraged teachers to expose students to experiential learning in a world that is often "information rich but experience poor" (Sims, 2019). Because the body and the mind are synchronized in breath, neurology plays a role in the resilience that derives from activating the parasympathetic nervous system, balancing it in homeostasis, and creating connection. Such connection is crucial to our nation's future; in a world where we are wired more to technology, we are less linked to each other and to our own inner realities. Allowing deep communication, mindfulness is anchored inward, where one first connects with the self in a restorative practice that allows "little moments of reconciliation" (Sims, 2019).

The brain's ability to create the moments of inner reconciliation also can be constructive in building healthy external relationships with others. Dr. James Doty (2016), founder of the Center for Compassion and Altruism Research at Stanford, offers research that reveals that one of the most important corollaries of mindfulness is its ability to cultivate compassion. Though often we are not fully present in our relations with others, neuroscience shows that presence and connection are defining aspects of our humanity. Inner dialogues have profound physiological responses in the central nervous and cardiological systems, but mindfulness allows practitioners to change the internal discourse to compassion (Doty, 2016). It turns out that research reveals that compassion has its own natural healing benefits—though it is not always an automatic response, especially when daily life abounds with distractions and demands. However, studies have begun to indicate that we can foster a capacity for compassion. For example, a University of Wisconsin-Madison study discovered that people who engage in daily compassion-mindfulness training are more generous and experience greater activation in the nucleus accumbens (Weng et al., 2013).

This research suggests that application of mindfulness and compassion in the classroom is akin to the principles of ahimsa. Embodying *swaraj*, nonviolence education can help alter students' inner turmoil of stress, anxiety, and self-harm. Gandhi, who utilized mindfulness practices as *satyagraha* during the most demanding times of his life, lived and promoted a sturdy sense of grounded self, where empathy and nonviolence begin. As the chapters in this section disclose, teachers can give their students vital skills to bring their own nonviolent paths into the world, beginning with transforming the inner self-violence. Exploring the ways that nonviolence is linked to mindfulness and compassion, the contributors illustrate their varied strategies for integrating these practices into K-12 contexts. They show us how to foster stress management, empathetic response, social and emotional learning, self-awareness, and self-transformation.

In Chapter 7, "Mindfulness and Meditation: Personal Swaraj in High School Classrooms," Adam W. Dennis explains how he has employed Gandhi's nonviolent philosophies in his creation of a mindfulness class for high school students in Portland, Oregon. Inspired by his Ahimsa Center fellowship, he describes how he began teaching meditation in his English classes to give students a new life skill—stress management—as his way of bringing swaraj through personal transformation. Dennis reveals that meta-mindful practice improves not only daily connection to students but also allows the teacher-practitioner to apply nonviolent communication and empathetic response in such experiences as student feedback, dialogues with colleagues, meetings with administrators. His work in building personal swaraj has grown to an elective-credit Mindfulness and Yoga class, where he guides students through semester-long mindfulness learning.

In Chapter 8, "Art, Mindfulness, and Peacebuilding: A New Framework for Social, Emotional, and Creative Growth," Elizabeth Benskin, Director of Teaching and Learning at the Baltimore Museum of Art, describes how she developed a museum program to investigate a question inspired by an Ahimsa Center Institute: What can K-12 students learn about nonviolence by exploring art that expresses ideas about peace and conflict? This multi-layered program for elementary students integrates art history, studio art, storytelling, yoga, meditation, and neuroscience to develop a new pathway for student social and emotional learning. Benskin outlines how students not only explore gallery art related to conflict and nonviolence but also create their own art to express ideas of peace, visions for an ideal world, and their role as peacebuilders. She shares assessment results that reflect such outcomes as increased connection, growth in sense of belonging, a broadened concept of art, and demonstrations of empathy. These findings offer a promising start for measuring the effects of using art in a learning framework for nonviolence education.

In Chapter 9, "Mindfulness: Connections to Social-Emotional Well-Being and a Compassionate Global Citizenry," Peggy Sia explores how social-emotional education, character building, and mindfulness in school curriculum can promote a compassionate 21st-century global citizenry. Describing the research that she conducted with her 4th-grade class in Los Angeles County, she reveals that exposing students to the experience of mindfulness and providing them skills for social-emotional development can lead to increased self-awareness, concrete methods of articulating needs and thoughts, and proactive dialogue. With the daily practice of her social emotional curriculum, students gain a better sense of self-awareness and create a moral identity that guides them through interactions with others with compassion, leads them to a greater social consciousness, and helps them to become stewards of the earth. Sia also demonstrates how technology can enhance such a pedagogical approach, linking students with classrooms across the globe through online platforms.

Finally, in Chapter 10, "Transformational Journeys of Nonviolence," Esteban Hernandez asserts that while public education often teaches students about the nonviolent tactics used by Mahatma Gandhi and Martin Luther King, Jr. to create change, it fails to emphasize the personal journeys that transformed these exemplars into the heroes we admire today. While emphasizing the supreme morality these exemplars employed in their search for justice, he argues also that students need to understand that they are very much like these heroes of nonviolence—mortal, flawed, vulnerable people with the ability to transform themselves into great beings. Hernandez, an English teacher in California, shows how he has led high school students to uncover the relevance of Gandhi and King in their own lives. Describing his creation of a curricular unit on Transcendentalism, this chapter helps teachers see how students can mindfully access principles of nonviolence to begin a modest, incremental changes in their thoughts, words, and actions that will foster permanent change in themselves, their relationships, and their communities.

Each of the following narratives derives from a profound understanding of the "palpable human needs [that] walk through the door virtually every day" (Bryk, Sebring, Allensworth, Luppescu, & Easton, 2010, p. 96). Through the strategies of nonviolence, the pedagogical emphasis upon mindfulness and compassion points to the powerful way that education can change not only students' lives but also communities. The contributors in this section exemplify the ways that educators can be "transformative intellectuals" (Giroux, 2010). As they beautifully illustrate, when teachers are dedicated to creating transformative learning that brings healing and self-understanding to youth, they move away from conceiving their roles as simply technicians, skills-developers, or imparters of knowledge.

References

American Psychological Association. (2018). Stress in America: Generation Z. Retrieved from https://www.apa.org/news/press/releases/stress/2018/stress-gen-z.pdf.

Brown, D., Forte, M., & Dysart, M. (1984). Visual sensitivity and mindfulness meditation. *Perceptual and Motor Skills, 58*, 775–784.

Bryk, A., Sebring, P., Allensworth, E., Luppescu, S., & Easton, J. (2010). *Organizing schools for improvement: Lessons from Chicago.* Cambridge, MA: Harvard Education Press.

Canter, P., & Ernst, E. (2003). The cumulative effects of Transcendental Meditation on cognitive function: A systematic review of randomized controlled trials. *Wiener klinische Wochenschrift, 115*, 758–766.

Doty, J. R. (2014, November). The compassion imperative. Talk presented at the "Care, Compassion and Mindfulness" 2014 Ahimsa Center Bipin and Rekha Shah Conference on Nonviolence, California State Polytechnic University, Pomona, California.

Funderburk, J. (1977). *Science studies yoga: A review of physiological data.* Glenview, IL: Himalayan International Institute.

Giroux, H. (2010). Teacher as transformative intellectuals. In A. Canestrari & B. Marlow (Eds.), *Education foundations: An anthology of critical readings* (pp. 197–204). Thousand Oaks, CA: Sage.

Hanley A. W., Mehling W. E., & Garland, E. L. (2017). Holding the body in mind: Interceptive awareness, dispositional mindfulness and psychological well-being. *Journal of Psychosomatic Research, 99,* 13–20.

Hayes, S. C., Strosahl, K., & Wilson, K. G. (1999). *Acceptance and commitment therapy: An experiential approach to behavior change.* New York: Guilford Press.

Kabat-Zinn, J., & University of Massachusetts Medical Center/Worcester. (1990). *Full catastrophe living: Using the wisdom of your body and mind to face stress, pain, and illness.* New York, NY: Delacorte Press.

Mrazek, M., Mrazek, A., & Mrazek, K. (2017). *Presence of mind: A practical introduction to mindfulness and meditation.* Santa Barbara, CA: Empirical Wisdom.

Sims, Stacy. (2019, June). My journey to mindfulness and connectedness. Shankar and Malathi Narayan Ahimsa Public Lecture. Talk presented at Ahimsa Center, California State Polytechnic University, Pomona, California.

Treadway, M. T., & Lazar, S. W. (2010). Meditation and neuroplasticity: Using mindfulness to change the brain. In R. Baer (Ed.), *Assessing mindfulness and acceptance processes in clients: Illuminating the theory and practice of change* (pp. 185–205). Oakland, CA: Context Press.

Weng, H., Fox, A., Shackman, A., Stodola, D., Caldwell, J., Olson, M., . . . Davidson, R. (2013). Compassion training alters altruism and neural responses to suffering. *Psychological Science, 24*(7), 1171–1180.

Chapter 6

Mindfulness and Meditation

Personal Swaraj in High School Classrooms

By Adam W. Dennis

We cannot change the world until we change ourselves. Thus, perhaps the most significant of Gandhi's four principles is *swaraj*. From personal transformation can come outward change, and then *sarvodaya*, *satyragraha*, and *satya* may be achieved. More than anything else from the 2015 Ahimsa Institute that I attended, I held onto personal swaraj. For several years I'd been pursuing Nonviolent Communication and meditation personally, but those didn't make it into my classroom until I learned about Gandhi and Mandela. Seeing so many students exhibiting violent behavior towards themselves and others (especially themselves) in their words, thoughts, and actions, I felt a sense of alarm and wanted to bring something more real, more tangible to students.

Gandhi had the salt marches. He chose to do hunger strikes and followed vegetarianism and celibacy. He used actions to embody his philosophies. I would do the same. Meditation and mindfulness would be my way of helping students manage their day-to-day life stresses and maybe lead them to personal swaraj.

My Teaching Environment

The following is a sample high school student's eight-class schedule at my small, suburban school located southwest of Portland, Oregon:

C. A. Bracho and D. Dodson (eds.), Teachers Teaching Nonviolence, 91–101.

Monday:

Tuesday:

Period 1) 8:25–9:55 Chemistry

Period 1) 8:25–9:55 Physics

Teacher-student contact time)
9:55–10:10

Teacher-student contact time)
9:55–10:10

Period 2) 10:15-11:45
Calculus

Period 2) 10:15-11:45
Psychology

Lunch) 11:45-12:20

Lunch) 11:45-12:20

Period 3) 12:25-1:55
English

Period 3) 12:25-1:55
French

Period 4) 2:00-3:30
Art

Period 4) 2:00-3:30
US History and Government

On paper perhaps this schedule seems ordinary, even doable. It's only four classes per day. And starting the day at 8:25 a.m. gives students a chance to sleep more and to align their teenage body clocks better. There is so much this schedule does *not* say on paper, though. There is so much demanded of students found between the lines. It goes something like this:
— 1st period: Be excellent and outstanding for 90 minutes. Listen attentively and take copious notes. Turn in your fully completed homework. Ask questions and answer prompts from the teacher. Be organized and a leader but humble. Don't drink in class. Don't eat in class. Use the bathroom sparingly. Follow directions. Do all of this while sitting for 90 minutes.
— Leave class, go to the bathroom, check phone notifications, grab a snack, and rush to the next class: you've got five minutes, but be on time.
— 2nd period: Do it all again.
— Lunch: Find your friends and some food and relax among the entire student body of 1,300 students eating at the same time. You've got 35 minutes.
— 3rd period: It's time to be excellent and attentive again.
— 4th period: Repeat it all one last time.
— After school: Go to practice/ rehearsal/ game/ competition/ volunteering/ your tutor/ your job and give 100% for as long as it lasts, usually one to six hours. Eat dinner at some point. Do all your homework for all four

classes that you were assigned today or that is due tomorrow. Spend time with your family and make healthy choices. Do it all yourself. Don't plagiarize. Don't look up answers online. Get enough sleep but not before all that homework and studying is done.
— Then get up and do it again for a new set of classes.

Students do not have time to take a breath, nor do the teachers and other school personnel who live within this rigid structure.

The teenage brain, more connected to the limbic system (reward center) than the prefrontal cortex (judgement, emotional regulation, rational thought), is already primed for addiction and bad, unhealthy habits; in this environment those unhealthy and harmful habits look even more attractive as young people reach for something, anything, to mitigate the stress, anxiety, fear, and gloom they feel. How many schools across the country include mission or vision statements with the phrasing "career and college ready," "life-long learners," "prepared to be productive members of society," or "well-rounded"? I argue that we're achieving none of that by promoting the student life described previously. Added to that is the recent educational buzz term, "grade 13," wherein a student takes AP/IB/Dual-credit classes to accumulate a year's worth of college credit. This has pushed more and more students into higher level, faster-paced, more rigorous classes, which in turn create more stress and anxiety and work for those students. The sample schedule above is for a regular, college-track student who is not taking any advanced classes: the minority in my school.

This small, suburban school routinely scores highly on numerous measurables reported by various publications and school ranking systems. To dig deeper at these high scores, students graduate at over 93%, and over 92% of those go to a four-year college. They take and pass hundreds of Advanced Placement (AP) exams. The school has National Merit Scholars, champions in Speech and Debate, significant programs for Mock Trial and Model United Nations, and state athletic championships every year. Furthermore, for the past several years, each school in the district has made Adequate Yearly Progress (AYP). The district is a "5" according to *US News and World Report*, and the high school is a "gold school" according to state and federal rankings. Many students come from middle- and upper-class families with a tradition of higher educational degrees and upper management positions, which supports the school district significantly. These students are being prepared by their parents, community, and school district for white-collar, upper-management, leadership positions.

They are not being prepared for life.

They are not being prepared to find inner peace.

They are not being prepared to contribute to a peaceful, nonviolent world.

Nowhere do I see schools putting the emotional and mental wellbeing of young people front and center; it's missing from mission and vision statements; it's missing from school board minutes and superintendent speeches; it's missing from all the rankings and all the data that goes into those rankings; it's missing from most schools' curriculum and structure. Sadly, I have heard too many stories about what happens when we continue to, at best, pay lip service to student health, and, at worst, actively create paradigms that negatively impact student health. Here is one such story (names and other identifying characteristics have been changed).

Catalysts for Change

Jeremiah took an elective credit Department Aide period with me one semester during his sophomore year. I knew him well from his freshman year because my classroom served as a safe space for a new, insecure student. By sophomore year he'd fully integrated into the life at my school: rigorous classwork, hours of daily homework, intense pressure to achieve academically and to participate in extracurriculars. He'd gone out for track. One day, while filing some papers, Jeremiah casually said, "I started taking my friend's Xanax," and I looked up. "Everything is just like, so stressful right now, and I needed something."

Hearing this, I knew—something had to change.

Jeremiah had scars on his arms. He wasn't the only one. From one student I learned to notice the difference between older, fading lines and newer, redder ones on other students in most, if not all, of my classes, from ninth graders to seniors. Legs and arms turned out to be the most common areas. My emails to the school guidance counselors and the school psychologist became more frequent; however, one school psychologist served both high schools in my district and, therefore, had limited time to work with students. The next year the school cut the psychologist and employed college-student interns part time instead.

The school had no safe room, no safety plan for such at-risk students, no training for teachers.

Something had to change.

I found out Jeremiah went out for track because he wanted to lose weight to fit the attractiveness standard at the school. He had an alcoholic mother and at the age of thirteen had been mixed up in the seedy motel drug bust of a pedophile. He came to high school under heavy trauma and was thrown into a competitive academic world without any supportive resources or even communications to teachers about his situation.

Something had to change.

Two months into Jeremiah's sophomore year, a classmate had a panic attack in our English class and ran out of the room hyperventilating. All I could think to do was calm her breathing and give her water to sip. What was going on? A month later in a different class another girl had a panic attack. I sat with her in the hall and hoped my class was doing their work. She had four hours of ballet practice every day after school and had fallen way behind in her classes. Her body shook as she said, "I don't know what to do any more." She was 15.

Something had to change.

Students were missing class. They skipped school with and without parent approval, sometimes to see therapists. They had diagnosis for anxiety, for depression, for ADD/ADHD. Students had begun taking prescribed medication. They weren't sleeping, but they were self-medicating: something to help them concentrate and stay awake such Adderall, caffeine, or Red Bull. Then, later in the day, students were taking something to help them relax such as marijuana, leftover pain pills, alcohol, or vaping.

Something had to change.

There are students who stay away from all those things and bottle it up without any healthy release. There are students who talk with their parents or friends or other confidants, students who use therapy well, and students who are well-adjusted. I don't mean to be an alarmist or over-dramatize the state of the nation's young people like a prime-time news special. Teenagers have long been experimenting with risky behavior. To be young is to be moody and live in perpetual uncertainty. What I was seeing in my classes and in my school, what I was hearing from other teachers, was not the normal teenage struggles, however. In fact, we formed a student wellness committee made of 15 teachers all deeply concerned about the stress and anxiety of our students. The culture of school was making students sick, and something needed to change.

In a larger context, current research is clear that this is not only an issue at my school. Young people are suffering through a pandemic of emotional and mental health challenges, and mindfulness may be one of the best antidotes to avoid potential catastrophe. In her article "Why Teaching Mindfulness Benefits Students' Learning," Tina Barseghian (2013) quotes from Dr. Patricia C. Broderick's (2013) book, *Learning to Breathe: A Mindfulness Curriculum for Adolescents to Cultivate Emotional Regulation, Attention, and Performance*:

> The landmark report in 2000 by the U.S. Surgeon General…revealed that one in ten of our young people suffers from a mental health condition that meets diagnostic criteria, and one in five suffers from problems that significantly impair day-to-day functioning, including academic achievement and social relationships.

> **One in ten** students have mental illness?
> **One in five** students have academic and emotional issues that are seriously impeding their daily lives?

These numbers are *staggering*, and something must change.

Nonviolent Communication

In 2009 I started studying Marshall Rosenberg's empathy-based communication framework, Nonviolent Communication (NVC). After five years I decided it could be something to help students and teachers. I was learning Buddhism and meditation along with NVC and seeing significant benefits in my personal and professional lives. How could I bring this to my students and to my colleagues? For years I'd dreamed of training staff on it, with NVC as the communication paradigm that teachers and students would use to relate with empathy to each other and themselves. The first part of NVC is learning self-awareness, recognizing our own emotions and actions and the needs behind them. If students could learn that, they might also learn to make healthier choices, I reasoned. If teachers could learn that, they might lessen their burnout, increase their patience and understanding, and relate better to their students.

The problem I faced with students was twofold: there are no published resources for teaching NVC to teenagers, and it fit nowhere in my curriculum. Still, in the fall of 2014, I forged ahead. First, I began teaching NVC during professional development to other teachers in my district. Second, I used it as character analysis in my English classes. For example, I used the NVC feelings and needs lists to examine George's needs in *Of Mice and Men* and to understand why Curley's wife behaves as she does. Still, it wasn't enough. Our student wellness committee would meet and share concerns about losing students because things were getting worse, not better. We were all worried about losing students. I received positive feedback about the staff workshops I led, but nothing seemed to be changing for the students.

One day I hit upon an idea to give students an outlet. I put an 11 x 17 piece of paper on each of the seven round tables in my classroom. Rather than starting class by covering the day's agenda and homework, I told the students to use the paper to write down anything they needed to vent about school, about their stress, about anything at all that was on their minds. No censoring, no grading, just five minutes to release, and I left the room to protect their privacy (I left the classroom door propped open). I stood in the hall and heard their voices start to bounce around the room and then laughter. When I stepped back in, the papers were covered with words and drawings, and the students were chatting and laughing with their tablemates.

I was onto something.

Ahimsa 2015

During the 2014–2015 school year, a colleague suggested I look at a summer institute focused on studying Gandhi and the application of his nonviolence philosophies to our teaching, knowing I was already working with NVC. What I learned in that 2015 Ahimsa Institute on Gandhi and Nelson Mandela made a significant impact and contributed to something of a mini-career re-focus.

Each man spent years fighting for change outward before looking inward. What I admire most is the way Gandhi changed from a career-focused lawyer to a crusader for social change. He embraced an ascetic life, daring to change his profession, change his clothes, change his eating habits, and change every other facet of his life. Before his long exile in prison, Mr. Mandela resorted to violence in fighting apartheid in South Africa, but he emerged from his horrific imprisonment freer because he replaced bitterness and violence with compassion and nonviolence. He changed and became a symbol of peace.

I learned all this from the Ahimsa Institute. But more than anything else, I learned about the concept of personal *swaraj* or, as The Swaraj Institute describes it, "a genuine attempt to regain control of the 'self'—our self-respect, self-responsibility, and capacities for self-realization." It is necessary for teachers to develop this sense of self in students if we are to guide their growth and learning and create a peaceful world ("What is Swaraj?"). Students, of course, could benefit as well, but that seemed much more challenging and abstract. I saw a need for a better way to align our inner compasses so that they always pointed to true north; in other words, by learning ourselves we stay grounded, we stay centered, and we do not react in violence to ourselves and others in our words, thoughts, actions, and beliefs. We transform ourselves. If teachers could do this, if students could do this, we could change the world. As Mr. Rogers (2014) wrote, "When you combine your own intuition with a sensitivity to other people's feelings and moods, you may be close to the origins of valuable human attributes such as generosity, altruism, compassion, sympathy, and empathy" (p. 47).

Teaching and learning need presence. Presence needs self-awareness.

Presence and self-awareness are not taught in any teacher-training program I've heard of; they aren't part of any university curricula, and they are most likely not on the radar of mentor teachers and administrators. To fully see, hear, and understand our students, we need to fully show up and be able to stay grounded amid the thoughts and emotions that surround us.

I needed more tools; I needed greater understanding. I found it through Peace in Schools, a Portland, Oregon nonprofit that brings Mindfulness Studies classes to Portland public high schools. I attended their summer three-day retreat for educators and their eight-week evening class, all focused on mindfulness for educators, both for ourselves and our work environments.

Mindfulness

My work with colleagues shifted to mindfulness and anxiety in the classroom and away from NVC. The workshops I offered for professional development changed so that I could help teachers with mindfulness in the stressful moments of teaching, showing them what student anxiety looks like and how to best work with students to alleviate it. Both are aligned much more with swaraj. We transform ourselves first and help students do the same.

I learned the need and use of a daily meditation practice, but more than that I saw that meditation could be used in any moment of life. In my workshops I teach belly breathing to activate the parasympathetic nervous system that can be done anywhere, any time. There is mindful walking, which any teacher (or student) can do as they go around a classroom or school. There are personal mantras that bring us back to center and the accessory things such as coloring meditation or bubble meditation (i.e., using adult coloring book pages or blowing bubbles while belly breathing).

For my own mental space and for my students' mental health, I now start class with five minutes of meditation with micro-mindfulness lessons about self-awareness, slowing down, and being in the *here and now*. The 2015 Ahimsa Institute inspired me to find a way to bring Gandhi's principles into my classroom and meditation became one path. I start on the second day of class by showing one short video on why we do it, followed by reading the class an article about a Harvard research study. The study declares that after eight weeks of mindfulness meditation participants' brains showed notable increase in grey matter and a less active amygdala or fear center of the brain. I do this so that the more science-oriented or skeptical students can see that meditation is not dogma or spiritual traditions but, instead, an evidence-supported life skill. Before we meditate, I show one last video on how to meditate, and then we start. I play a singing bowl to start the one-minute meditation and guide it myself with a simple breath awareness; to end the meditation I ding the singing bowl three times. Eventually we work up to five minutes of meditation. Sometimes I play instrumental meditation music from YouTube in the background; other times I find short guided meditations and play those. At the end of the week, the students get to do what they call "fun meditation," for which I've invented a buffet of choices: coloring pages, bubble blowing, Lego playing, Jenga pieces, Play-Doh, walking outside, gratitude note-making, and others. I poll students several times a year, and on average 92% report they want the meditation time to continue or increase, and only 4% or fewer want it to stop. I do tell students they are not required to participate and may opt-out by sitting quietly, reading, or sitting in the hall if they need to. This has been so successful that I now lead professional development workshops showing other teachers how to do something similar in their environments.

In 2017 I started co-teaching a Mindfulness and Yoga elective class wherein I could finally take all of these tools and concepts and hone them in one space, one curriculum: NVC, mindfulness, meditation, Eckhart Tolle, Jon Kabat-Zinn, and so much more. Students need this class in every school, and every community needs the shift that goes along with recognizing how important this is for students and teachers. The class has 60 students split into two groups of 30 who attend yoga for 40 minutes and mindfulness for 40 minutes. I have the incredible fortune to guide students to understand themselves, each other, and the world, to get that long-sought after space between stimulus and response. It's what we strive for in mindfulness. It's what we all wish we had more of in life. How can we live with our emotional experiences and not let that guide our interactions?

We learn presence. We learn patience. We learn self-love. We learn how to pause. We learn to breathe. We learn perspective. We learn here and now. We learn our conditioning. We learn our habits of being. We learn what serves us and what does not. We learn forgiveness. We learn how we want to show up in the world.

We learn mindfulness.

Conclusion

I believe Gandhi's nonviolent revolution, his *satyagraha*, is achievable and possible through personal swaraj. It happens every time we learn to pause and breathe instead of reacting, instead of saying the thing, doing the thing, thinking the thing that projects our emotional experience. It happens when we use mindfulness to transform our inner selves and, thus, remake the world around us. It happens every time we meditate in class, every time my students are coloring or blowing bubbles in the sun or walking in silence, every time we catch ourselves and make a different choice.

I didn't know what to say to Jeremiah when he told me about the Xanax, about the cutting. I didn't know what to do when the students had panic attacks in my classroom. I didn't know what to say to the administrators who spoke of "grade 13" and AP numbers while I was worried about students self-destructing. I have a better idea now.

It's clear that the high-stakes atmosphere is not going away as the decision-makers focus on data and numbers to tell the stories of "successful" schools. They must report to supervisors too. What is also clear, though, is how much we can do in our schools, in every classroom, starting with how we create the environments by how we create ourselves. I'm not sure how there can be space for both high-achievement and mental/emotional health foci, but giving both equal weight is a start. A math teacher can still give an exam, for example, but could also do a calm breathing exercise before the test starts. Maybe ninth graders don't have to take the PSAT and, instead, can have an introduction workshop to mindfulness.

A few years ago, I saw His Holiness the Dalai Lama speak, and he said when the Buddha first gave teachings thousands of years ago no one knew anything about science. Now that we do, he went on, the teaching of Buddhism needs to change to accommodate our new scientific understanding of the world. I see the same thing for modern education in the United States. We know students who take schedules like the one that started this chapter are more likely to graduate, go to college, and graduate with a degree. We know college degrees mean higher earnings. We also know students are experiencing incredibly high stress, anxiety, depression, self-harm, and self-doubt. While I'd like to call for a radical upheaval of the entire school system in the U.S., I'm more realistic and pragmatic. In the current paradigm of global competition, we must prepare young people for that world while also giving them the tools that embrace inner strength and calm abiding.

Sometimes we can make changes to the system from within. Gandhi removed himself and made bolder changes from the outside. As teachers we hold unique positions to promote the mental and emotional wellbeing of our students in ways that counter many other educational mandates and ideologies. A real education teaches students to intentionally choose who they want to be and how they can consciously respond to life moment to moment, what David Foster Wallace (2009) describes as "true freedom" (p. 73). Mindfulness helps students shake off the dust and cobwebs of projection and rumination, leaving space for the empathy soft-wired into the human brain to emerge. It's time we prioritized students learning ways of being that wake them up and develop consciousness awareness.

If students know their own inner wholeness and how to find that groundedness in any moment of life, they are closer to the ultimate independence of swaraj.

May we all breathe that true freedom.

References

Barseghian, T. (2013, September 12). Why teaching mindfulness benefits students' learning. Retrieved from http://www.kqed.org/mindshift/31291/why-teaching-mindfulness-benefits-students-learning.

Rogers, F. (2014). *The world according to Mr. Rogers: Important things to remember*. New York, NY: Hachette Books.

Wallace, D. F. (2009). *This is water: Some thoughts, delivered on a significant occasion, about living a compassionate life*. New York, NY: Little, Brown.

What is Swaraj? (n.d.). Retrieved May 28, 2019, from http://www.swaraj.org/whatisswaraj.htm.

Chapter 7

Art, Mindfulness, and Peacebuilding

A New Framework for Student Social, Emotional, and Creative Growth

By Elizabeth Benskin

In the spring of 2017, my colleagues and I in the Education Department at The Baltimore Museum of Art (BMA) were discussing a pattern that the Manager of School and Teacher Programs and the volunteer docents were noticing among students participating in Close Encounters, our multiple-visit program for Baltimore City Public School (BCPS) fourth-graders. The program consists of five sessions: a visit by the docent to the classroom for an orientation, three thematic tours in the galleries, and an art-making experience in the BMA Education Studio. One of the tours, "Moods and Feelings," was proving to be somewhat challenging, as students were frequently attributing a range of facial expressions to anger. In one artwork, A *Quick Nap* by Walter Henry Williams, a young black girl leans on a fire escape railing. Even though her face is hidden as she rests her head on her arm, students were confident that she was angry.

The conversation immediately made me think of work I had read about children who had experienced trauma; they consistently saw a range of facial expressions (some of which did express anger) as angry (Van der Kolk, 2014). In these circumstances, students are primed for conflict because they read many facial expressions as anger and, thus, as a threat. I had been thinking for some time about the emotional lives of the audiences with whom I worked, including teachers and young visitors. With youth, statistics from the Baltimore City Health Department show that approximately 30% of students have experienced significant trauma according to the Adverse Childhood Experience (ACE) scale (Wen, 2017). Assuming that many

C. A. Bracho and D. Dodson (eds.), Teachers Teaching Nonviolence, 103–114.

children come to the museum with significant hidden trauma, we asked ourselves, "What could we offer that would allow students the time, space, and resources to authentically connect on an emotional level with themselves, their classmates, the artwork in the galleries, and their own creative capacities?"

The Path to the Experiment

Traditionally, art museums have not focused on the emotional needs of their visitors, save for assuming that interested individuals will have positive personal responses to the aesthetic experiences evoked by viewing works of art. Having worked in the field of museum education for over eighteen years, I am happy to say that this attitude has changed considerably. Museums are recognizing their potential as sites of wellbeing and community connection. However, this is much more prevalent among programs for adults than for Pre-K-12 programs.

Contemplating the question that came out of the discussion with my colleagues, I reflected on the many avenues that I thought might prove worthwhile to explore in addressing this complex issue. This seemed integrally linked to a nonviolence course I took at the 2007 Summer Institute at California State Polytechnic University Pomona's Ahimsa Center called "Gandhi, Nonviolence and 21st Century Curriculum." This immersion in the work of Mohandas K. Gandhi and his approach to nonviolence fulfilled an interest I'd had since junior high school, when a teacher introduced me to Gandhi's work through Richard Attenborough's film *Gandhi*. (I now recognize that Attenborough took significant artistic license in his telling of Gandhi's life story, but as an 8th-grade student I was transfixed by the depiction of personal transformation and moral force. In fact, we watched the film at a special evening school session, and, relatively early in the film, I began experiencing fever and chills. Even though I was coming down with a bad case of the flu, I was so engrossed that I sat shivering through the movie until it was over.)

This early introduction to the religious traditions of Asia led me to study East Asian religions as an undergraduate and the history of Chinese Buddhist art as a graduate student. While working at a museum of Asian art, I was presented with the opportunity to participate in the Ahimsa Center's 2007 Institute, where I researched how the Buddhist and Jain artworks in the museum's collection might be used to explore the topic of nonviolence. Although the programs I envisioned never came to fruition, developing an in-depth understanding of the concepts of *ahimsa* (nonviolence) and *satyagraha* (soul force) would prove to be central to the development and content of the BMA program.

Now at the BMA, I began to experiment using meditative techniques in teacher programs based on my own growing knowledge and practice of meditation. A concept began to emerge: an intensive program that combined investigation of art with mindful practices for students at an age when they were becoming invested in questions of identity and social justice. Fifth grade seemed the ideal time—a stage where students are still open and curious but can also grapple with complex concepts. Students would learn about the workings of their own brains, so they had the tools to recognize the role their nervous systems were playing in feelings of anger and hostility and to be able to deescalate negative interpersonal interactions. As someone highly influenced by the groundbreaking work of the Reggio Emilia early childhood education methodology, I wanted to foster a sense of respect for every individual student and to create a safe space for practicing leadership, engaging in authentic emotional discussions, and demonstrating creative capacities. In this program, adults and students alike would be considered both teachers and learners.

Exploring artworks and making original works of art would be central to the program. Students would look closely at and discuss art in the galleries—experiences that complement the mindful aspects of the program as they invite the student to slow down, examine carefully, and craft meaningful responses to the work. These in-gallery conversations are also important because individuals can diverge in their opinion about an artwork, but they result in productive tension rather than hostile disagreement. Finally, making art would be key—not only to allow students to explore questions of identity, peace, and violence through their own unique lens but also because, as in the in-gallery discussions of artworks, it supports the mindfulness framework of the program. In fact, making art reduces levels of the stress hormone cortisol (The International Child Art Foundation, 2017).

The program that I was beginning to envision was highly ambitious—it would bring together art history, studio art, conflict resolution, neuroscience, and contemplative practices to create a new framework for student social, emotional, and creative development. I called the program Art, Mindfulness, and Peacebuilding (AMP). I realized that the complexity of the work and the success of the program would require an entire community of experts. Though hopeful of finding the right people, I did not anticipate the powerful results of their generous collaboration.

Building the Community

Once I felt that I had a grasp on the concept for the experience, I turned to the question of which partners would best support the outcomes that we hoped to achieve with the students. Working in art museums, I have found that it has always been critical to develop collaborative relationships with experts outside of my own field to create the kinds of experiences that transcend traditional art historical instruction. Although I was unaware of it at the time, I was fortunate to be within a few miles of two essential partners—Holistic Life Foundation (HLF) and Donna Basik at the Maryland Institute College of Art (MICA). A Boston-based third partner, Beyond Conflict, was serendipitously working at the time with BMA leadership on strengthening the museum's role as a center of civic dialogue.

The Peacebuilders

Beyond Conflict is an internationally recognized organization that facilitates peacebuilding efforts and research worldwide. Its extensive work in conflict resolution includes supporting the peace negotiations in Northern Ireland, and it was instrumental in the development of the "truth commission" concept in South Africa as it transitioned from apartheid. Having studied the Truth and Reconciliation Commission at the 2007 Ahimsa Institute, I was excited to connect with the founder, Tim Phillips, and his colleagues to see how I could incorporate their knowledge of peacebuilding into the program.

A form of powerful storytelling is one of the models used by Beyond Conflict in its work. The Shared Experience model is based upon the understanding that people can change, and authentic stories of change can help them do so. In their experience working with war-torn countries, they found that the leaders of those countries could not envision what peace might look like, which allowed violent conflict to continue. When Beyond Conflict brought in leaders of other countries who had been able to establish peace to tell their stories, eventually those leaders of countries experiencing violent conflict began to see that peace was possible. The stories of conflict resolution began to spark hope and, ultimately, a willingness to engage in the difficult task of building peace in their own context.

More recently, Beyond Conflict has brought together a team of pioneering neuroscientists who are researching the neuroscience of conflict and applying the findings to address violence, dehumanization, and social exclusion. Tim generously talked with me on multiple occasions about my ideas and the ways that the work of Beyond Conflict could support tangible positive change for the students. Through these discussions, I felt confident that using the Shared Experience model, and some key information about the neuroscience of conflict, would be invaluable to the program.

The Yogis

Located a short walk from the BMA is the Holistic Life Foundation, a Baltimore-based organization that uses contemplative practices such as yoga and meditation to improve the quality of life for children and adults in the Baltimore region and beyond. Two of the cofounders, Ali and Atman Smith, are brothers from West Baltimore who grew up practicing meditation and rediscovered its many benefits as adults. They decided to share their knowledge and have since worked with a wide range of adults and children—they are frequently in demand for conferences and retreats, such as those at the Omega Institute. The programs they had already successfully enacted in BCPS were proven to reduce suspensions and conflict.

As I looked for partners to lead the yoga and meditation experience, I was immediately impressed with their model. After meeting with Ali, I was convinced that they were the right source for the yogis we wanted for the program—local yoga practitioners (most of them yogis of color) with experience in and understanding of Baltimore's citizens, a demonstrated philosophy of working effectively with children from across the socioeconomic spectrum of Baltimore, and a palpable respect for the youth they teach.

Ali identified Akewi Karamba as the best fit for the program. A Baltimore native and poet, he is professionally experienced in working with individuals who have sustained traumatic injuries such as gunshot wounds—Akewi would play a pivotal role in the success of AMP. He would not only become the yoga and meditation instructor but would provide a deeply personal narrative that touched on the key themes of the program.

As a child, Akewi was frequently bullied; when he reached junior high school, he joined a gang for a sense of safety and to bolster others' respect for him. He skipped school on a regular basis, spent time drinking alcohol, and began selling and using drugs. After a confrontation with someone in his neighborhood, he quickly acquired a gun and shot the individual. Akewi was tried and convicted of attempted murder and, at age sixteen, found himself incarcerated. While in prison, he began to take on opportunities to lead, including tutoring other incarcerated individuals so that they could earn their GEDs and taking the lead on a step (dance) team at the prison. When he was released seven years later, he became a yoga and meditation instructor for Holistic Life Foundation, sharing his knowledge and supporting students across Baltimore City.

Clearly, Akewi's journey from low self-esteem and violence to peace and leadership would be ideal to share with students, along the lines of the Shared Experience model of Beyond Conflict, but with an emphasis on preventing violence. As we began to talk about the program, I asked him candidly whether he felt comfortable sharing his story with the students. Without hesitation, he agreed. His openness and generosity in sharing this deeply personal and painful experience would prove to be a transformative element in the program.

The Artists

I consider Donna Basik, a professor in the Master of Arts in Teaching (MAT) program at MICA, one of the midwives of the program. I was introduced to Donna by a mutual friend in the Baltimore education community who had previously been Director of MICA's MAT program. Knowing my interest in mindfulness and its applications in education, she connected me to Donna, who had been integrating contemplative practices into her teaching for quite a while.

We immediately recognized that our common interests in mindful practices could be the basis for a fruitful collaboration. At the time we connected, Donna was just about to begin a year-long sabbatical, and she offered to work on the program as part of her own exploration of how mindfulness and related practices can be used effectively in Pre-K-12 teaching in visual art.

Seeing this also as a mentoring opportunity, Donna identified current MAT students who could come and support the program throughout the pilot year. Key among the people she invited was David Ramos, a graduate of MICA's MAT program, who had worked as an art teacher in a Baltimore City public school, but whose experience had been so disappointing that he had lost interest in teaching altogether. David began to attend, observe, and then lead activities in the program. Initially very quiet and reserved—even politely skeptical about being asked to teach again—he soon jumped in with enthusiasm, working with Donna and me to co-develop experiences for the students.

The Pilot

The pilot program began in the fall of 2017 with a clear framework:
- The Shared Experience methodology of Beyond Conflict: that people can change, and that stories of transformation can help them do so

- The basic neuroscience of peace and conflict, inclusion and exclusion
- Creative and contemplative exploration of artworks from the BMA that communicate important ideas and personal experiences about peace and conflict
- Individual and collaborative art-making experiences focused on ideas of peace and conflict
- Mindful movement, breathwork, and mindfulness meditation

With our inaugural class in the fall, we found that, despite having planned to use specific artworks and activities, it was productive to leave space for adjusting and adapting so that we could be responsive to student interests and needs. Following each session, we would gather to debrief and then begin crafting the experience for the next session. In the six program sessions, students

- Engaged in yoga, breathwork, and meditation—sometimes leading the experience when they felt comfortable
- Listened and responded to Akewi's story of the violent experiences he had as a young person and how he made choices that led him to a life dedicated to service and nonviolence
- Learned about the amygdala and its function as the fight or flight center
- Explored a variety of artworks in the BMA galleries
- Created a range of artworks to explore ideas of peace and conflict, including paper devices that could be used to "pop the bubbles" that humans make to avoid meaningful connections to people unlike themselves
- Participated in other activities such as poetry writing, sketching, and creating an illustrated spiral that reflected a journey from violence to peace in response to collage works (featuring spiral shapes) by the artist Al Loving (1935–2005)

The Outcomes

Pre- and post-assessments were designed for students to measure the following: subjective sense of belonging, levels of empathic concern, and emotional regulation. Teachers were also provided pre- and post-assessments that reflected the above-mentioned outcomes as well as an opportunity to provide information on any changes in academic achievement. For students, the challenge was to design an evaluation instrument that would capture known indicators of the three key desired outcomes. Thus, questions included adaptations of assessments designed to gauge these domains in children, specifically.

The Class of Fall 2017

Each class in the AMP program has reported unique outcomes. The students in the class of fall 2017 showed the greatest self-reported growth in levels of empathic concern. They shared a range of responses that reflected what they considered to be the most impactful aspects of the program, including "yoga is very good for calming down," and "art can show you something important about yourself." They also referenced Akewi's story and the ability to regulate their own emotions; one student's response was "How to stop my anger."

In the final session, when students were asked how they could each be peacebuilders in their classroom and communities, they discussed caring for each other, finding ways not to escalate conflict, ignoring negativity, avoiding conflict, working on their own anger, avoiding outbursts, and noticing if a classmate was isolated and actively inviting the classmate into their group. The classroom teacher cited greater class cohesion and connection as the most notable shift amongst the students, but also supported the students' assertion that they were demonstrating more empathy towards each other: "One student began questioning another student about being hairy. Another student overheard the question and immediately stopped it by saying, 'Don't say things you wouldn't want someone asking you.' I feel like before, that kid would not have stood up for the other student."

The Class of Spring 2018

The spring class had a significant difference from the fall class—Akewi was not available to teach, so students were not exposed to his story. This would prove to have a notable effect on the outcomes, which emerged when the same teacher brought the fall 2018 class for the program and the results were significantly more aligned with the desired outcomes. In their evaluations, the spring 2018 class reported the most growth in their sense of belonging amongst their classmates.

In the final reflections, when asked how they could be peacebuilders in their classrooms and communities, students mentioned listening to each other and being their authentic selves in the wider world. This seems to have been supported by one of the class teachers who perceived greater class cohesion.

One of the most surprising outcomes from the pilot was the students' expanded sense of the possibilities of art. One student said, "I learned that art can be any—and everything. I learned that art is going to be always different." While I had anticipated that they would come to feel more confident both investigating original artworks and making art of their own, I had not realized how much their ideas of art and artmaking would broaden. In addition, David Ramos, who had lost interest in teaching, expressed a newfound satisfaction in working with students again.

The Second Year

In anticipation of the second year of the program, Donna, David, and I reflected on successes, challenges, and necessary shifts. With Donna returning to classes in the fall, I hired David as the lead teacher for the program. Donna and I also agreed that we would work together so that four MICA MAT students could participate in AMP to fulfill one of their internship requirements. This included an extension of the spring program with three in-classroom sessions in which the interns would lead lesson plans they had developed. Finally, I revised the student pre- and post-evaluations so that they were simpler and shorter, and I made sure that they had images next to each question to illustrate the concept.

The Class of Fall 2018

In the fall, we began with a class taught by the teacher who had been in the lead in the spring of our pilot program. This was the first time that these students had worked with Akewi; reflecting on the outcomes for the fall class, I believe it made a palpable impact on the student experience. Students' responses to the evaluations revealed more introspection ("I learned that I could be myself no matter what") and a sharpened focus on the neuroscience and mindfulness learning ("I learned how to do yoga and I learned about the amygdala").

The teacher reported significant gains in emotional control, empathy, class connection, and cohesion—including demonstrated inclusion of students who were previously excluded and increased academic performance. "I have one student who's always been excluded, and I've witnessed him having more friends in class and working with other students on projects as well," she noted. She also recounted an occasion when one of the participating students was punched in the face, hard enough that the student began bleeding. Given the teacher's experience with this student, she fully expected to see him punch back. Instead, he took a moment, approached the teacher, and asked if he could go to the bathroom to clean his face.

The Class of Spring 2019

The spring class of the second year was a new experience for us as it was a self-contained special education class of 11 students. Not having worked on long-term experiences for students with special needs, I reached out to the teacher to find out more about the class and how we could offer the best possible experience for them. The student academic levels were approximately two to three grade levels behind their peers.

The student feedback indicated a slight uptick in empathy. In the post-assessment and follow-up conversations, the teacher expressed that while she did not observe that the students met the desired outcomes related to empathy, emotional regulation, and sense of belonging, there were some notable positive outcomes. She referenced how much the students liked and trusted the adult facilitators of the program, and how excited they were when program sessions approached. She also commented on how surprised she was at the many things that students remembered from the program when asked to reflect on their learning.

The teacher and I discussed some of the noteworthy moments of the program. For me, one of the most profound demonstrations of student engagement came in one of the classroom sessions when students shared their thoughts after the art-making component. Students had looked at and talked about a mosaic from fifth-century Antioch (in present-day Turkey) depicting a lion and an ox facing each other, separated by a tree with the Greek word for "friendship" written on it. The students and I had a conversation about what a lion might typically do in the presence of an ox (attack and eat it) and how the mosaic was conveying the message that even "natural" enemies can overcome differences and build connections.

The art-making assignment required each student to choose an animal he or she would like to be if they could be an animal, find a partner, and then collaboratively make a drawing showing how the two animals could come together in a positive way. One student (I will use his first initial, D.) was in a three-person group with a classmate and the teacher. He had previously resisted coming to the program because he was extremely uncomfortable with new people and environments. When each pair/group presented their drawing and their stories, D.'s group talked about what they had represented in the picture, a lone tree with three animals around it. The story was that the tree was the last of what used to be a forest of trees that granted wishes. Over time, people had come and taken the other trees for themselves. When the animals approached the tree, they made wishes for themselves—for instance, the squirrel wished for some nuts. But the animals were aware that people were approaching and felt they needed to protect the tree. At this point in the story, the teacher pointed out that D. had come up with the conclusion. The animals decided that, rather than saying "no" to the people who had come for the wishing tree, they would let the people take some of the acorns from the last tree and give them out so they could plant their own trees and the last tree could remain. When I heard this, tears sprang to my eyes. This was a win-win solution that few adults could conceive. Yet D. had found a positive path forward for animals and humans alike.

Next Steps

Under ideal circumstances, I would look to expand the program for students. However, that is not currently possible due to a challenge well-known to museum educators—lack of space. Given that limitation, the number of students participating in the program will remain the same.

To disseminate the program, I began developing a written curriculum at the Ahimsa Center Seminar called "Leading Nonviolence Change Projects." Time at the seminar was particularly helpful in incorporating the stories of peacebuilding exemplars such as Martin Luther King, Jr. and Malala Yousafzai. The curriculum will be tested with teachers in the 2019–2020 school year.

In the summer of 2019, I also worked with David and Akewi on a week-long AMP institute for teachers. This institute largely paralleled the student AMP format but addressed the intersection of teacher well-being and student wholeness and success. By centering teacher social-emotional needs, I hope we can begin to change the paradigm of professional development for Pre-K-12 educators by demonstrating that these needs are not outside of—but rather at the heart of—effective teacher training.

Final Reflections

When I embarked on this project, I had no idea whether others would be interested in working with me on this initiative and whether we would meet any of the desired outcomes. What I discovered was that not only was the program effective for the young people involved, but also the process had enabled me to bring together a community of compassionate, giving, and committed individuals working together to create a program that is most definitely greater than the sum of its parts. It also reinforced for me the importance of my own practice of *satyagraha* as I persisted in bringing together this unorthodox program for an art museum. When I speak of AMP to anyone in education now, the first response is "Tell me more!" The next is usually "How can I be involved?"

References

The International Child Art Foundation. (2017, July–September). A safe space to be a kid: Heart—Save the children. *Child Art*, pp. 8–9.

Van der Kolk, B. (2014). *The body keeps the score: Brain, mind, and body in the healing of trauma.* New York, NY: Penguin Books.

Wen, L. (2017). State of Health in Baltimore [White paper]. Retrieved June 15, 2019, from https://health.baltimorecity.gov/state-health-baltimore-winter-2016/state-health-baltimore-white-paper-2017

Chapter 8

Mindfulness

Connections to Social-Emotional Well-Being and a Compassionate Global Citizenry

By Peggy Sia

The Dalai Lama believes that the education of the heart is just as vital as the education of the mind. Despite the demand for rigor, current events suggest that we need more than academics for the well-being of individuals. To ignore such an important component is a detriment to humanity. Schools across the country have come to realize the need for social-emotional curriculum, which was adopted in my school district.

In recent years, the global rise in nationalism has surfaced unapologetically. This social climate stunts creative growth and threatens the existence of all inhabitants of the earth. In a time where social media can claim space rapidly, people connect to each other and to ideas across the planet. It is essential for this human-to-human connection to bridge rather than divide. Because of this great dilemma, social-emotional education and mindful practices must now be an integral part of the school day.

As a public-school teacher, in this chapter I will present how opportunities to experience mindful moments and to provide skills for social-emotional development lead to increased self-awareness. I will also illustrate concrete methods of articulating thoughts through proactive dialogue. Explicit teaching of social-emotional curriculum proves rewarding, and the effects are notable within a school year, if not earlier. The participants for this research consisted of fourth-grade students in a self-contained classroom in a public school in Los Angeles County. The "Most

C. A. Bracho and D. Dodson (eds.), Teachers Teaching Nonviolence, 115–125.

Significant Change" (MSC) Technique was the methodology used to gather authentic assessments of the effectiveness of social-emotional education and mindfulness training.

Some may call what we do in our classroom community "non-cognitive skills" building; others may label it as "soft skills" curriculum. No matter the term, most experts believe that it is essential that teaching skills aim towards a cultivation of good character. Even as far back as 1788, Noah Webster stated, "'The virtues of men are of more consequence to society than their abilities; and for this reason, the heart should be cultivated with more assiduity than the head'" (as cited in Kamenetz, 2017). During the Ahimsa Center Conference on Care, Compassion, and Mindfulness, Dr. James Doty (2014) noted that scientists have measured the fact that compassion and cooperation "will lead to long term survival of species. It is the survival of the most sympathetic." Accordingly, science will give voice to mindfulness, but it is our own individual experiences that will be as the foundation for a better world.

As an educator of young (not small) minds, how did I come to this place of mindfulness and its implications on positive social-emotional well-being and global citizens? It began with my own unexpected encounter with Mahatma Gandhi at the Ahimsa Institute at Cal Poly. Gandhi is considered the father of nonviolence because of his capability to propel *ahimsa* as a weapon against injustice. Through his examples, I experienced a meta-awareness. Because of my work and participation with the Ahimsa Institute, I discovered I could harness some of my natural abilities, such as empathy and introspection, in a more focused and helpful manner. Though I have been practicing mindfulness for many years, I still have a long journey; however, because of this practice, in the classroom my personal experience helps guide students to their own experiences with mindfulness.

The Purpose of Mindfulness

What is mindfulness? Some of my students weigh in on that question. Eva states, "Mindfulness is about stillness and to breathe." Experiencing troubles as a young child, she has learned to carry all the heaviness that comes with instability early in life. Eva has tremendous difficulty relating positively to peers and is not socially accepted by them. Although our year together has seen its ups and downs, she has often led the mindfulness sessions in our classroom community, and she has also begun to participate in self-reflection to improve herself. Eva credits her mindfulness practice with helping her to gain control of thoughts and actions: "Mindfulness is everything to me. I would lose my mind. I get aggressive with people and say things to people I regret [later]." Similarly, in the *Bhagavad Gita* (Gandhi's "spiritual reference book"), Krishna tells Arjuna, "'When the mind is still…the True Self begins to reveal its nature'" (as cited in Cope, 2014).

Some may feel uncomfortable incorporating mindfulness techniques in the school setting. However, I have come to realize that the practice is easier when I am acknowledging the truth within me. In my call to teach, I see that the pebble I aim to cast will initiate ripples of self-knowing from my students. This starting place is how they will know to unfold their own paths. It is not uncommon to hear a teacher ask students, "What do you want to be when you grow up?" That simple question can evoke various responses. With students who practice mindfulness regularly, this question can become a present and future cosmic collision. Mindfulness in our classroom aims to gently remind us to engage in our purest selves through awareness, possibly revealing a path. We then make plans to get to where we decide we want to go. Our plans begin in the present: in the classroom. Suddenly, questions about why we must engage in the sometimes-laborious tasks of academics become clearer and more encouraging. Likewise, providing students with techniques for mindfulness in tandem with our school's social-emotional curriculum empowers them because I attempt to open the curtains to a world where they make choices that navigate them toward their best selves.

Resources to Support

When we use the district social-emotional curriculum, there are opportunities for students to watch scenarios of a circumstance they may encounter. Within that lesson, we focus on a skill based on the scenario. For example, "listening with attention" is a skill that I teach to promote positive relationships. Although the curriculum primarily emphasizes peer-to-peer interaction, we always remind each other that all relationships are valuable enough to nurture and to cultivate. This could include family, other citizens, and the natural resources of our earth.

The curriculum sets the stage for our week, or weeks, with communal vocabulary and prior knowledge. As we experience the skill(s), additional tools are infused into our school day to serve as reinforcement and as an opportunity to reset and rejuvenate. Our focused mindful practices occur after break, which means that we practice twice a day. A fellow Ahimsaka, who works as the Director of Mindfulness at Legacy Early College, offered suggestions to enhance our sessions with gradual increase of time and use of instruments such as singing bowls. Having the opportunity to discuss our classroom's practice reminded me to always pay attention to the beating heart of the classroom and to allow it to guide our flow. Practicing and living the mantra of "being present" brings forth integrity and reward.

Since our mindfulness sessions are based on the ebb and flow of our class, I introduce various techniques. Initially, sessions are guided by my voice and an online platform, *Go Noodle*. When my voice leads the sessions, my own breath guides the rhythm of our practice for that moment. Little by little, other students volunteer to guide our practice with breath and sometimes with gentle body-flow exercises. In addition, *Go Noodle* provides kinesthetic opportunities for the body and mind to unwind; during these sessions, I use the channels pertaining to "Flow," character building, and yoga. In that sense, our mindfulness sessions are not what some may deem traditional, but they have benefited us. Music and silence are also incorporated into our practice. My goal is to create a gentle, focused flow as I train myself with students to create harmony and balance. I have discovered that I can accomplish this vision through the examples of Gandhi's life and teachings.

Gandhi in my Classroom

There may be hesitancy to bring Gandhi into an elementary school classroom due to possible factors such as the need to address standards, the heavy weight of history that could be too much for students so young, etc. I would argue, however, that inviting Gandhi inside my classroom has only empowered me and unfolded a path of exploration, thereby enabling me to have a more positive impact. Gandhi related to others in the most honest way, even those who were at odds with him. Near the eve of his now famous Salt March, which was a nonviolent protest against the British tax on the making and selling of salt, he wrote an amiable letter to the viceroy of Britain detailing reasons for India's need for independence. One could imagine the battles of emotions swirling within, passionate and heated, when trying to overcome another's systematic obstruction of the cause. However, it was not in Gandhi's nature to succumb to the more violent dispositions of human beings. Instead, he appealed to their light. His actions were pure truth to me, leaving me brimming with faith and love for a better world. Fischer (1982) illustrates Gandhi's use of truth in his civil disobedience: "'Satyagraha': *satya* means truth, the equivalent of love, and both are attributes of the soul; *agraha* is firmness or force" (p. 35). In my classroom, I bring Gandhi along by using one of his most basic tenets— *satyagraha*. Thus, in our mindfulness sessions, I endeavor to make satyagraha the center of my work, emanating a hopeful love force to my students, imagining its rippling effects.

One of my own tenets is that there is goodness in everyone. When one is at odds with others or even the self, it does not always have to result in the end of a relationship, in violence, or in any other negative outcome. I believe these negative results, in many regards, derive from a temporary loss of direction within ourselves. Perhaps I oversimplify the complexities of life or ignore other important variables, but this is the truth that I see, which I have chosen to use to bring light to anyone who might want to receive it. It is not always easy, even in myself; sometimes the darkness temporarily gains control. Thankfully, Gandhi and other nonviolent exemplars have made such an indelible mark upon me that I return to that "space," as one of my students keenly noted, during my inquiry on mindfulness and its influence.

The student who termed mindfulness as a "space" is diagnosed with anxiety and a learning disability. Before she was in my class, I had already learned about her. Many years before, I observed this little girl in tears every morning before school. Her face was visibly distraught, and her crying was uncontrollable. I had heard that she was escorted to the office daily. When I discovered that she was on my roster, I prepared myself so that I could be at my best to serve her from day one. She confessed, "As I watched TV one day, I got really anxious, and talked to my mom and realized mindfulness helped me to be more aware of my thoughts." This youngster felt that mindfulness sessions gave her both the awareness to identify when her anxiety was looming and the tools to control it before it became too overwhelming: "I used to get anxious. I would cry and let it happen, but now I just do some mindful silence, [and] I don't get anxious." I cannot deny that, as an educator and a mother, one of my greatest desires is to know that someone has been able to live the most purposeful and meaningful life, which can only be defined by that individual. Nonetheless, I feel I am called to assist in any manner that can help others to achieve and navigate their own paths with the utmost vibrancy of a good life.

Mindfulness has the potential to make a difference in creating this good life. For example, another student explains, "Every time I go home I'm excited, I get to do whatever I want. The first thing I do is do some mindful silence so I don't destroy things. I do deep breaths." He has had difficulty in school due to his behavior. Some challenges included being argumentative, showing disrespect toward peers/adults, and acting uncooperative. This youngster's mother was aware of this, alerting me with both apology and helplessness. Although working with him had its share of ups and downs, I loved his presence in our classroom community. Like Gandhi, I practice to always appeal to the goodness in individuals. In doing so, I can form positive relationships and bonds that enrich my daily experiences with my students and, hopefully, vice-versa. He became more reflective on his behavior, soon taking responsibility for the choices he made. As a result, he experienced many more positive days in class. Also, there was tremendous home support to create continuity and consistency so that this young person could work on becoming his best self. At the end of the year, he summarized what he felt mindfulness is for him: "Mindfulness is something that helps you to calm down and not break stuff, be loud, and run around." As a student with high energy, he constantly yearned to be able to do what he wanted to when he wanted to. During this school year, this student recognized the importance of balancing his needs with respect and accountability. In our discussions, he used the vocabulary that we learned through both the social-emotional curriculum and our mindfulness sessions.

Mindfulness: A Journey of One

My experience with mindfulness began with the Ahimsa Institute, which put at my eager fingertips a variety of texts dedicated to nonviolent actions. A cherished book, *The Buddha and the Terrorist*, a parable about forgiveness, resonates deeply with me. Angulimala, an untouchable turned terrorist, torments his village committing horrendous acts of violence. An encounter with Buddha transforms him, and he abandons the violent life he led to follow Buddha. In the process of his transformation, he accepts the consequences of his actions when willingly confronting the angry citizens he had pained and harmed. Angulimala states, "To bring freedom to others, we have to be free within ourselves. So here I am. I await your judgement" (Kumar, 2006, p. 94). Students such as the one above long to move freely and to be unconfined and unconstrained. However, the question in our classroom community is always raised: How can I practice my freedom without impinging on another's freedom? Is it possible for everyone to live freely? These are some of the conversations that surface when students learn how to interact and relate to others. Inside this conversation, I allow my belief in the goodness of others to guide our conversation to a vision of a world where individuals actively live peacefully with all beings living and nonliving. Dr. Doty (2014) speaks of the mindfulness journey as an "inward journey of one." As my students engage in mindfulness, recognizing themselves without judgment, it is my hope that they achieve a sense of peace and acceptance of who they are in that moment.

During our social-emotional period, we discuss feelings such as excitement, sadness, anger, and frustration. We discuss the intricacies and complexities of human feelings, and I follow with the challenge of asking them to evaluate which emotions are positive and which are negative. In the end, our conversation rests on the idea that all emotions are neither "good" or "bad" necessarily. For example, a typically considered "good" emotion such as happiness could very easily lead one to react in an impulsive way—

shouting into neighboring ears. While one may have the freedom to express elation, respecting the space of others is something that must be kept in mind. Similarly, anger, typically considered a negative emotion, is a natural response to an event that one may not welcome. Thus, we talk about the skills and tools we can use to respond to situations, where response and action based on what one feels becomes the matter of good and bad. During our mindfulness session, there is freedom to practice for that moment in time with the understanding that personal choice does not interfere with the practice of others. Focusing on our own emotions and plunging deeper into their attributes can lead to an empathetic understanding of how others feel. Doty (2014), speaking of the inward journey that becomes a "transformation" of character, argues that the goal of mindfulness is not just to linger internally. The ultimate purpose is to take the inward journey into an "outward journey" in the form of service to others. That is when true transcendence can occur. The mindful path could lead to the cultivation of compassion for others. Doty ends his presentation with this idea about transcendence: "At the end of your journey, you can say you had purpose and that your journey is not that I made 1+1=2, but 1+1=infinity."

Becoming a Global Citizen

This idea of service to others and global citizenry is not a new one. The old South African belief of Ubuntu was exemplified during the Peace and Reconciliation hearings championed by Nelson Mandela. The Truth and Reconciliation Committee (TRC) possessed the daunting task of evaluating individual cases of culprits applying for amnesty for committing crimes of the most violent nature against others. The period of Apartheid destroyed communities, and its continual throbbing of anguish and devastation was ever present even in its aftermath. The TRC attempted to bring about accountability for the transgressions and to heal a deeply hurt community. Wanting to bring about a transformation in that spirit of community and common humanity, the TRC looked to a form of justice that restored humanity and its bonds to each other. Perpetrators admitted to their crimes during Apartheid in the hopes of being given amnesty, and victims of the atrocities were given a space to speak. With more than 7,000 applications for amnesty, the TRC listened to each story for a period of two years; in the end it granted amnesty to just under 1,000 applicants (Kendall, 2010). Although wounds so complicated and deep could not be repaired in just those two years of hearings, it was the beginning of healing with government support to help people move forward as best they could. The philosophy of

Ubuntu is "I am because we are." A reminder that we are all connected, and that one personal act can ripple across the human continuum, this is like Gandhi's idea of the Oceanic Circle. Comparatively, in developmental psychology, Urie Bronfenbrenner's Ecological Systems Theory shows how different environments create a child's experiences and character. Moreover, the ecosystems themselves, move, change, and influence each other, thereby producing a complex model of interactions and effects of a cyclical nature.

All in all, it is the connection between us that betters us. Our common humanity should not and cannot get lost in the sometimes disarray of life. In our classroom community, I like to extend the Ubuntu philosophy as "I am because we are, we are because I am." Each personal action affects another, and that is the reason for one to act with kindness and compassion with intention and purpose throughout the day. By examining the Truth and Reconciliation hearings, I listened to both the unimaginable stories of horror and the steady climb towards forgiveness, redemption, and healing. I cannot help but see flecks of humanity's light shining through that darkness. I am drawn to that light and inspired by it. It is this perseverance to overcome and to climb towards the summit that brings about the strength to create a world of great stories and triumphs.

Mindful Literature

In my effort to cultivate such connection of oneness in the classroom community, I use books as staples for our day. One book, How Full is Your Bucket for Kids, provides a springboard for a conversation about creating a supportive and positive community, and about how individual acts can affect others. Educating the mind and heart can hasten the transformation of individuals who intentionally connect to the knowledge of empathy and flow through a metamorphosis. How Full is Your Bucket for Kids reminds students that it is not necessary to charge into a burning building to save lives or to renounce the pleasures of the world in order to be considered great. Small and simple acts of kindness can make an impact surely just as great to those around us. Often, we underestimate the daily act that comes naturally, giving it very little value. However, my students remind each other every day that a smile, or a positive little note dropped in someone's mailbox, could bring about an immense turn-around for someone who may be experiencing a difficult day. In short, we emphasize that being a hero is in each of us, exemplified not by how loud or grandiose we can be, but how much heart we put into even the most inconsequential act for others and even ourselves. When a student is hesitant during a class discussion, and another student cheers with encouragement or applause, this act of kindness is truly the microcosm of satyagraha. My vision is that, in their own time, my students will find their niche and use the inner peace they have cultivated to bring about a positive change in the greater society.

Connection and Technology

While my students and I focus on the work inside ourselves, we simultaneously take our power outward to help others. Mark Twain once said, "Travel is fatal to prejudice, bigotry, and narrow-mindedness, and many of our people need it sorely on these accounts. Broad, wholesome, charitable views of men and things cannot be acquired by vegetating in one little corner of the earth all one's lifetime." The 21st century has enabled us to collaborate with others beyond the four walls of our classroom and to befriend others around the world. With student council and administrator/community support, students can take their kindness in action toward the larger society through campaigns such as anti-bullying and raising money in support of cancer research. Students of any age possess big hearts and want to help others. Providing guidance and illuminating social issues allows students to utilize knowledge and skills in the capacity of service.

For example, using UNESCO's 17 sustainable goals is one way a student can synthesize prior knowledge and needs to help improve surroundings. One example is the access to clean water and ocean ecosystems and sustainability. In this unit, older students worked with younger students with the sustainable goals as objectives. They had opportunities to explore how they could raise awareness using their interests and talents while guiding younger students towards these same goals. Nipun Mehta (2014), founder of ServiceSpace.org, states his basic tenets as: Ask Nothing; Gift Ties; Look for Service Opportunities; Inner Transformation. Mehta believes deeply that finding one's true authentic self involves reaching outward towards those who are in need. Moreover, in giving of ourselves in the service of others, we contribute to what Mehta calls a "gift ecology," fulfilled by deep ties with one another through mutual acts of generosity.

Such student activism does not have to remain only in textbooks and classrooms. Providing students access to others via online platforms illuminates how technology can be used for both entertainment and for meaningful research. Moreover, we can now create relationships much easier than in the past. During the past year, I connected my students to an atmospheric scientist via Google Hangouts, where they engaged in a conversation about atmosphere, pollution, and sustainability. The questions they asked during this session reflected what was most urgent in their minds, and their curiosity to want to understand the problems we face currently guided them toward a path for action. Creating a space for students to collaborate with peers is essential; furthermore, being able to create a space where students can collaborate with peers from another country yields benefits beyond standards and academics. Many platforms are available for classrooms to connect with others online. Empatico, UNESCO's DICE (Digital Intercultural Exchange) Learning Labs, and grassroots organizations such as Education for Global Peace's Classroom Connect are ideal for forming partnerships and collaborative projects with students across the globe. On one occasion, my students collaborated with students in Pakistan, where we began with greetings and introductions. As a teacher, I had an opportunity to work with a couple of teachers in Pakistan about their curriculum alignment, the accessibility of resources, etc. Students shared projects focused on Earth Day, and they eagerly awaited the next opportunity to communicate.

In the end, despite our distance and increased attention toward diversity, my students and I also learned that things we encounter such as hardship or triumph are universal. Of course, embracing the common threads of our humanity does not mean ignoring and isolating the different things with which we must contend. However, it serves as a reminder that celebrating together enriches our experience, and, simultaneously, working together to overcome obstacles makes for more strength and resiliency. As an educator, I now cannot assume the role of a bystander who witnesses acts of injustice, inadvertently modeling for my students an attitude of powerlessness. Quite the opposite: I want to exemplify how the power of inner peace and love for self can permeate outside of us in a powerful energy that can touch the hearts of individuals and move even political systems towards change for the better.

Conclusion

The research that I have described in this chapter is a small study with limited data. Nonetheless, it can spur further investigations of the practice of social-emotional education and mindfulness training as part of the curriculum of every school. My study also speaks to the effectiveness in promoting a compassionate 21st-century global citizenry.

Although human differences cannot be eliminated, bridges can be built to exemplify the interconnections of all things living and nonliving. These bridges can be built with the education of both the heart and the mind, serving as a reminder that "together we are stronger." Our mindfulness sessions aim to help individuals to become aware of inner dynamics and to learn how to self-regulate. By doing so, students become the masters of their own universe. A world of harmony and peace is the result of individuals who are at peace with themselves.

References

Cope, S. (2014, October 1). Gandhi and the Gita: The making of a hero. Retrieved from https://yogainternational.com/article/view/gandhi-and-the-gita-the-making-of-a-hero.

Doty, J. R. (2014, November). The compassion imperative. Care, Compassion and Mindfulness. California State Polytechnic University, Pomona.

Fischer, L. (1982). *Gandhi: His life and message for the world.* London: Signet Classics.

Kamenetz, A. (2017, August 14). Social and emotional skills: Everybody loves them, but still can't define them. Retrieved from https://www.npr.org/sections/ed/2017/08/14/ 542070550/social-and-emotional-skills-everybody-loves-them-but-still-cant-define-them.

Kendall, G. (2010). *Nelson Mandela.* Boston, Massachusetts: Wyatt North Publishing, LLC.

Kumar, S. (2006). *The Buddha and the terrorist.* Chapel Hill, North Carolina: Algonquin Books, 2006.

Mehta, N. (2014, November). A bridge from the Internet to the Inner-Net: Innovations in CCM. Care, Compassion and Mindfulness. California State Polytechnic University, Pomona.

Chapter 9

Transformational Journeys of Nonviolence

By Esteban Hernandez

While public education does teach students about the nonviolent means—such as protests, boycotts, and sit-ins—used by Mahatma Gandhi and Martin Luther King, Jr. to create change, it fails to emphasize the personal journeys that transformed Gandhi and King into the transcendent heroes we admire today. Although Gandhi and King exercised supreme morality in their search for justice, all heroes are imperfect and undergo internal and external transformation throughout their lives. Students need to understand that they are very much like Gandhi and King: mortal, flawed, vulnerable people with the ability to transform themselves into someone great. By studying principles and ideas of nonviolence, students will learn to appreciate their accessibility and relevance in transforming their lives. Many young people perceive Gandhi and King to be mythological figures armed with supernatural goodness that cannot be duplicated. While there will never be another Gandhi or King, there will always be good people who use nonviolence to better themselves. This chapter will focus on how students can access principles of nonviolence so that they can begin to make modest, incremental change in their thoughts, words, and actions, fostering permanent change in themselves, their relationships, and their communities.

Ahimsa Institute: My Transformational Journey

In the summer of 2015, I was fortunate to have the opportunity to attend, as a fellow, the Ahimsa Institute at Cal Poly Pomona. At the institute we examined the empowering journeys that Mahatma Gandhi and Nelson Mandela made toward nonviolence. After a week of seminars, lectures, and

C. A. Bracho and D. Dodson (eds.), Teachers Teaching Nonviolence, 127–137.

thoughtful discussion, I realized that Gandhi and Mandela were not born the transcendent heroes whom we study and admire today; instead, they transformed themselves into social and political champions by embracing principles of nonviolence. This embrace did not happen overnight. Rather, it took a lifetime; it was a journey. As part of the Ahimsa Institute, I wrote an essay that explored how American professor Joseph Campbell's monomyth serves as an omnipresent archetype structure that emphasizes the stages of hero's transformational journey. After reading Dr. Tara Sethia's *Gandhi: Pioneer of Nonviolent Social Change* and Gillian Kendall's *A Life Inspired: Nelson Mandela*, it was clear that Gandhi and Mandela experienced Campbell's monomyth in real life. They traveled to hostile places, struggled with social and political violence, confronted and collaborated with allies and enemies, and dealt with guides and knaves. Their journeys not only symbolize the ebbs and flows of life that we all experience, but they also, more importantly, represent growth and change. Much like Gandhi and Mandela, we—students, parents, teachers, myself—have the power to transform ourselves by embracing journeys of nonviolence. We are no different than Gandhi, Mandela, or Martin Luther King, Jr. Just like them, we are imperfect, vulnerable, and mortal individuals with the ability to become kind, mindful citizens.

As the institute came to end, I realized that by practicing principles of nonviolence, we can transform our relationships, our communities, our country, and ourselves. I learned that nonviolence is not about changing the world, although it does; nonviolence is about making small, incremental changes within ourselves. As I began my transformative journey of nonviolence after the institute, I wanted my students to experience it with me, so I also began to consider ways to transform my teaching to include elements of ahimsa. This personal and professional transformation is ongoing, challenging, yet rewarding, not only for myself but also for my students.

Transcendentalism: The Power of the Individual

For my students and me, our transformative journeys begin at Los Altos High School in our classroom, C-4, with the 11th-grade curriculum, specifically the unit on Transcendentalism, which focuses on the power of the individual. Although limited by grade-level alignment and ambitious pacing guides, I tend to emphasize and to extend this unit despite these limitations because it offers a logical segue into studies of nonviolence. At the institute I learned about *swaraj*, or "self-rule," as a way to discover and manage the self—including one's self-respect, self-responsibility, and aptitudes for self-awareness. Much like India struggled for swaraj, many young people struggle to find emotional and spiritual independence from a society saturated with influence. Transcendentalism encourages swaraj by encouraging inner exploration and allowing us to access and to embrace our conscience and our individuality.

Ralph Waldo Emerson and "Self-Reliance"

Our Transcendentalism unit begins with Ralph Waldo Emerson and his essay "Self-Reliance." I begin with this text because Emerson focuses on the power of the individual, a power that nonviolent heroes like Gandhi and King realized. If we want to be transformed, we first must know who we are. In "Self-Reliance," Emerson writes, "Accept the place the divine providence has found for you, the society of your contemporaries, the connection of events. Great men have always done so." In other words, we cannot resist our individuality if we want to achieve swaraj. In a society inundated with pressure, students ignore their identity, ignore their voice and conscience, and try to be someone they are not. The first step in the transformational process is figuring out "who am I" and "what are my guiding principles." The answers come from listening to and embracing our conscience and honoring our intuitions; this, Emerson believes, makes us one-of-a-kind. Self-discovery does not come from listening to society but, rather, listening to our conscience, which Gandhi and King did continually. Eventually, once students establish their identities, they can use nonviolence to put their principles into practice.

To encourage self-discovery in the classroom, in addition to a close read, thoughtful reflection, discussion, and writing on "Self-Reliance," students prepare a one-pager, an AVID activity that requires them to fill up an entire page, in this case a poster, with the following information about themselves, leaving no blank spaces:

— One quote that best represents who you are
— Three to five guiding principles
— These sentence starters: I am…, I believe in…, One goal I have is…
— Images that define you
— Creativity

With this exercise, not only do students get to express their creativity, but they also fill up the page with information that allows them to reflect on who they are and what they believe. When they present their posters to the class, in addition to realizing that ALL my students are good people who know right from wrong, I also realize how different and unique each poster is, symbolic of their diverse, imaginative spirits and personalities. Recalling Campbell's monomyth, or heroic journey, this exercise reveals the truth that all heroes must, at some point, reflect on who they are and how they can use that information to impact the world around them. We end our unit with by reflecting on and writing about Emerson's message that our transformational journeys begin with ourselves. Similarly, Gandhi and King were unapologetically themselves and projected that integrity into the world, which is what I want students to understand from studying "Self-Reliance." I want them to discover their truths, their guiding principles, and stay loyal to them.

Ralph Waldo Emerson and "Nature"

But how do we discover and live our truths in a world with so much noise and so many distractions? As part of our Transcendentalism unit, the second Emerson text that we explore is "Nature," which I use to emphasize the power of disconnecting. In order to contact our conscience and to discover our guiding principles, we must have quietness, stillness. In "Nature" Emerson states, "To go into solitude, a man needs to retire as much from his chamber as from society. I am not solitary whilst I read and write, though nobody is with me." He understands that not only is nature keeping him company but his thoughts are too. Using Emerson's challenge to disconnect and to reflect, I require students to complete three nature-writing assignments throughout our Transcendentalism unit. The instructions are as follows:

> Transcendentalists felt that people could be inspired by nature. They felt self-discovery, inner exploration, accessing our aboriginal self could be achieved through interacting with nature in a genuine way. Like accessing our individuality or potential, building a relationship with nature takes patience and a conscious effort. For this assignment, produce a piece of writing (poem, free write, short story, "journal" entry, etc.) that you will share with the class. There are no specific instructions, besides allowing nature to guide your inspiration. The requirements are as follows:

> - You must leave your phone in the class.
> - You must sit by yourself.
> - Don't make contact with anyone.
> - Observe your surroundings and your reaction to this activity.

Using these instructions, students retreat into our spacious quad, separate, and sit quietly to produce a piece of writing.

In a similar manner, Gandhi and King prioritized meditation and prayer to disconnect from society and connect with their consciences. These practices aided them in their transformational journeys. Although students are not required to pray or meditate, sitting alone with their thoughts is something they rarely do. Of all the work and activities that we do throughout the year, students remember this assignment the most. Not only does it produce some of the best writing of the year, but also students and I both authentically enjoy sitting in the quad, a place normally reserved for socializing, laughing, and selfies, to listen to our thoughts, observe our setting, feel the wind, etc. My students not only begin to develop an appreciation for their campus; they also begin to realize qualities about themselves. They see the value of getting in touch with the conscience through separation. We complete three nature writing sessions throughout the unit. As part of the assignment, students are required to share their work with the class. Some write poems, some write narratives from the point-of-view of a tree, some write personal reflections, and others make a list of words. Either way, students all produce authentic work that is inspired by their conscience and nature, allowing them to realize their individuality and creativity, an important step in the transformational process and in achieving swaraj.

Principles of Nonviolence

Our Transcendentalism studies serve as an empowering unit that encourages students to embrace their individuality by accessing their conscience through self-reflection. This self-reflection is designed to encourage students to explore their guiding principles, understand their potential, and exercise their voice with confidence. Transcendentalism provides them with the social and emotional tools to begin this transformational process. Once this is established, students are prepared to learn about how principles of nonviolence can both facilitate further personal transformation and help them transform their relationships and communities.

Our study of nonviolence begins with learning about the theory of ahimsa by completing a close read of various texts, such as excerpts from Henry David Thoreau's "Civil Disobedience," excerpts from King's "Letter from Birmingham Jail," Frederick Douglass's "Letters to His Master," and readings from *The Mind of Mahatma Gandhi,* a compilation of excerpts from Gandhi's writings. Unfortunately, not all these texts are included in the instructional path, so I have had to create this curriculum independently, which is why I have selected a range of texts from various time periods that address different historical and social conflicts, emphasizing how accessible, durable, and applicable nonviolence is. While these texts reinforce Emerson's teaching on personal transformation, the focus is to learn how we can use them to transform our relationships with family, friends/peers, community, and country.

The key quotations from Gandhi found in *The Mind of Mahatma Gandhi* make the book an accessible, manageable introduction to the basic principles of ahimsa. Although there are more comprehensive texts that address the history, philosophies, and social impact of Gandhi's life and work, I have to consider stringent pacing guides, grade level alignment, and other professional limitations, staying conscious about how much time I dedicate to this unit without going completely "rogue." Therefore, I focus on excerpts from *The Mind of Mahatma Gandhi* because it provides readable, effective chunks that students can read and understand in a timely manner. We start by exploring these basic principles:

- Nonviolence is an active force.
- Nonviolence requires matchless bravery.
- Nonviolence does not separate means and ends; both are inseparable.
- Nonviolence focuses on the deeds, not the doer.
- Nonviolence begins with our thoughts, which dictate our words and actions. We must stay mindful of our thoughts, words, and actions.
- Forgiveness and apology begin the healing process.
- Relationships require empathy.

Although there are other important principles of nonviolence not listed here, we focus on these because I want students to feel encouraged about applying these principles in their lives by presenting nonviolence in manageable increments. Even if they connect with just one of these principles and apply it in their lives, it's a win for everyone.

To examine these principles, since students sit in groups of four, I assign each group an excerpt from *The Mind of Mahatma Gandhi,* which they will read closely with their group and complete a mini-presentation that they will use to "teach" their section to the class. My instructions for "The Mind of Gandhi—Close Read" mini-project direct the group to complete a close read of an excerpt and then create a presentation that addresses the following:

- *Word Smith*: Identify and define the positive words from your section, explaining how the word choice impacts the excerpt.
- *Main Ideas*: Explain what your passage is saying.
- *Sentence Starters*:
    a.   This passage reminds of...because...
    b.   This passage makes me think about...because...
    c.   One important idea that stood out to our group was...because...
- *Images* that symbolize the passage: Explain the connection without using words.

In conjunction with the close read and presentations, I show segments from the movie *Gandhi* to highlight Gandhi's transformational journey from inexperienced lawyer to mahatma. After all the groups give their presentations and take notes, students read and annotate the complete text to make the lesson comprehensive. The presentations always provide powerful insights and interpretations that lead to impressive discussions about nonviolence and how Gandhi used it to transform himself and India. After this lesson, students begin to understand that no transformation, whether of a self or a country, happens overnight. Whatever we are trying to change takes time, effort, patience, self-suffering, discipline, courage, and much more. I want students to feel inspired by Gandhi and India's transformation and know that they too have the power to transform their lives through nonviolence.

In addition to the close read, we complete a Gandhi snowball fight as way to analyze and write about important Gandhi quotes. Each student gets a Gandhi quote and must respond by using guiding questions. After ten minutes of writing about the quote, students crumple up their quotes and throw them aimlessly across the room. We repeat this activity four times. By the end of the activity, students will have read, written about, and discussed four different Gandhi quotes. The snowball fight and the close read, coupled with the presentations and film, offer the foundation students need to consider application. How can they apply principles of nonviolence in their lives? To answer this question, students write a short essay explaining the following:

> What principles of nonviolence that we learned about could you apply in your own life? Explain why these principles stood out to you the most. How do plan on implementing these principles? How do you think these principles will transform yourself, your relationships, or help solve any conflicts you might be experiencing? Include specific references to the text. Also, you will be required to share your essay with the class.

As part of the writing process, I always require students to share their work, either in small groups or with the whole class, depending on the assignment. However, because assignments like this are so important, I want students to hear how other students plan on integrating principles of nonviolence into their lives, so sharing their work is essential. At the end of our nonviolence unit, students report back and share how their experiments with nonviolence have impacted their lives.

Now that students have seen how Gandhi used nonviolence to transform himself, those around him, and India, we begin to examine other texts while continuing to complete critical and creative assignments that allow students to explore and experiment with elements of nonviolence.

Civil Disobedience

After studying Gandhi's efforts and successes with mass civil disobedience, we flashback to analyze Henry David Thoreau's influential essay *On the Duty of Civil Disobedience*. Because this text is part of our core curriculum and it directly inspired Gandhi, we dedicate several days working with *Civil Disobedience*. Unlike our lessons on Transcendentalism and Gandhi, which we used to emphasize personal transformation, we analyze this text to learn how we can confront social and political injustices that affect our communities. Although personal transformation is laborious enough, how do we begin to address the political and social problems that overwhelm our daily lives? Many of these problems seem out of our control, students say; however, after reading, discussing, and writing about Thoreau's essay, they begin to realize that change begins with one person. "Be the change you want to see in the world" is the Gandhi quote that is reiterated throughout this lesson. The chart below identifies key quotes and the main ideas from those quotes that emphasize Thoreau's teachings. Students complete similar charts on graph paper that they present to the class in groups.

Quote:	Interpretation:
"[The state is] not armed with superior wit or honesty, but with superior physical strength. I was not born to be forced. I will breathe after my own fashion. Let us see who is the strongest. What force has a multitude? They only can force me who obey a higher law than I."	Governments cannot and should not force us to do anything, especially if it is something immoral or against our principles.

"It is not desirable to cultivate a respect for the law, so much as for the right."	We should not obey laws blindly; we should obey truth, or what's right.
"if one thousand, if on hundred, if ten men whom I could name,—if ten honest men only, —ay, if one HONEST man, in this State of Massachusetts, ceasing to hold slaves, were actually to withdraw from this co-partnership, and be locked up in the county jail therefore, it would be the abolition of slavery in America. For it matters not how small the beginning may seem to be: what is once well done is done forever."	One honest person can change an unjust state or community if they have the courage to stand up to it.

After breaking down this text, students write an explanatory essay that highlights the way Gandhi used Thoreau's ideas in his mass civil disobedience campaign. The goal is for students to understand that change, whether personal, social, or political, can start small. If we overwhelm ourselves by tackling every problem at once, we're of course more likely to fail. But if we can concentrate on one problem at a time, our transformational journey has become more manageable. Thoreau refused the government his money to protest an unjust war. Gandhi applied this idea by organizing similar protests in his country to fight injustice. The transformational journeys of both Thoreau and Gandhi involved having the courage to do what was right despite the consequences. If we embrace this mindset, we too can become political and social heroes.

Letters of Nonviolence

As students begin to understand the power of nonviolence, we turn our attention to transforming our relationships, whether with family, friends, or country, by understanding the power of empathy, constructive dialogue, forgiveness, and apology. Most students think of nonviolence when confronted with physical violence, which is important. But while most students, fortunately, do not experience physical violence regularly, it's important they understand that nonviolence can be used not only to transform relationships into healthy, meaningful kinships. They also can come to understand that nonviolence can be used to resolve conflicts with peers, teachers, co-workers, and anyone else who does not recognize truth.

For this unit we exam Gandhi's letter written to the Viceroy in 1930, Frederick Douglass's letters to his master, and Martin Luther King, Jr.'s "Letter from Birmingham Jail." In analyzing these letters, we focus on three elements: logical and emotional appeal, use of diction, and tone. For example, the authors' tone of humility and respect despite the violence and injustice they have experienced reinforces the ahimsa principle—focus on the deed, not doer. Gandhi starts his letter by suggesting he has no problem with Englishmen; he has a problem with British rule of India. His tone and diction create a mood of optimism and unity in addressing the Viceroy, which creates room for dialogue. Because Gandhi was mindful of his words and how he presented them, the doors for communication remained open, for the most part.

Similarly, Douglass, despite all the violence his master committed against him, harbored no malice or hatred towards his former master. Like Gandhi, he wrote his letter with a tone of reverence and tolerance. Douglass writes, "There is no roof under which you would be more safe than mine, and there is nothing in my house which you might need for your comfort, which I would not readily grant. Indeed, I should esteem it a privilege, to set you an example as to how mankind ought to treat each other." Douglass goes so far as to offer protection and comfort to his former master. He completely forgives him!

After dissecting all three letters, we learn that the way we communicate our ideas, especially with those with whom we have conflicts, matters. The words we use, and the way we say those words, determine the outcome of our relationships. In addition, students and I realize that in order to transform any relationship dialogue must happen, which requires speaking and listening to others critically. Furthermore, dialogue might require apologizing, admitting that we were wrong, forgiving, or helping someone see the truth without provoking by placing blame. Once we have written about and discussed how these ideas relate to principles of nonviolence and the letters, students write their own letters to someone with whom they have had a conflict:

> Prompt: Write a letter of forgiveness or apology to someone that has wronged you, or to someone you have wronged. You are encouraged to give that person the letter as a sign of peace. If you feel comfortable, you're also encouraged to share your letter with the class. Remember to stay conscious of your tone and diction. Tones of anger, resentment, judgment, etc. can trigger similar feelings in your reader, so be mindful of what you say and how you say it.

This is another assignment that continues to blow me away. Not only do I learn invaluable information about my students' social and personal lives, but I also learn that they have the courage to either forgive or apologize for serious conflicts they've experienced. This assignment gives me comfort in knowing that if students are willing to use nonviolence to address major problems, maybe they will consider using nonviolence for minor ones too.

Conclusion

While this unit has an end, our transformational journeys do not. Because we are imperfect and so is the world, our journeys of nonviolence will never end. Gandhi, King, and Mandela realized this, which is why they never stopped trying to improve themselves or the world around them. At the Ahimsa Institute, I realized that Campbell's monomyth captured the transformation that led to salvation and prosperity for themselves and their countries. Although they exercised supreme morality, making them seem perfect, they were flawed and underwent internal and external transformation throughout their lives. They committed themselves to the change that they wanted to see in themselves and in the world. Both the Ahimsa Institute and Emerson taught me that personal change begins with swaraj. Once swaraj is established, we can concentrate on *sarvodaya*, or universal progress, using principles of satyagraha to purify our relationships and communities. In his article "Self-Transformation and the Hero's Journey," David Bookbinder writes, "Through his struggles, the hero is transformed from an ordinary person into something larger. His guiding principles—altruism, compassion, and self-sacrifice—serve as a model for his people even after he passes." I want both my students and me to feel the rapture of life by committing ourselves to journeys of nonviolence so that we too can transform into something larger, something meaningful!

References

Bookbinder, D. (2007, December 12). Self-transformation and the hero's journey. Retrieved from https://www.beliefnet.com

Emerson, R. W. (2015). *Self-reliance and other essays.* New York: Dover Publications.

Gandhi, M. K., Prabhu, R. K., & Rao, U. R. (2007). *The mind of Mahatma Gandhi.* Ahmedabad: Navajivan Pub. House.

Thoreau, H. D. (2012). *Walden and civil disobedience.* New York: Sterling Publications. (Original work published 1854).

SECTION 3

Subverting Curriculum through Nonviolence

Section Overview

Subverting Curriculum Through Nonviolence

By Danita Dodson

Gandhi's personal life reveals his commitment to development, progress, and subversion. In *Hind Swaraj* (1909) he articulates the understanding that the future must be held consistently in our social vision, indicating that transformative practices are essential in leading society toward more liberated structures that eradicate the perpetuation of confinement and inequity. Educators happen to have critical opportunities to create real change that transforms the future by imploding outdated and unjust methods, as seminally argued by Postman and Weingartner (1969). Gandhi used the term *sarvodaya* to emphasize that, to be effective, any institution must aspire to the wellbeing of all. The application of this concept to education suggests that traditional structures and standards-based plans in classrooms today—aimed at creating competitive and achievement-oriented students—can undermine the future. Educational research has begun to document the pejorative effect of such scripted programs in schools (Ede, 2006; Crocco & Costigan, 2007). Critics describe the current realities of traditional schooling as "regimes of accountability, a standardized and packaged curriculum, and a lock-step pedagogy that are combined with a focus on privatization and regulations that hold teachers and administrators' feet to the fire of competition" (Apple & Beane, 2007, p. 36).

In response, innovative pedagogy works to create experiences that fulfill Gandhi's vision of the Oceanic Circle (Gandhi, 1946); opposing the confining hierarchal structure of the Pyramid, this Gandhian image of fluidity suggests the value of building apertures of transformative learning, growth, and elimination of division. Myles Horton (1990) has similarly asserted that true

C. A. Bracho and D. Dodson (eds.), *Teachers Teaching Nonviolence*, 141–145.

education is organically holistic, advocating that new educational practices must create experiences that subvert the formalized and "dehumanizing" segmentation of the learning process. Drawing upon the tradition of nonviolent activism, the educators in this section examine their capacities for impacting the future and enacting social change through the subversion of standardized curriculum. In altering the teaching of texts or concepts through a nonviolent lens, they discover possibilities for challenging systems of power and elevating voices of resistance through innovations in social studies, language arts, art, and storytelling courses. Their narratives also testify to the resulting shift in student agency. Such unscripted curriculum exemplifies the possibility of what Mihaly Csikszentmihalyi (1993) calls the "fellowship of the future," a place for collaboration, unity, and nonviolence. This type of vision requires inventive approaches. In an Ahimsa Center Conference presentation about modernizing the struggle for change through strategies in the age of social media, Patrisse Khan-Cullors (2018), co-founder of Black Lives Matter, posed this challenge to the educators she addressed: "What kind of curriculum are you creating to remind students that their lives matter?"

Rising to such a challenge of transforming prescribed curriculum, the following four narratives provide examples of new practices that can contribute to emancipatory, critical, multimodal pedagogies. They show strategies such as artistic expression, self-grading, storytelling, and dialogue. In the time of accountability and standardization, they prove that, even within the constraints of dominant educational systems, teachers can critically reflect on their own practices and create more inclusive learning communities. As students become judicious readers and writers of new media, questioning meanings and agendas in text, these subversive practices support critical thinking and literacy (Freire, 1968) and maintain skeptical reflectivism (McPeck, 1990). Ledwith and Springett (2009) show how such participatory pedagogies allow learners to tap into deep inquiries and experiential knowledge that open their minds to multiple truths and a more holistic way of perceiving the world. As examples of "deschooling" (Illich, 1983) that critically model ideas about tweaking teaching practices and designing lessons for connected learning, the narratives in this section suggest that classrooms created outside of prescriptive curriculum are significant.

In Chapter 11, "Reframing the Study of South Africa," Donna Hill, a retired high school teacher in California, discusses how the Ahimsa Institute inspired her development of a ground-breaking program at Cleveland Humanities Magnet in Los Angeles. Her narrative explains the measures that she and her team of teachers took to implement a ninth-grade global studies curriculum that features a South Africa Unit on nonviolent social activism. Hill describes the subversive methodology that integrates social studies, English, and art history to create diverse approaches that engage and inspire all students. Beginning with a springboard of multiple perspectives on violence, the unit follows with a lesson on how Gandhi's nonviolent strategy arose from his transformative experience with discrimination in South Africa. Hill delineates ensuing lessons on the history of Apartheid, instruction that leads learners to engagement in simulated protests to represent various voices of the resistance. Through the reading lenses of plays, films, non-fiction excerpts, short stories, and songs, students are shown how to deconstruct multimedia texts about violence and nonviolence and then create their own expressions of resistance.

In Chapter 12, "Shifting Content, Sparking Agency: An English Language Arts Curriculum of Nonviolence," Karin Rose, an educator in Colorado Springs, shows the "continuing ripple" of the Ahimsa Institute experience in motivating her to create inventive curriculum, modifications in pedagogy, and change in her students. Viewing teaching through a lens of nonviolence, she describes how the transformation in content in her lessons caused a resultant shift in the focus of the classroom design. Offering students the opportunity to see the world where powerful words allow them to become agents of change, Rose describes how the shift in her language arts approach involved the study of short stories, texts, speeches, poems, and other writings that use the principles of nonviolence. She charts how this curriculum subversion altered the reflections, conversations, and relationships that students experienced daily, moving them away from a teacher-directed system and toward a space of choice, voice, and advocacy. This narrative provides valuable information for teachers who are interested in creating a positive shift in classroom culture to create both student agency and agents of change.

In Chapter 13, "Voices of Young Women Leaders: Swaraj and Satyagraha through Digital Storytelling," Jode Brexa, a retired teacher in Santa Fe, documents the unfolding path that led her from the Ahimsa Institute to Free State—the former center of the Apartheid in South Africa—to facilitate a digital storytelling project, a pedagogical innovation that combines words, photos, and music in multimedia artifacts. She contextualizes her narrative in the educational imperative to meet the needs of all students in 21st-century classrooms, moving them toward the future by building a culture of inclusion through transformative curriculum that addresses the achievement gaps that exist in a diverse student population. Intersecting her exploration of Gandhi's *Hind Swaraj* with her journey in post-apartheid South Africa, Brexa's narrative spans the navigation of politics and power, the ethical issues of working with students of different cultures, and the creation of a subversive approach that captures the stories of twelve South African students who challenged the violence of poverty, drugs, and sexual abuse in their families and schools to become young leaders of change in their communities.

In Chapter 14, "Design for Good in the Classroom," Travis Sevilla, a high school art teacher in San Diego, discusses how the profound experiences of the Ahimsa Institute influenced his teaching practice, sparking a pedagogy that he has named *Design for Good*. This appellation alludes, on one hand, to his daily interactions and relationships with students—which involve creating space for daily meditations and making subversive shifts in mundane tasks like grading to create a more compassionate method of assessment. His second meaning of this term lies in the projects that he assigns in digital art and design classes; these are anchored in an agenda of applying the principles of nonviolence by collaborating with corporations that have a positive impact, such as surf industry companies that use recycled materials, companies that provide mobility access to people with disabilities, and environmental organizations. In an effort to create content that stimulates social activism, Sevilla's chapter provides inspiration for teachers who would like to create a similar program that not only teaches content but simultaneously helps learners see that their choices matter and that they have the power to make a positive impact.

Through their descriptions of inventive ways to subvert harmful traditional strategies, these narratives view education as a space of hope and vision. When the future is in educators' minds and hearts, they make strides toward a world that is more nonviolent by leading students to visualize a more just future. In their emphasis upon critical pedagogy, both Paulo Freire (1968) and Giroux (2011) have argued that active education must inspire imagination so that it can envisage a better world. By courageously subverting curriculum through nonviolence, this section's contributors encourage teachers to create situations for students to become "critical agents" (McLaren, 2007, p. 310). This pedagogical action paves the way for a better future.

References

Apple, M. W., & Beane, J. A. (2007). Schooling for democracy. *Principal Leadership, 8*(2), 34–38.

Crocco, M. S., & Costigan, A. T. (2007). The narrowing of curriculum and pedagogy in the age of accountability: Urban educators speak out. *Urban Education, 42*, 512–535.

Csikszentmihalyi, M. (1993). *The evolving self: A psychology for the third millennium.* New York: HarperCollins Publishers.

Ede, A. (2006). Scripted curriculum: Is it a prescription for success? *Childhood Education, 83*(1), 29.

Freire, P. (1968). *Pedagogy of the oppressed.* New York: Seabury Press.

Gandhi, M. (1946). Gandhi's political vision: The pyramid vs. the ocean circle. In A. Parel (Ed.), *Gandhi: 'Hind Swaraj' and Other Writings*, Centenary Edition (pp. 181–183). London: Cambridge University Press.

Giroux, H. (2011). *On critical pedagogy*. New York, NY: Continuum Press.

Horton, M. (1990). *The long haul*. New York: Doubleday.

Illich, I. (1983). *Deschooling society*. New York: Harper Colophon.

Khan-Cullors, P. (2018, October). Modernizing the struggle: Strategies in the age of social media. Transformative power of education: Lessons from Gandhi, King, Chávez, and Mandela. Talk presented at 2018 Ahimsa Center Conference, California State Polytechnic University, Pomona.

Ledwith, M., & Springett, J. (2009). *Participatory practice: Community-based action for transformative change*. Bristol, England: Policy Press.

McPeck, J. E. (1990). *Teaching critical thinking: Dialogue and dialectic*. New York: Routledge.

McLaren, P. (2007). The future of the past: Reflections of the present state of empire and pedagogy. In P. McLaren & J. Kincheloe (Eds.), *Critical Pedagogy: Where are we now?* (pp. 289–314). New York, NY: Peter Lang.

Postman, N., & Weingartner, C. (1969). *Teaching as a subversive activity*. New York: Dell Pub. Co.

Chapter 10

Reframing the Study of South Africa

By Donna S. Hill

Throughout my teaching career, I have been committed to social justice curriculum. As a light-skinned black woman, I have struggled with identity and the socialization that comes with living in American society where I have encountered racist, anti-racist, and unaware people from a variety of racial backgrounds and ethnicities. Based on my experiences, I have purposely dedicated my teaching career to supporting students in their struggles to understand themselves and the society in which we live. In my own life I practice yoga, tai chi, and meditation as I journey to becoming more aware and self-reflective. I also try to instill in my students a value for empathy and compassion for themselves as well as for people who are different from them. Because of this background, in the summer of 2005 at the first seminar of Ahimsa fellows, I felt that I was fertile for a deepening understanding of a nonviolent way of life.

The theme for the first institute was "Nonviolence and Social Change," a perfect topic for me. Not surprisingly, I was attracted to the concepts and implications of Gandhi's principles and strategies as Dr. Martin Luther King, Jr. applied them during the Civil Rights Movement. I was especially interested in *satyagraha* because both Gandhi and Dr. King, believing in the "truth" of their causes and willing to make personal sacrifices, embraced nonviolence in order to change both the hearts of their oppressors and/or people in the public who could pressure those in power. Although everything I learned in the seminar was profound and relevant to me, the most significant book we read, followed by a film version, was without a doubt *A Force More Powerful*. For the first time I was awakened to the understanding that nonviolence is a strategy requiring planning, training, and careful implementation. Additionally, I was exposed to the reality that there have been incredibly successful nonviolent revolutions globally.

C. A. Bracho and D. Dodson (eds.), *Teachers Teaching Nonviolence*, 147–156.

Returning home, I realized the value of what I had gained both personally and professionally. However, I had a few lessons to learn about introducing nonviolence curriculum to a teaching team that felt ownership of curriculum they had developed over many years. My teaching environment, Cleveland High School Humanities Magnet, is a remarkable public high school; it is one to which I have devoted almost thirty years of my life as a teacher, and it is now a school I continue to serve, after retirement, as a substitute teacher. In 1989 I was recruited to the magnet to coordinate the ninth grade. This first year of high school focuses on Global Studies, with students learning about diverse cultures as well as the evolution of humans interacting with nature and each other. In fact, the theme for that year was powerful: "Gaining awareness of our increasingly interdependent and globalized world, and taking responsibility for ourselves, others and the environment."

My absolute joy in being a part of the creation of this school's curriculum started with an introduction to Neil Anstead, the first coordinator and visionary of our writing and thematic-based interdisciplinary program. Mr. Anstead guided us by one prevailing belief: teachers must teach to their passions. If we developed our own curriculum rather than resorting to textbooks and scripted lessons, then we would be invested in what we taught and become life-long students ourselves. The investment would lead us to be enthusiastic about our subject matter, and this zeal would automatically be transferred to our students. The magnet has become a model school for Los Angeles Unified School District because of the dedication of our teachers and subsequent commitment of our students to the program.

When our four member ninth-grade teaching team (Vitaly, Ariane White, Susana Barkataki, and I) returned to school that next fall from the 2005 Institute, we could not wait to share what we had learned and to include nonviolent philosophy and history in our curriculum. However, the other teachers were stubbornly unconvinced to make any changes. We thought it would be obvious why high school students need to be taught nonviolence as a way of life. Unconvinced, some of the other team members did not have that same understanding; they equated nonviolence with being passive and ineffective. Unfortunately, we did not take the time to create staff developments to inform the team of the insights we had gained at the Institute. That was a hard lesson, but our group decided to include mini units based on nonviolence principles in our own classes and share what and why we were teaching those ideas. Since then, team members (Co-coordinators Marisa Del Pino and Grace Kim-Oh, members Hala Dillsi and Joe Kim, along with new member, Stacy Endman) have increasingly become open to teaching nonviolence and seeking information for themselves. This chapter describes how the South Africa curriculum at our school was reframed around a focus upon nonviolence

A Glimpse of How the Team Teaching and Interdisciplinary Instruction Work

The magnet has a unique way to schedule classes. Students have the same English class all year because this is the foundation class for the writing-based program. However, the Social Institutions (SI) and Art/Religion (A/R) classes alternate during the next period. Let's say, for example, that the South African Unit is sixteen days long. During period five, there are two English classes. The first English class is paired with period six SI for the first eight days, and the second English class is paired with A/R. At the beginning of the next eight days, the first English class changes to pair with A/R, and the second English class is paired with SI. There are also X-Days that block out the two hours to show a film or to give time for a simulation. Because these classes are integrated thematically, they are called Core.

I have chosen to share the South Africa Unit in this chapter because it reflects years of developing its thematic approach and subject integration as well as the concepts of inclusion and principles of nonviolence that my colleagues and I learned from the Ahimsa Institute. The unit is a case study ending a more comprehensive Africa Unit that explores pre- and post-colonialism with the theme "A Struggle for Power: From Colonial Oppression to Self-Determination."

Introduction to the Africa Unit: English Class

Before the students start the South Africa Unit, they move through several assignments that set up the entire Africa Unit, beginning with listing what they know about Africa. Generally, student associations include starving children, wild animals, jungles, and primitive huts. Very little is known about the reality of African life. To help them address these stereotypes and misunderstandings, the students view Chimamanda Ngozi Adichie's TED Talk entitled "The Danger of a Single Story," where the Nigerian author and activist states a significant point: when there is a single story told about a race, an ethnicity, or a religion, misconceptions prevail and lead to stereotypes and biases. She explains that children are vulnerable to and influenced by what they read. As a young writer, Adichie had created characters and settings that reflected the British and American books she read rather than the people and places that she observed in her own life in

Nigeria. Her later discovery of African books exposed Adichie to characters who looked like her and places she recognized. She appreciated the diverse worlds open to her through the foreign books, but with African writers she was exposed to other stories, her stories. This single story about Africa leads to stereotypes that American children still believe today, even with media that can capture anything anywhere in the world in seconds. Therefore, one of the objectives of the Africa Unit is to tell some of the many stories, perspectives, and types of people who populate the continent.

Paired with the TED Talk is a short story written by Adichie, "The Headstrong Historian." In this story the unit theme and topics are explored as Adichie demonstrates several stories being told. The narrative involves the contrast between the customs and beliefs of an African culture with the changes brought by the missionaries and British court system. It perfectly establishes the unit's main ideas about pre-colonial traditions existing along with colonial changes. It also fits the theme: "A Struggle for Power: From Colonial Oppression to Self-Determination."

The first reading in English class is Les Blancs, a densely written, little-known play by an African American author, Lorraine Hansberry. This play offers more than six different perspectives, from both white and black characters, on the beginnings of the revolution against colonialism in a fictional, composite African country. These perspectives are rich for student discussions about how people react and think differently as both oppressors and the oppressed. To understand the positions of the oppressed characters, the RAW conceptual frame is used. RAW is an acronym that stands for resistance, accommodation, or withdrawal. Students apply these terms to the black characters in the play.

Les Blancs begins with a dying father whose son returns home to a small African village during the initial stages of a revolution to be waged against the colonial settlers. Each of the black characters represents a different point of view about how to handle the explosive situation. In contrast, the white characters demonstrate their reactions to the emerging conflict, which vary from becoming an ally to remaining a staunch racist proposing to keep the "blacks in their place." The play seemingly ends by advocating a violent overthrow of the white settlers in the struggle for self-governance, suggesting violence is the only strategy that can work. Therefore, the play perfectly sets up the South African Unit that introduces nonviolence as an alternative.

South African Unit

The South Africa Unit is part of the larger Africa Unit, so it is a case study utilizing the concepts students have been studying, and it fulfills two major objectives. The first is for students to begin to understand the dynamics of domination and resistance, the human reactions to oppression, and the ways that the oppressed might gain back freedom and dignity. The second objective is for students themselves to be empowered, to learn that their voices are important, and to realize that they can think critically and resolve conflicts.

South African Unit: English Class

To transition to the South Africa Unit, there are a series of readings that introduce the concept of nonviolence. The first reading is an excerpt from "Letter from Birmingham Jail" by Dr. Martin Luther King, Jr., which vividly describes his reaction to the often-heard white leaders' response of "Wait" to black people's demands for full citizenship and the privileges that go with it. Dr. King eloquently lists many ways black people have been oppressed by racism in this country and have been kept at second-class citizenship. He goes on to explain that the oppressor is not willing to give freedom to the oppressed without some pressure being exerted. This claim echoes the famous quote by Frederick Douglass: "If there is no struggle, there is no progress." Thus, for Dr. King, there is no waiting; the time is right for using a "type of constructive non-violent tension" or direct action to coerce white institutions and leaders into negotiating in good faith. However, to remain nonviolent, the idea is to counter hatred with love and bring about change by appealing to the conscience of the oppressor.

A short reading that summarizes Dr. King's strategies is "Six Steps to Kingian Nonviolence." This is a one-page list of the steps: information gathering, education, personal commitment, negotiation, direct action, and reconciliation. Students discuss their understanding of each step as they refer to the "Letter from Birmingham Jail" and/or any personal experience to further understand the terms. The purpose of this reading is to begin the discussion of how nonviolence resistance must be strategic and organized.

The third and fourth readings are from *Long Walk to Freedom* by Nelson Mandela. The first narrates when young Mandela speaks before the court after he is arrested in August 1962. At this point he recognizes that the nonviolent strategies of the ANC have seemingly made no advancement in the freedom struggle of his people. He admits to helping form the Umkhonto We Sizwe, an organization that begins to contemplate violent resistance because of the fear the country "was drifting towards a civil war in which blacks and whites would fight each other." Because of the scars left by the Anglo-Boer War and the great loss of life, the organization believes that sabotage and guerrilla warfare strategies would be most effective.

Following this reading is the second from *Long Walk to Freedom*, an excerpt taken from the day of Mandela's inauguration as president of South Africa. This time Mandela speaks of overturning the Apartheid system and replacing it with freedom for every individual, regardless of race. He thanks all his comrades who gave him the courage to continue in the face of overwhelming odds, as he has learned that courage means conquering fear and not the lack of it. Mandela also thanks his people for the remarkable courage and sacrifice that they demonstrated in decades of resistance to the Apartheid system. Lastly, he discusses his personal sacrifice of not being able to spend time with his family in order to stay true to his commitment to his people.

The fifth reading is an example of nonviolence at work in post-Apartheid South Africa with the Truth and Reconciliation Commission (TRC). The commission was "to investigate the violations that took place between 1960 and 1994, to provide support and reparation to victims and their families, and to compile a full and objective record of the effects of apartheid on South African society." There are many articles written about this commission's work. One particularly relevant story for American students is Amy Biehl's. She was an American from California on a Fulbright scholarship who chose to go to South Africa. Although Amy was a fierce supporter of black South African freedom, in 1993 she was murdered in a township by an angry mob of youths who saw a white lady and turned their wrath on her. Four youths accused of her murder were sentenced to eighteen years in prison and went before the commission to ask for forgiveness. The commission released the young men from prison after serving only four years, and Amy's parents, who also forgave them, approved of the release. Since then Amy's parents have kept in contact with the men and have founded the Amy Biehl Foundation.

Finally, students read a one-page definition of Ubuntu, the philosophical concept that Bishop Desmond Tutu often speaks about. It is from a Nguni Bantu word that means "humanity," or the "quality of being human." Students can better understand the importance of dignity and worth when confronted by racism and discrimination.

Following the readings, students watch a segment of the film *Gandhi*. It begins with a panoramic view of the train that takes Gandhi to South Africa and ends when he boards the ship to India. This powerful segment illustrates the basic nonviolent principles and practice of satyagraha. Students are shown images of bravery and activism inherent in Gandhi's methods and beliefs, so they understand that nonviolence is not equivalent to passivity. What this excerpt demonstrates is that nonviolence takes planning and strategizing; it is far more courageous to act nonviolently than violently, and the intent is to change the mind and heart of the oppressor by appealing to morals and the law.

After showing and debriefing the film, the follow-up is a short story called "The Bench" by Richard Rive. It is a perfect example of the empowering nature of nonviolent resistance. The story begins with the protagonist, Karlie, at a rally where he is inspired to make an individual stand against an oppressive law of the segregated Apartheid government in Johannesburg, South Africa. He chooses to sit on a bench for whites only and does not move even when a white man confronts him and when, finally, a policeman comes to arrest him. His dignity and courage are enhanced by this personal act of civil disobedience to an immoral law. For him, it becomes the act of a man with convictions and commitment. However, students realize that his act obviously does little to make changes in the society. These observations lead to a class discussion that centers on the differences between individual acts of protest and mass demonstrations of resistance. Students understand that it took collective consciousness and action to end Apartheid, a system that seemed impossible to overthrow.

The English class ends with a weeklong writing workshop that prepares the students for their Interdisciplinary Unit Exam called an IUE. This essay exam is written during the two-hour block of the three Core classes, and it includes information from each of them.

South African Unit: Social Institutions Class

The Social Institutions class is half the length of the English class because it alternates with Art/Religion. The entire South Africa Unit in this class is a multilayered experience called the South African Resistance Festival (SARF). Students are divided into groups based on African leaders: Steven Biko, Nelson Mandela (as a young man), Nelson Mandela (the older man), and Desmond Tutu. The remaining students are in the Unconvinced Group. Readings for SARF are compiled in a packet called "Resistance Festival Reader." It is divided into four major sections: "Background Information," "Resistance Leader Biographies," "Primary Source Documents," and "Additional Information." The first major section begins with a historical background reading of the origins and development of Apartheid. Apartheid means "apartness" in Afrikaans and was instituted into law by the National Party in 1948. To reinforce the separation of the races, black Africans were removed from their homes and forced to live in townships, reserves, and Bantustans while being stripped of all their rights. The next reading is "Issues and Events to Resist," which summarizes the Apartheid laws of "No Vote" for black South Africans, "Pass Laws" to segregate the population, and "Banning" to silence dissenters. Major events included are the Sharpsville Massacre and Soweto Uprising. Completing the first section is a reading entitled "South African Resistance Strategies" that explains six strategies the resistance leaders used against Apartheid; among them are controlled violence, nonviolent direct action, divestment, and Black consciousness. The next two major sections contain biographical information about each student group's leader and one primary source written or orated by each leader. The fourth and final major section consists of timelines and important people, places, and ideas.

All these readings prepare the students for the culminating activities of SARF Day and a Socratic Seminar. The first individual assignment that utilizes the packet readings is a two- to three-page analysis paper that first summarizes the oppressive nature of the Apartheid system. Then the student addresses the resistance strategy/strategies and beliefs of the leader chosen for that group, moving to a consideration of how that leader would want South Africa to heal and move forward. The paper ends with the student's reflection on which strategy seemed the most effective and why. In addition to the paper, each student writes at least two critical and thoughtful questions to be used in the Socratic Seminar. There is also a group assignment to make one mural to be hung on the classroom walls during SARF DAY. The reason for the mural, besides adding a visual backdrop to the festival, is that many people living in townships did not receive an adequate education; therefore, murals with few or no written words were often used to educate and inspire them to continue the struggle.

On SARF DAY students come to school dressed in business-like clothing. They know that the purpose of their campaign is to spread the word about their leader and his vision for South Africa. The group actively tries to educate other students, particularly the Unconvinced Group about their leader's resistance strategy(s). Students are given flexibility to present their leader in any creative or engaging manner: demonstrations, spoken word, song, protest, or skits. Moreover, each group is expected to make, at some point, a two-minute presentation to the class (that involves every member), highlighting the main ideas of the campaign.

The final activity in SI is the Socratic Seminar that takes two days. The first session opens with an introduction to each of the SARF resistance leaders and Unconvinced Group. The Unconvinced Group then addresses each leader with a series of questions: How do we resist? What is the most effective way to resist? How do we move forward? During this questioning, all students are expected to stay in character. In the second session, students are given the opportunity to discuss any points or arguments that they want to emphasize or clarify.

South African Unit: Art/Religion Class

Alternating with Social Institutions is Art/Religion, where students watch *Amandla: A Revolution in Four-Part Harmony.* The wonderful film is examined section by section as it documents almost every phase of the struggle against Apartheid in South Africa. A major component of that struggle comprised the hundreds of songs that were similar in use and impact to "We Shall Overcome" in the Civil Rights Movement in the United States. These revolutionary songs were an essential part of the nonviolent resistance movement. In the 1950's the first songs protested the relocation of black neighborhoods to townships. Then songs were composed about the experiences of the men who were carried on trains to work in the diamond mines in Johannesburg, where they labored long hours for little pay. In addition, songs were composed and sung in opposition to the Pass Laws of the late 1950's and early 1960's that led to massive demonstrations, including the Sharpeville Massacre. There were also songs to free Mandela when he became a political prisoner after 1964, songs about black children resisting being taught in Afrikaans (the Soweto Uprising), and songs calling for the overthrow of Apartheid due to increasing numbers of funerals and people in mourning. Sung in solidarity, these songs inspired the continued resistance to decades of Apartheid rule from 1948 to 1994 when Nelson Mandela became president. After deconstructing the film, student groups compose and sing their own protest songs about anything that they sincerely agree needs to be changed in their own lives.

Concluding Statements

The English, Social Institutions, and Art/Religion classes all end with a review for the Interdisciplinary Unit Exam (IUE). Based on a review from each Core teacher, students write and memorize outlines for each discipline. Then in English class students review how to write an introductory paragraph and thesis in order to make connections and transitions throughout the essay. The IUE is the foundation of the writing-based program for all four years.

As I mentioned in the introduction to this chapter, Core units have taken years to develop. Every summer for decades, teachers have changed and improved them. The Africa Unit, for example, is a living entity that has grown through multiple iterations. In its present form it consists of many different methods for teaching and evaluating students. I share here the unit because students can be fully engaged, inspired, and empowered by it! This is what we all want for our young learners.

References

Adichie, C. (2008). The headstrong historian. *The New Yorker*. Retrieved from https://www.newyorker.com/magazine/2008/06/23/the-headstrong-historian

Adichie, C. (2009). The danger of the single story. Retrieved from https://www.ted.com/talks/chimamanda_adichie_the_danger_of_a_single_story?language=en

Attenborough, R. (Producer & Director). (1982). *Gandhi*. [Motion Picture]. USA. Colombia Pictures.

Dean, S., & Markgraaff, D. (Producers). Hirsch, L. (Director). (2002). *Amandla: A revolution in four-part harmony*. US Import: ATO Pictures.

Hansberry, L. (1994). *Les Blancs: The collected last plays*. USA: Vintage Books.

King, M. (1963). Letter from a Birmingham jail. Retrieved from https://www.africa.upenn.edu/Articles_Gen/Letter_Birmingham.html

The King Center (n.d.). Six principles of nonviolence. Retrieved from https://thekingcenter.org/ king-philosophy/

Mandela, N. (1995). *Long walk to freedom: The autobiography of Nelson Mandela*. New York, NY: Little, Brown and Co.

Reid, F. & Symons, J. (Producers). Hoffmann, D. & Reid, F. (Directors). (2000). *Long night's journey into day* (Truth and Reconciliation Commission). Iris Films/Cinemax Reel Life. Retrieved from http://www.newsreel.org/guides/longnight.htm

Rive, R. (1963). The bench. Retrieved from https://mrsgewitz.weebly.com/uploads/1/3/4/7/13476108/the_bench.pdf

York, S. (1999). *A Force More Powerful*. Films for the Humanities

Chapter 11

Shifting Content, Sparking Agency

An English Language Arts Curriculum of Nonviolence

By Karin Rose

Change can be difficult to see all at once, like a pebble dropped in a pond creating cascading ripples outward. My experience attending the Ahimsa Center Institute has felt like a continuing ripple, first in my curriculum, then in my pedagogy, and in the change that I continue to see in myself and in my students. Viewing my teaching through a lens of nonviolence has not only changed the emphasis of the coursework, but it has also shifted the focus of my classroom as I have worked to employ the practices of nonviolence with my students and with myself. The academic, social, and emotional needs of students are ponderous because many often come into classrooms feeling as though they outweigh the resources available. I cling to the hope that by offering students the opportunity to see the world as a place where change can occur, I can show them that with powerful thoughts and words they may be advocates and agents for change.

My participation in the Gandhi, Sustainability, and Happiness Institute in 2013 was a transformational experience in my teaching career. I saw how academic topics overlapped the discussions about the relationships and the everyday challenges that both students and the community face. More than anything, I learned to give myself permission to add emotion, and to challenge students themselves to add emotion, to the fact-based academic instruction required at each grade level. As I began conversations that challenged me and my colleagues to reconsider the content and the ways that we frame challenging dialogues with students, I experienced

C. A. Bracho and D. Dodson (eds.), Teachers Teaching Nonviolence, 157–166.

professional growth. The shift in my own perspective began to spark agency in my students.

Shifting Perspective: The Influence of the Ahimsa Institute

While attending the Institute, my first feeling of actionable momentum was after we read *The Buddha and the Terrorist* by Satish Kumar. Through this short and accessible allegory, I began to see how the principals of nonviolence can be shared and discussed through literature. The parable shows the impact of violence on individuals and a community. Kumar identifies the challenge for individuals in the face of violence: their desire for either revenge, forgiveness, or reparations, and the ripple of each decision. Expertly paired with the discussions we had in the Institute and the in-depth study of Gandhi and his journey for freedom through nonviolence, Kumar's story brought all these ideas into focus in a way that felt manageable in my novice but eager hands. Had I read independently, I would not have been able to see how the principles of satyagraha and ahimsa could be put into my teaching practice.

The Ahimsa Institute presented the ideas of *satyagraha* and *ahimsa* as Gandhi used them historically and in other broader contexts: "Gandhi's originality lay in his innovative synthesis of the two concepts to create a powerful paradigm of revolution and social reform" (Sethia, 2012, p. 47). My own perceived role as an educator began to shift as I began to hope for students to have the principals of satyagraha as they encountered challenges in their own lives. The idea that my time with students could empower them to become seekers of truth and nonviolent change was very motivating as I looked at what I wanted to pursue in my career. Gandhi was clear that education was an instrument and, therefore, could be used or equally misused. He emphasized in *Hind Swaraj* that the purpose for education was to support the overall independence of individuals with skills they needed as well as to build character. The idea that the acquisition of academic skills is not the sole indicator of a successful student was not new to me. As I contemplated the process of teaching academic skills, I began to see that the ways we worked could be a part of the critical character-building that all students need. I began to understand that teaching is my passion, not my job. Seeing the role of both the educator and education itself through the lens of Gandhi's work brought new depth to my profession. Being able to teach in a way that produces character and happiness is vital.

Through thoughtful and powerful discussions with other educators at the Ahimsa Institute, I began to see the opportunity to have discussions about how individuals encounter violence, about the impact on the community, and about the opportunity for each individual to choose nonviolence. When framed as a bigger picture of nonviolence, the question became how I could begin to shift not just individual lessons but whole units or areas of study into helping students become curious about ahimsa. During the first three years after the Institute, I continued to teach elementary school, finding stories and historical areas of study to begin to build the conversations about nonviolence in my classroom. The passage of time was another ripple of change as I continued to be curious and reflective about what I learned at the Ahimsa Center Institute.

As my personal and professional interests continued to shift, I moved from elementary education to teach as an English Language Arts teacher in middle school. Having considered this change for several years, I struggled with leaving the elementary classroom and the powerful community that is nurtured in such a special instructional ecosystem. Change is a powerful force. By changing first to middle and then to high school, I have been allowed a chance to start fresh with what goals I set for my classroom instruction and environment. I knew I would need to make serious shifts in instruction as I worked with young teenagers, who are full of opinions and ideas but who are also gaining more and more experience in their communities. Now six years separated from my time at the Ahimsa Center Institute, I have worked to transform the lessons in both my middle school and now my high school classroom, not only to have academic purpose but also to serve as an outlet for students to process their own stories and grapple with the ideas of nonviolence. With the help of collaborative colleagues, flexibility in curriculum options, and supportive administrators, I have been able to find or create whole units, spanning most of the school year, that challenge students to consider the historical, practical, and emotional aspects of nonviolence in multiple contexts.

Shifting Content: Curriculum of Nonviolence

As I moved from isolated lessons anchored in practices of ahimsa to a year-long focus on nonviolence, I wanted to introduce students to a more reflective and empathetic way to look at the world. The elementary, middle, and high schools where I have worked are all located in a community with a demographic of diverse students, whose needs have shifted significantly over the last ten years. The need for dialogue and support of students beyond the academic content has increased as well. As I began to see the impact these conversations and reflections had among students, I recognized the opportunity to shift my entire curriculum with short stories, texts, speeches, poems, and other writings that use the principles of nonviolence.

With each text, classes have explored the impact that nonviolence has on the self and on a community. Short stories such as "The Gold Coin" and "Thank You Ma'am" have been critical vehicles for introducing the principals of ahimsa and for helping students see alternatives to violence and destructive behavior. Students read *A Long Walk to Water* by Linda Sue Park, the story of the Lost Boys of South Sudan who worked together to survive. They also read *Lyddie*, a fictional narrative about life in a factory town in Lowell, Massachusetts, during the 1840s and the struggle for workers' rights, unionizing, and fair treatment. Paired with this book, my classes read César Chávez's "Commonwealth Club Address" and excerpts from his 1986 "Wrath of Grapes" speech to identify persuasive techniques and to gain understanding about the effect of unionizing and boycotts in history. My classes also studied several speeches from the Civil Rights Movement as well as poetry about Dr. Martin Luther King, Jr. and other civil rights leaders.

One of my goals at the beginning of the year is to make sure my classes have a collective experience with several texts so that we can refer to them as a class throughout the year. These anchor texts have proved to be so powerful throughout the year to help students understand and build a framework for what nonviolence can look like in many different situations. I appreciate the brevity and succinctness that Alma Flor Ada uses in "The Gold Coin." As students engage in rigorous Socratic Seminar discussions to consider the ideas of honesty, crime, and reparations, many can see how the text has some themes common in contemporary, local, or personal stories they encounter. This text is very academically accessible for most students to read and understand. Because the challenge is not about the text's complexity, they are then able to consider the themes and bigger principles at play in the text and discuss it with passion. I encourage students to focus on the themes and text for a portion of the discussion, but I also motivate them to bring in personal and real-world examples of the themes of honesty and repentance and to be curious about "what if" when considering a new topic. Students always impress me with the depth and complexity of the connections they make to their own world. My classes have often remarked how much they enjoy having these types of discussions because of the opportunity to share about their lives and to learn about each other. Given the right framework, young people seem to always rise to the occasion and have discussions about complex and challenging topics.

Working through various academic skills while reading the short story "Thank You, Ma'am" by Langston Hughes, my students quickly make connections to "The Gold Coin" as they begin to see themes of poor economic conditions, rule-breaking, forgiveness, the role of a community, and the importance of rebuilding trust. Almost all students can relate easily to such universal concepts, and my classes spend several days discussing, finding evidence, and supporting details as we compare texts. My goal is to introduce them to the ideas surrounding restorative practices while affirming the complexity of these situations. Without explicitly stating that we will be learning about restorative practices at the beginning of the reading, students experience the productive struggle in trying to understand and to name the concepts in both texts. This idea of profound truth, even as literary characters faced difficult circumstances, is a way to begin incorporating the ideas of satyagraha into the classroom. We end our discussion with an empowering idea: "what if" we and our class use some of these same practices in the classroom throughout the year?

The first major unit of study is focused on stories of survival. The goal for this unit is for students to see the profound strength and soul-force that characters struggled to achieve amidst their struggle for survival. Students are often highly engaged by the powerful characters and powerful stories of endurance in the face of insurmountable circumstances. Students self-select novels with themes of survival: *Long Walk to Water* by Linda Sue Park, *Outsiders* by S.E. Hinton, *Island of the Blue Dolphins* by Scott O'Dell, *The Pearl* by John Steinbeck, and several other novels. Classes can have powerful discussions about the impacts of violence on individuals and broader communities as characters struggle to survive. One powerful task is for students to categorize the internal and external character traits of their protagonists. As they lead discussions about the internal changes that characters experience in the face of a variety of challenges, they make powerful literary connections as well as connections to the wider world around them.

While reading the novel *Long Walk to Water,* my classes also read several historical and non-fiction sources about the conflict in South Sudan and the devastating impact of the civil war on the region. As we continue to read source after source, students begin to build a technical understanding and empathy about the complexity of violence in the book. Understanding the context of tribal culture, geographic barriers, colonialism, and historical events establishes a beginning foundation for a more comprehensive picture for students as they work to understand the impact of violence on a group of children.

Another in-depth unit of study, "Working Conditions: Then and Now," directs students to toward historical accounts and a fictionalized novel about working conditions. The goal of this unit is to build understanding and empathy for the economic and social injustice that various groups have faced, especially through their employment. Throughout the quarter, students read a coming-of-age novel, *Lyddie*, by Katherine Paterson. The author gives readers a window into the conditions for young women working in textile mills in Lowell, Massachusetts, during middle of the 19th century. I am blown away with the perceptive reading and questions that students propose as the characters encounter low wages, lack of education, dangerous working conditions, sexual harassment, personal losses, and the struggle to rise above.

During this unit, students also study several speeches made by César Chávez as he advocated and fought for the farm workers' rights at the end of the 20th century. While developing their rhetorical skills and strategies, they are impressed with the argumentative writing style Chávez employs in the fight to improve working conditions. Many students are surprised as we learn about Chávez; they had never heard of him or his work. Because this is an unknown topic for most of them, in many ways their engagement in the unit soars as they read to find out how history treated another group of individuals who utilized principles of nonviolence. After reading "The Wrath of Grapes" speech by Chávez (1986), many students express that they, too, are willing to boycott grapes if it can help influence the working conditions. With a careful re-reading of the title, they find that this boycott occurred a generation ago, but they also begin to independently research products sold today that are harvested or made amid poor working conditions. As students begin to see their own power as consumers, their own analysis and writing become sharper and more focused.

In addition to this curriculum shift, this year I worked with my colleague to develop an in-depth unit on poetry analysis and writing. Students read and discuss dozens of poems, while building a collection their own poetry to prepare for a class poetry slam and then a school-wide poetry slam. We read several poems, songs, speeches, and other texts about the Civil Rights Movement in the United States during the 1950s and 1960s. Students are at first slow to engage in their learning, often arguing they have already read and "know" about this topic. However, as we begin to read poems that discuss this time period, they become curious and notice the powerful language choices and complexity of facing violence and choosing to respond with nonviolence. Many of them anchor pieces of their own poetry in the ideas reflected in the Civil Rights Movement, making compelling poems relevant to their own personal concerns. Students are peer-selected to share their poems for our school poetry slam, and I notice that each class enthusiastically receives the poems that are written as reactions, responses, or calls to action related to social injustice; their response to each poet demonstrates value for the individual student as well as the ideas expressed in the poem. Not only am I encouraged to see them expressing themselves well with the poetic skills that are the focus of our work, but I also see them take the ideas and conversations about nonviolence, care for our community, and difficult topics and then weave them into their own words and voices.

Building Student Agents of Change

I end every year with asking students to reflect on their own learning and growth and to share with me insight or thoughts based on our class. As I prepared to write this chapter and its reflection on my instruction and experience with the Ahimsa Institute, I also asked students about our units of study and how it impacted their thinking. As a statistic, 98 of my 114 students responded to the survey. Several students did not want to respond and have their answers included in my writing here, and others were new and had not completed most of the work from the year. Of those who responded, the following data represents their reflection:

— It revealed that 97% of students felt that they knew the difference between a peaceful and not peaceful protest.
— It showed that 70% of students said that they liked reading examples of stories (or history) where people used nonviolence to work to solve problems.

Students were given a prompt: "Reading examples of people who use nonviolence to create change makes me____." Among their responses were as follows:

— "want to make change"
— "inspired"
— "more thoughtful"
— "want to help do something that will make a change for people who are struggling"
— "thankful"
— "I wonder how they made change, and if they ever used violence in their life"

— "What else needs to change?"
— "I realize that violence is not the only answer, and that by working together you may get through problems"
— "wonder why people don't use it as a solution more often"
— "think of how we as a country can do better"
— "I want to do non-violent protests"
— "feel all good inside and they [sic] I say LET'S MAKE A CHANGE!! I then go sit on the couch and watch YouTube or something"
— "bored because when they don't use violence it is less drama"

I also asked students what they see about their world that they might not have otherwise noticed:

— "By reading these poems and speeches about the unfair conditions it got me to think about it more. It shows me that we are a strong country when we fight for the greater good. I also noticed that they make the biggest changes peacefully."
— "We get scared and blame the DIFFERENT people for our own problems."
— "I think people should get to vote for president even if they are under the age of 18 because younger people should get a say in their state. A lot of younger people have strong opinions of stuff that happens in their state."
— "There are still bad working conditions in the world that I hope can get better because without good jobs a lot of people can't live a decent life."

One of my biggest points of reflection is the need for student agency. Overwhelmingly, students had profound and meaningful responses to the work we did. Additionally, students expressed enthusiasm for issues of the past as history has reported them, but they did not know how to engage or to take actionable steps in their current conversations and issues in their lives. This is where I find myself with work to do as I begin to teach high school, seeking ways to continue to integrate the ideas of satyagraha into my curriculum but then seeing how to support students as they put these ideas into practice in their own lives.

Sparking Agency

The shift to curriculum content that centered on nonviolence changed the conversation that students experience every day in class. My classroom has also shifted toward a space of choice and student voice, moving away from teacher-directed systems and moving toward student advocacy for learning. At first this shift in student agency seemed unrelated to the shift in curriculum. However, as I listened and read what students understood, I realized the positive shift in classroom culture goes hand-in-hand with what students are learning. Each time we read about a character making a difficult, courageous decision, I saw the spark of courage in students as they see themselves as agents of change. Each time students had choice in what they read or how they presented their learning, their willingness to engage in their own learning increased. The academic skills remain rigorous, but they allow students to have choices and flexibility engages and excites them in a new way.

Students encounter the real world every day; therefore, by giving space in my classroom to learn and see stories that are important, they are eager to engage in the learning. In one of our most complex assignments of the year, students were required to write an argument essay. As I was steeling myself for the job of introducing this assignment in addition to all the technical requirements, I was pleasantly reminded about how passion and purpose can serve as intrinsic motivation. Even my most reluctant writers and students who struggle with academics had strong opinions and evidence about the working conditions we had read throughout the unit.

Students consistently astound me with their willingness and need to share about their own lives. Time and time again, they had powerful opinions and experience about topics we were reading: conversations about families who had been victims of violence, concerns about economic conditions, and those who knew firsthand the impact of jobs with low wages or heart-breaking conversations about the threats of school violence at our own school or around the country. I heard them relate how their hope for a better world required a need for change. I found that, as the year continued with a community of students, these conversations grew from a veiled conversation of "what if" to an outright conversation about how violence impacts individuals and their community. By trying to find literature and units of study to integrate the principles of nonviolence, I quickly began to realize that I was really finding opportunities for them to share the everyday concerns and challenges that many face in their own lives. For many students in my classes, the challenges of economics, mental health, race, violence, displaced families, or limited opportunities are not something to consider; they are daily realities.

As an educator, I see my role not only as teaching and introducing academic skills but also as providing students with the social-emotional skills to navigate their world. I am passionate about literature because it gives readers a lens to see a new world, or to see their own world in a new way.

As students grapple with the text and academic rigor, I have found that the text and assignments are one cord in the braid of building true comprehension. They can see how the text acts as a window into another world and how each individual is impacted by another. For them to be able to see how learning impacts their own world, I make the intentional inclusion of social emotional skills in lessons a priority in my instruction. I ask myself a series of questions: How am I giving students an opportunity to see their world in what we study? How can characters and story arcs model a different way to see and react to the world?

As I began to see the need to work with many students in a different way, I also wanted to encourage other staff members who encountered many of the same challenges in their classroom. I began to read several books by Bruce Perry and Maia Szalavitz, including *The Boy Who Was Raised as A Dog: What Traumatized Children Can Teach Us About Loss, Love and Healing* and *Born for Love: Why Empathy is Essential—and Endangered*. The idea that students who have or are experiencing trauma struggle to learn was nothing new, but the language to have this meaningful conversation had been lacking from my vocabulary. I advocated to my team and administrators that our staff needed more support with some of our most challenging students, and this year our whole staff had professional development about trauma-informed care.

Time and time again, when I work to build relationships with students, build rapport, and take time to know their stories, the academics often fall into place. I have never regretted learning more about a student, taking time to talk to him or her more! When we use the phrase "person-first," I have to remember it isn't just a careful use of syntax, but a concept that education is really an opportunity for people to come together to seek truth about who we are and about how we can positively impact the world.

Reference

Sethia, Tara. (2012). *Gandhi: Pioneer of nonviolent social change*. New York, NY: Pearson.

Chapter 12

Voices of Young Women Leaders

Swaraj and Satyagraha through Digital Storytelling

By Jode Brexa

It's January 2014, the beginning of the academic school year at the University of the Free State in Bloemfontein, South Africa. As a visiting American teacher in Free State on a five-month Fulbright to collect stories of undergraduate women leaders, I have been welcomed to Welwitschia—one of the young women's residence halls on campus. The foyer of the dorm smells of the long-stemmed white roses placed in a tall vase to welcome the freshwomen—First Years—to the residence. Sumien, a blue-eyed longhaired blonde on the Leadership Team responsible for First Years, sits down with a stack of black and white glossies of the future Welwitschia residents, and says, plaintively, in a lovely South African accent, to the Residence Head Elize Rall, "Tanni, we can't take any more white girls." I am curious: issues of equity are challenges in my public high school back in Boulder, Colorado—though the conversations there have never been stated so explicitly as black and white.

"Why can't the Residence Hall take any more white girls?" I ask. Sumien launches into an impassioned explanation about the University's integration policy. University residences were formerly segregated by color; now, under the leadership of Rector Jonathan Janssen, each residence is targeted for fifty/fifty black/white integration. The success of the policy varies with each residence. There are residences with white/black ratios of 90/10, 80/20, and 70/30, and the reverse ratios with black majorities/white minorities. Word has it that incoming First Years know the ratios and

C. A. Bracho and D. Dodson (eds.), *Teachers Teaching Nonviolence*, 167–177.

request their preferred residence on applications based on how comfortable they think they will be with the diversity ratios.

The previous year—2013—Welwitschia won the university's award for reaching a 50/50 balance of racial integration. This year, ninety percent of freshwomen applications are white, but Sumien is committed to protecting the integration policy. On the bulletin board in the foyer where we sit, successful diversity is apparent in color photos of each of the Leadership Team. In addition to Sumien, the stunning nine are freckled and strawberry blonde Melissa; thousand-braided Montseng; pink-cheeked Chantelle; petite, brown-eyed, blonde Roelien; statuesque, chestnut-haired Karen; dark beauty Refemetswe; lithe, lean, blonde Cherise; and serious, raven-haired, black-eyed Eugené. These are the young women who, over the course of my five-month Fulbright, I befriend and support in their exploration of the engaged methodology of digital storytelling. Through the technology project, each of these women creates digital stories about her residence leadership experience on the University of the Free State campus. Through narrative, each woman leader explores her commitment to social action as a leader, each her civic duty of guiding the young women under her responsibility; thus, each might be said to exemplify Gandhi's concepts of *swaraj* and *satyagraha*.

Swaraj and satyagraha have infused my professional work as an educator. Accordingly, this chapter explores the initial challenge of equity in my public high school; gives references to and an interpretation of swaraj and satyagraha as related to educational leadership; provides background, literature review, method, and participants for my Fulbright Capstone Project; and a delivers a summary of three digital stories that exemplify Gandhi's idea of soul-force and the accompanying moral imperative for nonviolent civil action in the world.

My Context

I taught for fifteen years in an alternative high school on the outskirts of a white suburban community with student demographics of 60.5% Hispanic, .7% percent Native America, and 1.4% African American—the highest percentage of culturally and linguistically diverse students in a middle or high school in my district. 72% of the population had free and reduced lunch. Early Childhood Education on campus served 17 teen parents (and their babies) in onsite childcare. 34% of the population represented English Language Learners. Therefore, addressing issues of race and class was the biggest challenge there. My high school was often seen as the "dropout" school where students open-enrolled to retrieve credits for courses they failed in traditional schools. My cultural and linguistically diverse students—many adjudicated—faced issues of abuse, poverty, homelessness, and unwanted pregnancy. I faced an educational challenge to find nonviolent means to address cultural, racial, and class inequities.

Summer Institute 2013

When I applied to Ahimsa Center's Summer Institute in 2013, I was seeking to meet the challenge of creating inclusive classrooms where the voice of every student is heard, especially those marginalized by race and class. There I learned about Gandhi's rationale for civic engagement by Indians under British Rule in his seminal work *Hind Swaraj* and how it might provide a rationale for civic action by youth leaders in educational contexts worldwide. *Swaraj* embraces both self-realization and social justice in the world. Gandhi asserts, "It is Swaraj when we learn to rule ourselves" (Parel, 2009, p. 71). In the historical context of his work, he encourages Indians to seek the self-rule of India as well as through the "moral regeneration" of the individual (Sethia, 2013, p. 58). In the context of the individual's discipline of Self, Gandhi calls swaraj "the internal moral transformation of the individual" (Sethia, 2013, p. 58). Specifically, he demands self-discipline. Such swaraj has "to be experienced by each one for himself" (cited in Parel, 2009, p. 71). Thus, it is no less than an awakening to self-transformation.

In the realm of the spiritual, swaraj is rooted in Truth or God: "a self-existent, all-knowing living Force which inheres in every other force known to the world" (cited in Parel, 2009, p. 182). Truth, in Gandhi's concept, is pluralistic. If framed in a Christian context, it would "reference grace or divine revelation" (Sende, 2004, p. 14). For Gandhi, this Truth is not a fuzzy philosophical abstract concept but is action manifested in the world. He coined the term *satyagraha*, or civic nationalism, which he believed is grounded in one's own inner strength: "The power of satyagraha, known as the concept of truth force or soul force awakened in the Self, leads to imperative moral action in the service of social justice" (Parel, 2009, p. xxiv.). Gandhi's philosophy, which combines the spiritual awakening of the unconscious Self and the historical, political awakening of Indians to the limitations of modern civilization under British rule, can guide personal transformation and the resulting commitment to nonviolence, an imperative for 21st-century educational leaders.

South Africa

The 2013 Summer Institute ignited my search to explore transformative educational approaches, particularly within the cultural and historical paradigms of racism and classicism that contributed to achievement gaps among multicultural and multilingual groups (Tileston & Darling, 2008). I sought out South Africa—the country where Gandhi had experienced firsthand racial oppression under British rule. I hoped to learn how democratic South Africa—like India post-independence—had transitioned from its oppressive colonial history.

In 2014, I was awarded a Fulbright Distinguished Award in Teaching—a grant open to K-12 educators through the U.S. Department of State Bureau of Educational and Cultural Affairs. I traveled to Free State—the former center of Afrikanerism—to the University of the Free State (UOFS), where world-renowned scholar Professor Jonathan Jansen had become the first black Rector, at a time when racial tension on the campus was rife. The violence of the Reitz Four video made by male students at one of the campus residence halls had inflamed the students (Mail & Guardian, 2008). In his response to campus unrest, Rector Jansen (2014) had written that "university leaders, including student leaders, need to deal with expressions of racism systemically and not simply on an incident-by-incident basis." He called campus leaders to address "both symbols and substance of white supremacy in hiring practices, curriculum silences and the names of residences" (Jansen, 2014). In this "demanding" leadership role, Jansen saw—echoing Gandhi—a moral duty. He called on his campus youth leadership to "address wrongs and recognize rights, repair the damage to black people but as it does so, reconcile with white people on campus, laying the foundations for a just and reconciled future" (Jansen, 2014).

When I arrived at UOFS, Rector Jansen personally welcomed me to his campus and took an interest in helping me shape my Fulbright Capstone Project. With his approval, I would work with a leadership team of one of the residence halls to support his policy of reconciliation and enlightened integration. Through the engaged methodology of Digital Storytelling, I hoped to support young residence hall leaders is telling authentic stories of civic engagement.

Digital Storytelling as Method

The Gandhian 20th-century notion of civic engagement is parallel to the 21st-century concept of digital citizenship. Digital citizenship contributes to "civic life" by engaging in discussions and debates about political, social and cultural issues through digital media, necessary for millennial learners (Greenhow, 2010). Teaching practice must model and instruct students in emerging technologies (Sadik, 2008). Digital Storytelling (DST) is an approach that develops 21st-century technologies, provides a way for youth to construct identity, gives storytellers an authoritative role, and allows stories to function as symbolic tools for identity construction (Davis, 2005). As a result, the act of narration shapes a sense of self that can, in turn, lead to self-understanding.

I arrived at UOFS with the engaged methodology of DST in my educational toolbox, and my initial Fulbright Capstone Project proposed to document South African students' experiences in a racially integrated rural high school. In DST, personal narrative, photos and videos, and music are combined in short multimedia pieces, giving voice to unique perspectives. I had hoped to encourage digital literacy with students in a high school in Thaba N'chu, a former township some sixty miles from Bloemfontein. However, I discovered that, in post-Apartheid South Africa, I held little agency as a white outsider in a black community. As well, internet access (necessary for the execution of the DST software) was limited to one modem mounted in a locked metal cage high on the wall in the Teacher's Workroom/Library. My Americentric vision of transforming an underprivileged school through digital technology needed to be grounded in a reality where "the material conditions of a significant section of society are still excluded and marginalized" (Mahlomaholo, 2006, p. 45). Thus, understanding the realities of an under-resourced rural school overturned my belief that, as an American teacher with six laptops, I could use my "privileged position to create opportunities for learning and advancement" (Mahlomaholo, 2006, p. 44). I needed to re-frame my project.

In a meeting with Rector Jansen, I proposed Welwitschia (wired with internet) as the learning environment for my technology project, where new skills could be built upon an existing foundation of digital literacy. I had agency there through my relationship with the Residence Head Elize Rall. I shifted the focus of my Capstone Project from working with South African high school students to working with South African young university women. I hoped my facilitation of DST would support the young women leaders in combining narrative imagination, audio recording, and photos in three-to-four-minute multimedia pieces to tell their unique stories of residence house leadership. Also, I hoped that viewing the finished artifacts through the lens of Gandhi's conceptions of swaraj and satyagraha might give insight into the evolution of the young women leaders' commitment to social action.

The participants in the project were the nine members of the leadership House Committee I'd met on Welcome Day. Each held Portfolios—areas of responsibility—and provided leadership based on the five values of the residence: Integrity, Responsibility, Reliability, Respect, and Unique [sic]. These young women lived, worked, problem-solved, and socialized together in a leadership community grounded in Christian practice. One of the house leaders and I met to co-construct a workshop approach and a timeline for the DST project that fit into the demanding schedule of second- and third-year varsity students who served on the House Committee. These young women self-selected to participate in the DST project. Only women were invited as the residence hall is a female-only accommodation, but the group represented diverse ethnicities and socioeconomic levels. Anonymity was not a condition of the stories; in fact, the converse is the norm: the highly personal nature of these narratives serves as powerful acknowledgement of the authors' identities and leadership roles.

The Digital Storytelling project was not framed as academic research; however, because I was conducting the process in a campus residence hall, the participant selection, approach, and timeline had to be reviewed by the Assistant Director of Residence Life. Since I was inviting the personal stories of undergraduate women enrolled at UOFS, Ethical Guidelines were also required and submitted. Before the project was initiated, Ethical Clearance was granted on behalf of the Dean of Student Affairs, and the proposal was filed with Student Affairs at the College of Student Affairs Research Desk at the University of the Free State.

Women Telling Their Stories

The DST process was conceptualized in two parts. The first centered on the narrative imagination through writing, editing, revising, recording, and sound editing the storyline. The second part was conceptualized around facilitating learning of a software program that would provide a structure with capabilities to construct a multimedia piece with photos, music, and thematic transitions to enrich the storyline.

The first three-day workshop was held in early April. A sub-group of five women engaged in viewing digital stories and overviewed the scope and sequence of the project. Media release forms were signed—one for Fulbright publicity and the second with options for permission to give access to my school and community in the United States, to the UOFS community, and for future academic research.

I posed the question "How do you as a young leader express the moral values (Integrity, Responsibility, Reliability, Respect, and Unique [sic]) of your residence hall?" Though I did not frame the question in the context of Gandhi's philosophy, I believed the digital work would show how the young leaders shaped their identities and their moral imperative towards service. In the first meeting, the young women clarified they wanted to tell their "life stories." As participants' authority is key to ownership of the DST process, my role as facilitator was to support the stories the young women chose to tell.

During the first day of the workshop, the university women brainstormed in journals the themes in their lives related to the residence's five values, shared ideas, overviewed a graphic analyzer on the structure of a narrative, and began writing their "life story." On the morning of the second day, the young women shared their stories with each other and with me, then peer-edited and timed their spoken narratives, exploring ideas in a group story circle on the process of revising a "whole life" into a three- to four-minute piece.

The following week, I met individually with each of the initial five young women to revise and practice their narratives, then set up recording equipment at Welwitschia to record and edit their sound files. Through the month, I facilitated one-on-one workshops with the additional four women leaders, following the same process. Nine digital stories were completed and exported in May 2014.

As a group, the university women decided to share the stories with each other and with their Residence Head. In a celebratory forum in the Welwitschia gazelli, the digital stories were showcased to interweave themes: "Life as I Have Experienced It" by Refemetswe Dimbaza; "Journey" by Annika va Schalkwyk; "Setting the World on Fire" by Roelien vd Westhuizen; "Where There's a Will, There's a Way" by Sumien de Bruin; "Endurance" by Melissa Taljaard; "The Deeper Purpose" by Karen Faasen; "Blessings" by Montseng Matlotlo; "Eduna: My Reason for Breathing" by Eugené Visagie; and "Being Truly Me" by Chantelle Fekete.

Voices of Young Women Leaders is a collection of intensely personal narratives. The stories the young women chose to tell are framed in an arc from childhood and adolescence, through secondary school matriculation and university enrollment; these stories articulate crisis and change, ending with the challenge and moral imperative of values-based residence hall leadership. Each explores an external challenge (poverty, divorce, violence, and abuse) and early self-destructive behaviors (drug use, self-cutting, acting out sexually). Transcending challenge, each story describes an awakening to "truth," framed in the context of Christian divine intervention, and a resulting commitment to responsibility, stewardship, and leadership. In the following, I summarize three of these digital stories and reference my understanding of swaraj and satyagraha in the South African context.

"Eduna: My Reason for Breathing" by Eugené Visagie

Eugené Visagie (2014) shares the story of the death of her father when she was an adolescent. She narrates how she experiences "inner rebelliousness, pain and rebellion." The response to her grief is to act out sexually. She becomes pregnant and enters motherhood long before she is prepared. An unwed mother, she returns to high school, graduates, and then enters university. Though she initially rejects her role as a mother, her moral regeneration occurs through her faith in the "living force of the Creator." She says, "I cannot neglect my duties," and from this moral stance she develops "a personal sense of responsibility" for her daughter. With deep self-exploration, she attests, "My responsibility is to correct the mistakes I've made in the past." Awakened to her Truth in "the words of the Creator who has never forsaken me," she overcomes her fear and moves from personal responsibility to civic responsibility, a contemporary swaraj manifested as taking a leadership role in the Welwitschia Residence.

"Setting the World on Fire" by Roelien vd Westhuizen

Roelien vd Westhuizen (2014) narrates the challenge she faces following her parent's divorce and her mother's remarriage. Custody of her and her siblings is given to her father. Not only was there "not food and not space" in her broken home, but, when visiting her mother, she witnesses her stepfather's violence. Roelien narrates how she seeks comfort in acting out: "I partied and drank and did too much [sic] drugs." After an experience of awakening to the Truth of God's "sheer grace and mercy," she develops "self-discipline, self-restraint, and self-control." As a result, she narrates, "I learned to address others, learned that others had hardships, learned to be myself in God's eyes instead of the eyes of the world." She identifies her essential Truth as "integrity." With this understanding, she—like Eugené—embodies a moral imperative: in her words, to "take responsibility for my own work and my own failures." And she asserts she will strive to persuade others to do the same. In Roelien's own words, "And now that I know who I am and where my life comes from, I can go forth and set the world on fire."

"Being Truly Me" by Chantelle Fekete

Chantelle Fekete (2014) narrates her childhood story of a dysfunctional home and financial challenge. Characterizing her world, she says, "Everything around me felt restricted." As a result, she says, "I isolated myself from deep true relationships." She leaves home to "discover herself." Chantelle finds her Truth—as the others have—in her Christian faith, noting "I found Jesus Christ inside of me." Through that internal transformation, she understands that she is "part of a bigger plan and purpose." Her call beyond the self to social action she names "stewardship." She ends with a paraphrase of perhaps a contemporary understanding of satyagraha: "I want to have the integrity to rise to a challenge, the courage to face the unknown, and the honesty to express who I am."

Storytelling as Swaraj and Satyagraha

These stories of transformation embody themes of swaraj and satyagraha in the modern South African context of a post-apartheid university campus. Each of the stories shows a journey through personal awakening and self-transformation with a resulting imperative towards moral action for social justice. Initially, each woman's personal crises—loss, divorce, poverty, violence, isolation—catalyze a story of finding the force of her inner spirit, her personal swaraj. In her story, each woman narrates coming to self-understanding, authoring her own identity. As Gandhi's Truth is the "all loving living Force which inheres in every other force" (Parel, 2009, p. 182), Eugené's faith in "the living force of the Creator," Roelien's acceptance of God's "sheer grace and mercy," and Chantelle's discovery of "Jesus Christ inside of me" all represent Truth in the context of Christian faith. Through an awakening of her own uniqueness—her "soul-force"—each woman moves beyond the self to the moral imperative of commitment to nonviolent social action—each to responsibility, service and stewardship. Thus, theirs is a contemporary satyagraha: the drive towards civic duty of residence hall leadership. Interestingly, through their leadership, they meet Rector Jansen's moral imperatives by supporting enlightened integration in the only racially balanced residence on a racially troubled campus.

Through the medium of DST, then, we have gained insight into the evolution of commitment to social action. Here we have a lens on how shaping one's most authentic identity is an example of contemporary swaraj while the moral imperative towards service is exemplary satyagraha in a modern world.

The Way Forward

Kouzes (2007) notes, "You can only be authentic when you lead according to the principles that matter the most to you.... To act with integrity, you must first know who you are. You must know what you stand for, what you believe in, and what you care most about" (pp. 47–50). As Gandhi called his fellow Indians in the 20th century to their own transformation of the Self in the service of civic action, Kouzes calls to us in the 21st. Each of us— teachers, principals, community leaders—must be catalyzed by our values. We can learn from the young women leaders at the University of the Free State, who tell us what they stand for and what they believe in. Though these courageous women who shared their unique stories in 2014 have graduated from the University of the Free State and stepped into careers and professional work in South Africa, their stories continue as testaments to the evolution of self-transformation and values-based leadership in the 21st century. Each of us, too, must find the roots of our inner strength and self-realization—our individual "soul force"—to carry on the educational work of this century. Each of us must first tell our own story to discover our identity as a transformational leader. With the engaged methodology of Digital Storytelling, our own stories may come alive to be shared not only in our schools and local communities but also—through the Web—with like-minded teachers and leaders worldwide. Fearlessly, as teachers with the understanding that comes from self-knowledge, we must then encourage our students to write and narrate their own unique stories of "truth-force." We can hope that as they understand and learn to rule their own behavior, they, too, may find the moral courage that Gandhi advocates to engage in nonviolent social action for a more inclusive and a more just world.

References

Davis, A. (2005). Co-authoring identity: Digital storytelling in an urban middle school. *THEN: Technology, Humanities, Education, and Narrative*. Retrieved from http://thenjournal.org/ feature/ 61.

Fekete, C. (2014). Being truly me. Personal narrative in a Fulbright Digital Storytelling Workshop. University of the Free State, Bloemfontein, South Africa.

Greenhow, C. (2010). A new concept of citizenship for the digital age. *Learning and Leading with Technology, 37*(6), 24.

Hlalele, D., & Brexa, J. (2015). Challenging the narrative of gender socialisation: Digital storytelling as an engaged methodology for the empowerment of girls and young women. *Agenda: Empowering Women for Gender Equity, 29*(3), 79–88. Retrieved from http://www. tandfonline.com/eprint/iwamlk8KCAReb4ZDgVTF/full

Jansen, J. (2014). Racism on campus: Jumping around "like mad hatters." Retrieved from http://www.thejournalist.org.za/spotlight/racism-jump-around-like-mad-hatters.

Kouzes, J., & Posner, B. Z. (2007). *The leadership challenge*. San Francisco, CA: John Wiley & Sons, Inc.

Mahlomaholo, S. (2012). *Culture, education, and community: Expressions of the postcolonial imagination.* London, UK: Palgrave Macmillan.

Parel, A. J. (2009). *Gandhi: 'Hind Swaraj' and other writings.* New York, NY: Cambridge University Press.

Racist video surfaces at the University of the Free State. (2008). *Mail and Guardian.* Retrieved from https://mg.co.za/article/2008-02-26-racist-video-surfaces-at-the-university-of-free-state.

Sadik, A. (2008). Digital storytelling: A meaningful technology-integrated approach for engaged student learning. *Education Technology Research and Development, 56,* 487–506. doi:10.1007/s11423-008-9091-8.

Schmoker, M. (2006). *Results now: How we can achieve unprecedented improvements in teaching and learning.* Alexandria, VA: Association for Supervision and Curriculum Development.

Sende, P. et al. (2000). *Presence: human purpose and the field of the future.* New York: Society for Organizational Learning.

Sethia, T. (2012). *Gandhi: Pioneer of nonviolent social change.* Boston: Pearson Education.

Tharp, R. G. et al. (2000). *Teaching transformed: Achieving excellence, fairness, inclusion, and harmony.* Boulder, CO: Westview Press.

Tileston, D., & Darling, S. (2008). *Why culture counts: Teaching children of poverty.* Bloomington, IN: Solution Tree Press.

Villa, R., & Thousand, J. (2005). *Creating an inclusive school.* Alexandria, VA: Association for Supervision and Curriculum Development.

Visagie, E. (2014). Eduna: My reason for breathing. Personal narrative in a Fulbright Digital Storytelling Workshop. University of the Free State, Bloemfontein, South Africa.

Wagner, T. (2006). *Change leadership: A practical guide to transforming our schools.* San Francisco, CA: John Wiley and Sons.

Westhuizen, R. (2014). Setting the world on fire. Personal narrative in a Fulbright Digital Storytelling Workshop. University of the Free State, Bloemfontein, South Africa.

Chapter 13

Design for Good in the Classroom

By Eusebio T. Sevilla

I had no idea what to expect when I applied and was accepted to be an Ahimsa Institute Fellow in the summer of 2011. In the ensuing weeks, I was informed of the books that I was to read ahead of attendance, and thus began my introduction to Mahatma Gandhi and the people he influenced (King, Chávez, and others). During my time at the Institute, my colleagues and I heard from speakers and experts on topics related to Gandhi and César Chávez. We discussed nonviolence as a group of educators, and in our temporary housing we shared and worked out our thoughts about how to integrate this new knowledge into our practices. What I learned in that two weeks has been profound and life-changing for me as an educator and as a person. I now start each class with a mindfulness meditation. Also, I am a better and more compassionate person and teacher. Most profoundly, how I approach the nature of my class has changed. In this chapter I hope to describe the immense influence that the Ahimsa Center has had on my pedagogy and the types of projects that I create with students.

The Power of Education

I will provide a little background first. I began teaching in non-traditional ways. As a young man, I taught rock climbing to kids and adults. Growing up, attending colleges and then art schools, I often taught things that I was passionate about to others. When I worked in the outdoor industry, I endeavored to educate people about the benefits of pristine ecosystems. As a bike shop employee, I provided instruction about the benefits of non-automobile transportation, teaching them how to maintain and care for their bicycles and how to advocate for cyclists in their cities and

C. A. Bracho and D. Dodson (eds.), *Teachers Teaching Nonviolence*, 179–187.

neighborhoods. At the University of California, Irvine, in my role as a graduate teaching assistant, I began a more formal teaching career.

Since then I have taught, and continue to teach, at the college level, working to help teachers get their credentials. I have been an invited guest lecturer, taught at a prestigious Los Angeles private school, and worked at an internationally renowned project-based charter school. I currently teach at a comprehensive public high school in San Diego, where the student body is about 2700 students, where my average class size is 36, and where some teachers will see 41 or more students in their rooms. Our student demographic is defined by highly educated, affluent parents. On the surface this demographic might seem to indicate the students' inherent advantage in life, and in some respects that could be the case if we treat education like a form of emergency triage whereby educational resources are directed at the most socioeconomically "in-need" schools. However, I look at any student I encounter, including the students with the most advantage, and think that our goal as educators, and my own goal, should be in line with Gandhi's statement that "education is that which liberates" (Sethia, 2012, p. 124). Our mission as educators is to make sure that as students go forward in life, they use their advantage to do good for others. The longer I teach, the more interested I become in how we as a nation and as a species can put more emphasis on education in all its facets, which include vocational programs and everything else that we can offer to make kids excited about learning, curious about the world, and generally motivated to create a fairer and more enlightened society. It is in this light after attending the 2011 Ahimsa Institute that I started to make some very significant changes in how I run my classroom.

To provide a bit more context, I am an art and design teacher, so I already get the "he's a chill teacher" compliment from students in the hallways because of my luxury of teaching art. I have tattoos all over my arms, and I like fashion, so I score lots of points with students from the jump. I also love teaching and find that it is the pursuit that I have been doing the longest, though at first without even knowing it; teaching is the pursuit in which all my interests and passions coalesce into something that works for me and for my students. Despite all of this, I often wondered how to make my work more meaningful to me and to my students. Moreover, I wanted to structure my classes and my schools in such a way that allows the students to become fully realized in all their endeavors, to encourage them to be compassionate people, and to help them find balance amid all the distractions that turn their attention away from the positives in culture and society.

My contemplation of a more meaningful education has led me to the role of empathy in creating a more positive educational environment. Empathy is a primary aspect of Ahimsa and all forms of nonviolence from Gandhi, King, and Chávez. No nonviolent movement can exist without empathy for everyone, including one's enemy. This aspect—which can be clearly observed from reading Gandhi's "Hind Swaraj" or the writings of King and Chávez—is paramount in all things. Empathy is also the cornerstone of good design. As an art and design teacher, I am always encouraging students to understand this concept in order to truly understand the needs of their clients and the needs of people more generally. Looking to Gandhi's idea of empathy, I often think of his talisman and how it asks the reader to "Recall the face of the poorest and the weakest man whom you may have seen, and ask yourself, if the step you contemplate is going to be of any use..." (cited in Pyarelal, 1958, p. 65). These questions are perhaps the same ones that a designer must ask when working on a product. Can someone with arthritis use this tool? Will the label I am designing help consumers to make a better choice about their health or the planet? And, of course, if this litmus is applied to teaching, it reminds us as educators to think and act in ways that will benefit our students. This empathetic default is the approach that I employed coming out of my experiences at the Ahimsa Institute, and it informs how I look at why I made the changes in my pedagogy to this day.

A Journey Towards Empathy

One of the first things I did coming back to my school from the Ahimsa Institute was to start a daily mindfulness meditation. Keep in mind that the extent of my meditation knowledge was a history of thinking that people who meditate are all the hippy-dippy types who want to align your chakras. My only really practical meditations happened with guest speakers and educators at the Ahimsa Institute. There I began to understand the value of meditation and the way that it may add value to my students' lives and help to quiet the noise, so to speak. So I began doing a simple "one minute" of mindful breathing. I was still teaching at the progressive project-based charter school, so my students were game to try something new. I was met with zero parental resistance in implementing this practice. I simply invited the students who wanted to participate to do so, and for those who did not wish to participate, I invited them just to use the time to sit quietly and think about whatever they wanted, plan their day, contemplate their next classes, etc. This practice went on some weeks, and I gradually began to see marked change in students' focus and attention immediately following our meditations. I started to give students more time, eventually settling on a five-minute meditation each class period.

Meditation became a practice of personal empathy that my students really valued and enjoyed. More explicitly, in student feedback about the practice, I was receiving statements like this: "The class meditations are the only time I am not plugged into something or in silence," or "My homework and life at home are always so distracting, and the meditations give me a chance to just be for a minute and know that I'm ok." This became more frequently the type of response I was seeing from students. In class it became the way we all got settled and focused on what we had to do that day. It allowed me as a teacher to recalibrate the energy in the room and to clear my own head after every class change and the different energies that we, as educators, all know can occur in any given classroom environment. Due to the overwhelming positives I was witnessing, I began to read more about the science of mindfulness, and I started looking at all the different types of meditation and working in my own time to develop my own personal practice. In full disclosure, I still find it difficult to sit most days for more than ten minutes. Yet currently, meditation is an automatic part of my day at every school where I get a chance to work, especially in my own classes. It is the glue, so to speak, that holds everything else I do together.

Making the Grade

The second most profound change as an educator that I made after returning from the Ahimsa Institute came in the form of assessment. Looking at the teaching I received and the learning I was doing on nonviolence, I began seeking to find a way to invite students to complete high-quality work without the coercive force of traditional grades and points often given as a means of control than a meaningful feedback to motivate student growth. As I thought deeply about the role of a teacher, in my studies of Gandhi, I came across this quote:

> For the work of the teacher is to challenge us to a timeless, limitless task— that of being truly human. To awaken our higher sensibilities. To fortify us with the powers of our own intellect that lead to transcendence of ignorance, the mean and the mundane. To set us on the path to a balanced life that ennobles us. The task implies discipline and work, patience and a sense of inner direction. Most of all, of course, great love. (Kamala, 2006, p.13)

The idea of great love as the preeminent motivator in my teaching hit me instantly and deeply. Looking back at my own time as a student, the teachers who had that love in them and who shared it with students are the ones I remember most and whose teaching resonates with me still.

When I work with new teachers, and visit other school sites, I am on the lookout for this love. I also try to pinpoint the areas where I can see coercion, endeavoring to discover ways that I can possibly help others find their limitless human potential. I see the use of points to encourage or mandate "good behavior," and I cringe a bit. I do not judge those teachers who do this, however. I understand that there are a host of reasons why any school or department or classroom may have these types of rules in place. Even though my logical brain understands the reasoning behind these practices, I still feel there must be other and better ways to get kids to understand the content and to apply their knowledge in novel and meaningful ways. Therefore, with a newfound quest to be as non-coercive as possible in thought and deed, I got rid of grades in my classes.

Queue the sound of the record scratching and the music stopping! Queue also the teacher cries: "But how can I just not grade?" and "That will never fly at my school!" or "How did you get administrative support?" Valid concerns, all of them. To answer one of them, I just did it without asking or consulting anyone; the adage of begging forgiveness was the order of the day. I will attempt to describe what it means to not have grades in my classes. First off, there are grades assigned as required by the state and by my school to serve as a record and a transcript, etc. Instead of creating complicated grade books and multiple assessment points, I require students to submit a grade proposal, providing a place for them to argue and to defend their grades with evidence of the work done in the course and how that work was, or was not, up to a minimum standard of quality. This strategy works well in any class where students develop a portfolio of creative work, but it is not limited only to an art class. In a practical sense, I use an online tool to give students projects and their requirements. I teach, lecture, and demonstrate for the students, providing online resources for them, etc. When they turn in work, they get it checked off, which only means that they met the deadline and turned in the work to a minimum standard. Then at the end of the quarter and again at the end of the semester, the students respond to a series of prompts as to their work and performance in the course, and they submit that in conjunction with their portfolios, including any draft or supporting work that they want to be considered. This provides them a space to constantly improve any work that they do not feel is good enough, even after it is submitted.

This grading system also allows me to spend my class time helping students and providing kind, specific, and helpful feedback (KSH) to them. One of the things that I have found to be antithetical to nonviolence is the nature of grades being finite on any given assignment or project. Do not misunderstand, however. I am ruthless with deadlines. To be eligible for an

A in the course, the students must complete all the projects, but I never understood how a teacher is supposed to encourage a student to improve or learn from mistakes if failure is not an option. To me failure is the teacher! This schema provides a space where, even if work is not up to snuff, a student is not penalized and has room to improve his or her work; this ultimately leads to a deeper and richer understanding of content and a better application of knowledge and skills, which to me should be the point of education.

Establishing Ahimsa in the Physical Classroom Space

In addition to the meditations and grades, I began to think about all of the small and large decisions that affect the environment and flow of any classroom, from the art and decorations on the walls to the way the seating is arranged to either facilitate individual work or collaboration. I began thinking heavily about the physical space of classrooms and schools and the impact that the environmental design and architecture play in how we can educate students. This is a juggernaut of an issue when considering design for good because so many educators do not have much choice about the classrooms where they teach. Some classrooms exist in antiquated buildings or shared spaces, and schools often lack budgets to do the overhaul that is needed with regards to the physical spaces. Having said that, I still feel it is incumbent upon me to urge all teachers not to overlook this issue. We are, as educators, designing our classrooms, hopefully, in order to get our students to connect major ideas, develop empathy and understanding of the world and people around them, and spark creativity in all disciplines. Ultimately, we want them to learn to problem solve and to explore in a challenging, engaging, and safe environment.

My contemplation and experimentation with classroom and pedagogical design have led me to believe that I have a unique educational approach and philosophy inspired by ahimsa. At the 2018 Ahimsa Conference at Cal Poly, I was honored to share the stage with some influential and fascinating human beings doing amazing things in practices of nonviolence. In my role as a presenter, I was asked to share my thoughts on the impact that the study of Gandhi and the Ahimsa Institute has had on my practice, and in that capacity I spoke to my thoughts on "Designing for Good in the Classroom." The title has a double meaning. On the primary level as an educator and person, it alludes to how I treat, listen to, and feel compassion for my students and coworkers. How I approach even mundane tasks like grading, as I have described, has shifted to a more compassionate and meaningful method. And I have incorporated meditations to help students become more aware and compassionate in their own lives.

Praxis

The second meaning of "Design for Good" alludes to the types of projects we tackle in a design classroom, and really in any classroom. One of the major benefits of being an artist or craftsperson is the chance to pursue the things that are of interest to you. You get to seek out the knowledge of others, experiment, and work with your mind and your hands to fully grasp the concepts that you wish to communicate or to make functional objects that better the lives of others. This artistic or making approach to learning coincides deeply with what Anil Sadgopal (2013) writes concerning Gandhi's ideas for a new education. This approach, called "Nai Taleem," delineates ideas that accord with what some schools are implementing when they move towards a more student-driven and project-based approach to learning:

> When children learn through productive work, the Macaulayian practice of prescribing textbooks would become superfluous, just as Gandhi had passionately argued. Instead of textbooks, each school would have a reference library of resource material drawing from both local and global sources...prepared by the community and children themselves. (Sadgopal, 2013, p.175)

As artists and designers in my digital art and design classes, my students and I are the de facto culture-makers in society, creating all the visual forms of communication going out into the world. This is an area where I feel that putting theory into practice is paramount because the effects are real. In this capacity we have, for the most part, only tackled collaborative projects with businesses and organizations that have a positive impact on people in our communities and, more broadly, the planet.

"Design for Good" means that as creative producers we can make choices in the types of clients with whom we work in order to move forward an agenda of peace and nonviolence and to establish and grow community connections. By doing so, we can create a classroom environment where students have deep connections and passion for their work. As teachers of design and art, or really any subject, we can move toward a more aware generation of students by helping them to understand the reality of working for corporations, small companies, NGOs, and environmental groups that have major positive impact on the world. To date we have worked with surf industry companies that use recycled and up-cycled materials, companies that provide wheelchairs and mobility access to people with disabilities, and environmental and natural resource groups such as the Surfrider Foundation and our local watershed organization.

An example of one of our design class projects involved our collaboration with a company called Senior Mobility Aids or SMA. Senior Mobility Aids was represented by a man named Allen Newsome, who is part of the family that runs the business. This business involves providing wheelchairs to patients and people with disabilities or injuries to help them have access to a full life outside of their homes. Allen and his company advocate to the government the importance of getting insurance companies to provide the best wheelchairs possible so that the people who are in them can enjoy the highest quality of life. As he told our class during our design briefing, people who obtain cheap, mechanical wheelchairs are more likely to develop pressure sores or have limited access when their families or caregivers cannot push or move this style of chair. Additionally, SMA advocates for getting more access in public spaces, as they provide wheelchairs for venues like Sea World, etc. Allen has traveled to Africa to work on access issues and to help others. All in all, this is a tremendous small company doing really great things in the world, the perfect client for my students. What the business needed was simply a new logo and a graphic design style that would be more contemporary and communicate to their clients that they care about their quality of life. My students then took that briefing and began their iterative process, and then progressed by garnering feedback from each other, from me, and from the client. They looked at the different groups of people who would see the logo and ultimately came up with a great solution that is used by Senior Mobility Aids today. The students get to do some meaningful work with a client who does meaningful work.

Another great example of the types of projects I like to tackle with students was a recent design project with the San Dieguito River Valley Conservancy, or "SDRVC." This organization works to preserve a local natural watershed and is continually working to re-establish the continuity of the watershed from its headwaters to the coast, as well as provide access and recreation to anyone who would like to enjoy it via the "Coast to Crest" Trail. This trail currently connects about 70 miles of trail in five major sections in the North San Diego County area of California. SDRVC needed a patch design for the patches that are given to hikers who complete the Coast to Crest Trail. Additionally, this organization wanted a patch that represented its mission. Once again, I asked a representative from the SDRVC, Ana Lutz, to speak with the students and give them background on what they do, the local history, and the flora and fauna, as well as the two Native American tribes that have occupied this watershed. The students needed this information in order to be aware of all the vested interests and to develop their empathy research to make good design solutions. With this project, the organization took submissions from all my students and narrowed them down to two separate designs that they put into production. As of the writing of this chapter, if you complete the Coast to Crest Trail, you will get a patch design by a high school design student from my classes. These types of projects provide many real-world connections for students. Furthermore, when they are executed well, they develop a relationship between the schools, the classrooms, and the community.

Continuing the Vision of Design for Good

In our effort to create content that furthers the messages of these companies and organizations, the "Design for Good" program and projects like the aforementioned provide opportunities for students to learn and hone their art skills, to learn to communicate their ideas to each other and the public at large, to learn that their choices matter, and to learn that they have the power to impact the world in a positive way.

I do not by any means have this all sewn up, nor do I consider myself an expert in anything. Rather I am a continuous student following my own passions and questions and seeking to understand the world around me though continued, thoughtful experimentation. By using the meditation time and design-thinking approach in classrooms while developing visual communication skills and deep empathy through thoughtful exercises and projects, we can help students to bridge all the gaps they are perceiving in their education. We can develop a pedagogy that nurtures a student's compassion, creating school and classroom communities that foster and support the growth of students into intelligent and thoughtful stewards of the future of our world. We can encourage our students who suffer from adversity, and we can lead our students to work towards the common good by facilitating their interests and passions. We can inspire our students to make positive changes in their lives and in the world by using the tools at their disposal. We can design for good.

References

Kamala, S. (2006). *Yours faithfully, M.K. Gandhi*. Washington D.C: The Mahatma Gandhi Memorial Foundation, Inc.

Pyarelal, N. (1956). *Mahatma Gandhi: The last phase* (Vol. 11). Ahmedabad: Navajivan Publishing House.

Sadgopal, A. (2013). The pedagogic essence of Kai Taleem: Reconstructing its role in contemporary curriculum. In T. Sethia & A. Narayan (Eds.), *The living Gandhi* (p. 175). New Delhi: Penguin India.

Sethia, T. (2012). *Gandhi: Pioneer of nonviolent social change*. New York: Pearson Press.

SECTION 4

Students and Teachers Making Change

Section Overview

Students and Teachers Making Change

By Danita Dodson

Though he had a prominent role in shaping the last century, Gandhi is also still relevant in our time as an exemplar who teaches us much about making change happen. In fact, the word *change* is famously and synonymously linked to the Mahatma. True, there is no documented evidence that he uttered or wrote the statement most often attributed to him: "Be the change you wish to see in the world." However, his life's message testifies to the fact that he sought change, created change, and was change incarnate. Not the saintly figure in his early years that he will become before his transformation, Gandhi relates in his autobiography (1983) that he once had some anger-management issues, sported fashionable clothes like a coxcomb, and endeavored to act the part of an elite colonial lawyer. Nevertheless, after his experience with racism on a train in South Africa, Gandhi began to understand that if he wanted to change the world, he must first sublimate his own personal desires—leading him to eschew Western dress, enact fasts, and accept voluntary poverty. Also, as he encouraged his followers to protest their oppressors, spin their own cloth, and overcome prejudice and discrimination within their own culture, he moved them toward social change.

In *Gandhi: Pioneer of Nonviolent Social Change*, Tara Sethia (2012) states that Gandhi shows us the importance of "individual responsibility" as the first step in social change (vii). Though "Be the change you wish to see in the world" may not be formally attributed to him, there is evidence that he proclaimed, "If we could change ourselves, the tendencies in the world would also change. As a man changes his own nature, so does the attitude of the world change" (Gandhi, 1958, p. 241). Gandhi does not suggest here that personal transformation is enough in itself; instead, he implies its imperative connection to social change. To him the struggle to create a

C. A. Bracho and D. Dodson (eds.), Teachers Teaching Nonviolence, 191–195.

better world must involve not only strict self-denial and arduous personal devotion to the philosophy of nonviolence, but it also is indelibly centered upon an awareness that one person alone cannot transform anything, and that injustice can be overturned only when people work together steadfastly. The Gandhian rules for nonviolent social change hinge not only upon this collective action but also awareness of the present moment, forgiveness, mindfulness of the essential humanity in everyone, and commitment to growth.

As the contributors in this final section disclose, speaking truth to power is crucial in any movement toward real change. With transparency and vulnerability, these powerful narratives examine how the practice of *ahimsa* can encourage others to act, manifesting the principle that nonviolent social change begins with personal, local transformation and culminates in creating collaborative revolution. Highlighting stories about the steps that the educators themselves have taken toward becoming change agents, these authors emulate the Gandhian use of persuasive writing to prompt transformation in young people as well. Through powerful rhetoric to persuade and to promote community action, viewing writing as a tool of service and *satyagraha,* truth-force, Gandhi (1931) spoke to the necessity of youth engagement in the dialogic process of nonviolent social action: "If we are to reach real peace in this world and if we are to carry on a real war against war, we shall have to begin with children." The following chapters all similarly illustrate how educators, inspired by their own personal transformation, can provide space, time, and support to empower youth in envisioning and fashioning a better world.

Historical and current research documents that better schools—defined by nonviolence, empathy, and equity—happen through the efforts of stakeholders who share similar goals, visions, and values that are clearly articulated. Transformational curriculum can occur when participants in the educational process believe that "the school is the center of change" (Bezzina, 2006, p. 160). This transformational development begins with recognition of the problems and an ensuing awareness of the need for transformation (Grant & Murray, 1999; Heckman, 1993). The narratives in this section delineate how educators have worked with the school administration and their communities to create local and global programs of change.

In Chapter 15, "The Change Agents: How the Dream Began," Shara Carder, a 2nd-grade teacher and leader of the Change Agents Group at Collins Elementary School in San Diego, discusses the Ahimsa Institute's role in inspiring her to create a school club that leads children to become nonviolent "change agents." Narrating how this action-oriented mission sprang from her response to the shock and fear that she experienced after the 2016 presidential election, she recounts her endeavor to establish a pathway for inspiring young people to become engaged citizens through direct experience in developing, planning, and implementing projects of social change in their school, community, and the state. This plan for youth engagement developed into a group called the Change Agents, which launched such positive missions as Kindness Week, Art by the Trees, and Buddy Benches. Carder also describes how the students' dedication to nonviolence led them to a creative project to show support of the students at Marjory Stoneman Douglass High School after the tragic school shooting.

In Chapter 16, "Voices of Student Changemakers," Susan Milan similarly recounts her creation of a "Changemakers" class for middle school students, inspired by her transformational fellowship at the Ahimsa Institute. Rooted in a commitment to bring principles of nonviolence to youth—especially at time when they are overwhelmed by perpetual attacks on social and environmental justice—her narrative articulates a belief that educators must propel students into meaningful, productive actions that are guided and fueled by satyagraha. Advocating that educators can encourage and facilitate student choice, Milan provides a detailed example of how young people can excel beyond typical classroom assessments. Through their own voices, she reveals how her students conceptualized, developed, and led three action projects for social change, inspired by lessons about Gandhi, King, and other nonviolent leaders: reduction of food waste, provision of reusable water bottles to "boycott" single-use plastic bottles, and campaigns to promote a school culture that honors diversity and inclusivity. Providing vital information to other educators who wish to lead students toward establishing groups dedicated to change or integrating this system into the classroom structure, Milan encourages the creation of spaces that echo Gandhi's concept of constructive program.

In Chapter 17, "Navigating Tension to Develop a Practice: How a Teacher Transforms," Sarabeth Leitch, a high school language arts teacher and basketball coach in Portland, Oregon, explores her own personal and professional navigation through the tensions of her experiences to inspire her students and other educators to do the same. Narrating how the Ahimsa Center provided her both the language and the fortitude for satyagraha through the stories of King and Gandhi, she shares several poignant anecdotes about the process of her own commitment to nonviolent social change. In these personal stories, Leitch reveals how her emulation of models of resilience led her to important action: letters to administrators about ending racist policies, speeches at board meetings to save threatened programs that support marginalized youth, marches in the streets with families to mourn their loss, participation in a hunger strike, forgiveness when a student thief stole money from her desk, and courage to share with her students the story of her cousin's death from gun violence. This narrative of one teacher's pedagogical transformation shows how educators can become part of a social-justice revolution.

In Chapter 18, "DIY Revolution: Arts, Technology, and Nonviolent Social Change," Vikas Srivastava elucidates how his Ahimsa Fellowship motivated him to use digital storytelling to conceptualize classroom dialogues about violence and nonviolence, oppression and privilege, communication through the arts, the role of technology, and the purpose of engaging in social change. His narrative explores the integration of these elements into a multimedia format that creates the recipe for a DIY Revolution that can be incorporated into any subject matter and facilitated by student-centered learning, project-based instruction, and arts-integration. Describing the five phases of this unit plan, Srivastava demonstrates how educators can create dialogue-based classroom experiences that help students define nonviolence as active confrontation of violence, show them how support of violence is linked to privilege, and lead them to an awareness that nonviolent social change is centered in communication. Since technology is undeniably linked to contemporary pedagogical strategies, this chapter demonstrates the value of five-minute video projects that integrate visuals, text, and numerical statistics to define violence and to suggest nonviolent action for social change.

Finally, in Chapter 19, "Listening to a Sound Heart: Applications of Ahimsa in Education," Laura Hirshfield, School Site Coordinator for YouthBuild Charter School of California, explores her transformation as a teacher after participating in the Ahimsa Center Institute, which quickened her desire to bring experiences of positive change to others' lives. She describes three of these experiences. Recounting the conversion of her high school English classroom into a space that honored the belief that an education of the heart is just important as education of the mind, she describes her exploration of literary texts that emphasize nonviolence. Hirshfield also delineates her ensuing creation of a professional development program called Teaching for Peace, a summer immersion experience that takes educators to India to spend three weeks in an experiential and reflective study of practical nonviolence. Finally, she displays how the required exercises of *aparigraha* (non-posessiveness) and *anekant* (multiplicity of truths) in India equipped her to effectively manage the nonprofit organization for which she now works, CCEO YouthBuild, a leadership development program for young adults who have been pushed out of public schools.

The following chapters all reveal that these educators are concerned with more than the simple short-term goals of instruction, which as quick fixes do not consider the moral, social, and political ramifications of education. Instead, they reveal that teachers and leaders who view education as a path to positive social change must create transformational pedagogies and must articulate a framework that helps students see themselves as intelligent change-makers (Christiensen, 2009), contributors to a democratic society (Parker, 2005), and activists who resist environmental degradation and violence to cultures (Bowers, 2004).

References

Bezzina, C. (2006). "The Road Less Travelled": Professional communities in secondary schools. *Theory in Practice, 45*(2), 159–167.

Bowers, C. A. (2004). Revitalizing the commons or an individualized approach to planetary citizenship: The choice before us. *Educational Studies, 36*, 45–58.

Christiensen, L. (2009). Teaching for joy and justice. *Rethinking Schools, 23*(4). Retrieved December 7, 2019, from http://www.rethinkingschools.org/archive/23_04/joy234.shtml.

Gandhi, M. K. (1931). Young India. Retrieved December 14, 2019, from www.mkgandhi.org

Gandhi, M. K. (1958). General knowledge about health. The collected works of M. K. Gandhi (Vol. 13, p. 241). New Delhi, India: The Publications Division.

Gandhi, M. K. (1983). *Autobiography: The story of my experiments with truth*. New York: Dover Publications. (Original work published 1948.)

Grant, G., & Murray, C. E. (1999). *Teaching in America: The slow revolution*. Cambridge, MA: Harvard University Press.

Heckman, P. E. (1993). School restructuring in practice: Reckoning with the cultures of school. *International Journal of Educational Reform, 2*(3), 263–272.

Parker, W. C. (2005). Teaching against idiocy. *Phi Delta Kappan, 86*(5), 344–351.

Sethia, T. (2012). *Gandhi: Pioneer of nonviolent social change*. Boston, MA: Pearson.

Chapter 14

The Change Agents

How the Dream Began

By Shara Carder

In the fall of 2017, a group of students at L. P. Collins Elementary School, a typical public elementary school in the heart of the Silicon Valley, had a unique opportunity: these students gained direct experience developing, planning, and implementing improvement projects in their school and in the community at large. This date marked the beginning of the Change Agents Group but not its foundational ideas. These ideas were based upon a dream.

I am a 2nd-grade teacher at L. P. Collins and a co-leader of a group still active today on campus called the Change Agents. My passion for inspiring students to become social change agents began in 2011 when I attended a summer institute called "Journeys of Nonviolence: Gandhi and Chávez" at the Ahimsa Center at Cal Poly Pomona. Dr. Tara Sethia established this fine institute, whose core mission is to make nonviolence an essential ingredient in K-12 education. If we are lucky in this life, we are inspired by a cause or a dream, and we might have the opportunity to make this dream come true. It was at the Institute that I developed an understanding of Dr. Sethia's dream, and over the years it would become my own dream.

Applying to the Ahimsa Institute

It was a typical day during the winter of 2011, and I opened my email inbox to discover a unique opportunity: I might study about the lives, struggles, and contributions of two great exemplars of nonviolence, Mohandas Gandhi and César Chávez. Based on the study of two great exemplars, I would be

C. A. Bracho and D. Dodson (eds.), *Teachers Teaching Nonviolence*, 197–206.

expected to design curriculum that aimed at helping students develop an understanding of nonviolence and social change. At first, the thought of designing curriculum that I would eventually use to teach in my class seemed overwhelming! I was already expected to cover so much and to meet rigorous state standards. However, then I asked myself the following question: "What do I truly want to teach my students?" Deep down, I knew that I wanted to help my students develop a set of core values that might help them act kindly towards their fellow humans. Could the students I taught be the ones to change the world for the better? These upper-middle-class South Asian students are given classes and opportunities to develop academically shortly after leaving the cradle. However, they have great difficulties with solving interpersonal conflicts in class and on the playground. They are highly competitive, bickering over who is out when playing wall ball. With these ideas in mind, I submitted my proposal and was accepted.

As I prepared for the Institute, I found myself nervous and challenged: in addition to creating a lesson plan, I would be expected to create a digital story using a program called iMovie. Knowing that César Chávez did a great deal of work mobilizing field workers, I decided to film the vegetable garden at Emma Prusch Farm Park, a nearby farm and garden located in downtown San Jose. Little did I know that this practice of diving into a project without knowing exactly where it is heading would be an ongoing theme in my work to develop nonviolence projects about nonviolence in the years to come.

The Ahimsa Institute

I arrived at the Ahimsa Center in late July, excited to meet elementary and high school teachers like myself from all over the country. We came from diverse educational environments. I taught in a district (Cupertino Union) where students luckily know only the violence of the video game. A colleague at the Institute taught in a middle school in Boston where students were exposed to violence daily. Despite our differences, we were all deeply concerned about our students, and we shared a restless desire to give them more than purely academic instruction.

As the Institute progressed, we became interested, many of us personally moved, by the lives of César Chávez and Mohandas Gandhi. We wondered how our students might benefit from direct exposure to these great exemplars of nonviolence. I learned that César Chávez was a famous union organizer who mobilized the Mexican and Filipino grape pickers of California's San Joaquin Valley. As I studied his life, I became interested in his ability to employ risk and self-sacrifice.

Chávez was born on a 160-acre ranch, and his parents, Juana and Librado, made a living farming the land and growing vegetables. When he was ten years old, his parents lost the farm and lived as migrant farm laborers moving from town to town. Chávez, like most children of farm laborers, was forced to work long hours picking grapes in a stooped position "breathing the hot dust of the fields as sweat poured into his eyes" (Ingram, 1990, p. 98). In 1948, he married his childhood sweetheart Helen Fabela, but the couple continued to live as migrant laborers, and they dreamed of having a better life for their families. Then in 1952, Chávez and his wife moved to San Jose, California, because he was hired by Fred Ross to work as a labor organizer. For the first time, he was able to earn a living wage. Ten years later, he made the remarkable choice to give up this stable position because the organization was unwilling to accept the cause of the farm workers. Chávez returned to Delano as a migrant field worker, but he began meeting with other workers both in their homes and in the fields with the goal of forming in a union. His own family lived and worked alongside people who came from different parts of the world. Each family was extremely poor and often went without food. However, when Chávez's family was in dire need of sustenance, another poor migrant family often gave them food. Although one family might be Mexican, and another Filipino, they showed kindness and compassion toward one another. Perhaps this early experience built inside of him a very strong allegiance with the farm workers and a true passion for "La Causa," the cause to better their lives.

As I studied Mohandas Gandhi, I began to understand that he, like Chávez, was deeply committed to bettering the life of his people, this time the Indian population of South Africa and later of India itself. Gandhi, known throughout India as "Mahatma" or great soul, was most famous for using nonviolent civil disobedience to free India of British rule (1947). How did he, the son of a wealthy Indian diwan, or prime minister, become an astute nonviolent organizer capable of mobilizing thousands of Indians to join him on a 240-mile march to harvest salt from the sea, thus breaking British law? I considered this question as I learned about his life, soon coming to understand how he developed a language of nonviolent resistance. I learned that Gandhi was exposed to several values in his childhood, which may have led to the development of his unique conception of *ahimsa*, or the respect for all living things and the dedication to non-injury. As a young man, he studied law and then traveled to South Africa, having accepted a position to work as a legal aid on a civil suit. Shortly after he arrived, he experienced racial prejudice firsthand. Having purchased a ticket, Gandhi was seated in the first-class compartment of a train. When the white railway officials asked him to move back to the van section, where the Indian passengers were expected to sit, he refused. As a result, Gandhi was thrown off the train. Incidents like these awakened him to the prejudice that the Indian population endured in South Africa. Beginning a careful study of the Indian population in South Africa, Gandhi came to understand that he could become a spokesperson for his people. He began to write articles and editorials that supported the Indian community, using newspaper writing as a method to garner attention and dispel stereotypes. Experiences like these helped Gandhi to develop the concept of *satyagraha*, a Sanskrit word from the roots *satya,* meaning "truth," and *agraha,* meaning "insistence." This is defined as nonviolent resistance to a political injustice, but it also means a whole way of life based upon love and compassion.

During the last days of the Institute, I worked hard to write two lessons for primary grade students that would make the nonviolent legacy of these two great exemplars accessible to this age group. The first lesson, "The Power of Nonviolence: César Chávez and the Delano Grape Strike," focuses upon Chávez's early life and development as a creator of the grape workers union. I carefully defined the terminology, and my completed iMovie was embedded in this lesson because I wanted to inspire young students to take an interest in Chávez. I now understand that Dr. Sethia had carefully planned the lessons in accordance with her own dream: that those of us who have attended the Institute will return to our schools eager in some way to effect change. I left so excited about Gandhi and Chávez, their fascinating lives, and their hard-fought struggles. I found it difficult to talk or think about much else!

Returning to Collins School

I returned to teaching second grade at Collins School in August of 2014, having taken on the challenge put forth by Dr. Sethia that I might, as an educator, inspire other teachers within my school community to consider how the study of Gandhi and Chávez could be integrated into their class curriculums and beyond. Teachers across the grade levels had used the "Talk It Out" program to help students learn to solve interpersonal problems independently. Still, I observed that many at Collins were unkind to each other and that many students wandered at recess with no friends to play with. Learning about an exemplar like Chávez, who built his union by bringing in those who were different from himself (the Filipino workers), would benefit this population. To what better student population could there be to introduce Gandhi than one with 90% of the student body being South Asian? I planned a presentation for an August staff meeting, creating a PowerPoint on the lives and accomplishments of Gandhi and Chávez and then leading an open-ended discussion about how teaching students about these exemplars of nonviolence could be integrated into social studies and language arts curriculums at each grade level. My colleagues were cordial during the meeting but had little interest in changing their curriculums. Like teachers all over the country, they felt overwhelmed with the responsibilities already placed upon them, and they did not want to take on anything that was not required. Short of presenting myself as a resource on these two leaders, I did not know how to spark an interest in Gandhi and Chávez within the student body. Thus, my desire to effect change sat dormant inside of myself.

Then, seven years later, in the spring of 2017, my passion for social change bubbled to the surface once again. Donald Trump had won the U.S. presidency, and I shared feelings of shock and despair with my colleague Mary Tapec, a 3rd-grade teacher in the classroom next to mine. Ms. Tapec and I agreed that part of the problem in American society was that there had been a lack of civic and political engagement among youth and adults alike. We wondered how we might help the youth at our own school develop into the morally conscious leaders, or the "Change Agents," of tomorrow. We agreed that, as teachers, we had the unique opportunity to help young people develop not only the cognitive skills necessary to get a job and survive in the existing society but also the passion and interest in shaping society for the better. Here I had the opportunity to draw upon my understanding of what Chávez and Gandhi were like as leaders as I helped students become leaders themselves.

A New Idea Comes into Existence

In May of 2017, Ms. Tapec and I wrote a proposal for a student group called "The Change Agents" to meet during school hours. Our shared goal would be to guide the students as they worked to design projects for school, community, and state improvement. I had learned at the Ahimsa Institute how Gandhi had the ability to learn from his raw life experiences, no matter how challenging and shaming they had been. Specifically, he entered a period of reflection in times of hardship and was able to determine a logical, proactive course of action. Thus, the ideas for the "Change Agents" projects and the planning would come from the students themselves. Ms. Tapec and I would be there to steer the group, to encourage the students to reflect after a project was complete, and to celebrate their accomplishments. But would our principal Steve Woo be receptive to our idea? At that very time, Mr. Woo was confronted with a record number of arguments among the students during recess. They were quite competitive but had difficulty with kindness and inclusivity, frequently returning from recess still during a dispute. Some wandered aimlessly around the playground even though teachers had worked hard to build class community. A program called "Project Cornerstone" had been in place for several years, and students were exposed to a whole language promoting prosocial behavior. For example, they were learning how to be an "upstander" and to confront any student who might be bullying and treating another student unfairly. Still, there was more to be done. Our principal gladly accepted our proposal, requesting that students who were also members of a group called "Expect Respect" be a part of our group. (In accordance with the Project Cornerstone program, students chosen by their teachers to participate in Expect Respect actively confronted bullying and promoted kindness on campus.)

Now that we had approval from Mr. Woo, Ms. Tapec and I met to develop a concrete plan for the first year of our grand experiment. Our mission would be to give students the opportunity to develop leadership skills, qualities such as kindness and compassion, and to stir within them a desire to become engaged citizens willing to take an activist role in society at large. Specifically, we would first encourage the group to carry out two projects at Collins, then undertake a community project, and hopefully take on a statewide issue at the end of the year. I was distinctly aware that I was planning for something that has not been done before; therefore, I didn't know where the plans would lead. In creating and leading this group, Ms. Tapec and I were cast in the role of change agents ourselves. When Gandhi addressed the problems that the Indian community faced in South Africa, he quickly took on a leadership role and became quite visible. As a spokesperson for the entire Indian community, he used speeches and articles to call upon the dominant white society to reflect on their prejudice by considering their sense of ethics. Similarly, the success of the Change Agent group would rest firmly upon the shoulders of Ms. Tapec and myself. A large sector of the student community would take part in the Change Agents activities. The projects must reflect the students' creativity and ingenuity, but they would also need to be well-planned and well-run.

The Change Agents Group Begins

A group of approximately twenty enthusiastic 4th- and 5th-grade students, who were all members of Expect Respect, piled into Ms. Tapec's third-grade classroom during lunch on a mid-September day in 2017. Ms. Tapec and I each briefly described our background and our vision for the group. I was impressed that she had orchestrated the school fundraiser almost entirely on her own with only student support. She was a very strong leader. When I spoke, I told the students, "In this group, you will get to be the leaders. You will work together to choose, plan, and carry out the projects." Prior to the meeting, the students had participated in an Expect Respect planning meeting, which allowed them to begin to talk about things that they could do to make the school a better place. They excitedly shared their ideas, which centered around one general theme: to help students who were shy and lonely to make new friends. I was impressed that this group already had a high level of empathy. Next, Ms. Tapec and I engaged the students in a discussion about possible projects until there were four ideas and a great deal of enthusiasm for all of them. I was impressed with how easily this group engaged in discussion.

The project ideas were rough and would be further developed over the coming weeks, but they fell into three general categories. Specifically, many Expect Respect students wanted a Kindness Week: a week to promote friendliness and inclusivity at Collins School. Others talked about art or science activities that might be offered during recess time. The students were also very eager to lead games or, in some way, to help the kindergarten students during recess. Many of the fifth-grade students supported the idea of raising money for a field trip. Eager to share ideas, they had the social skills necessary to engage in an informal but focused discussion. Since we had originally planned on just two projects, we asked the students to vote for their top choice of project. We found that there was an even distribution of votes and interest in all projects. Ms. Tapec and I made the executive decision that there are other funding sources for the fifth-grade trip, so that idea was eliminated. At the end of the meeting, Ms. Tapec, who had recognized the students' enthusiasm, asked me, "Do you think we can manage three activities?" Perhaps honoring the students' passion and letting them bring all three ideas to fruition was more important than sticking to our original plan of completing state-wide, community, and school-based projects in the first year. Our dream was coming to life: we now had a group where the students made the decisions and were following their passions!

In the coming weeks, we broke into committees, and our projects took form: there would be Kindness Week, a week with a different activity each day promoting kindness; Art by the Trees, a monthly art projects for students during lunch recess; and Buddy Benches, a beautifully-painted bench in the kindergarten playground where a student with no one to play with could go to meet a new friend. Mrs. Tapec suggested that we create a survey both to determine how interested the Collins students were in each project and to give the student body the opportunity to give their input whenever possible. Helping the Change Agents understand the importance of the survey, she said, "Before you build a Macy's, you want to make sure that people will go there and shop." (I chuckle to myself, wondering what Gandhi, might have thought of this analogy. Still, it is right on target in helping students understand the importance of the survey!) There are many anecdotal comments on the survey, and it is difficult to know exactly what to do with the data, but results did confirm that the student body was eager to partake in the three core activities that the Change Agents had begun to plan.

As the year progressed, Ms. Tapec and I broke the students into three committees, and the students enthusiastically moved forward with their projects—writing letters, ordering materials, and requesting funds from Mr. Woo. We did our best to let the students decide what steps needed to be taken in the planning of each project, but progress was slow in two of the groups, and I had a growing sense of apprehension that some might not be completed on time. However, I observed that the students in all three groups were excitedly moving forward with necessary preparations. The Buddy Benches group decided to paint a cougar (the animal representing Collins School) surrounded by a rainbow and worked with Ms. Tapec on determining how much paint would be needed for the project. The Kindness Week group brainstormed daily activities that might engage the entire school community. The students in the Art by the Trees group were able to partner with the 4th-grade teacher who offered STEM based art activities to elementary school-aged students one time a month. The Change Agents undertook the responsibility for planning and teaching each monthly activity. I was happy and relieved that this project had come to fruition.

Then a very sad event altered the course of the group: in February, there was a terrible shooting at Marjory Stoneman Douglass High School in Florida. A group of strong and courageous students who attended the school visited the Florida State Capitol and ignited the debate over gun violence once again. They called upon lawmakers to understand the immediate need for stricter gun laws. Students from all over the country walked out of their schools for approximately 15 minutes in support of this group of students. Our principal took a neutral stance, wanting neither to encourage nor discourage Collins Students from participating in this walk out. However, he asked Change Agents to take leadership role in deciding how the Collins student community would respond. Although I was aware that taking on this project might push back the entire timeline for completing the Kindness Week and Buddy Bench projects, there was a fire inside of me about how the Change Agents could make this important decision for the entire school community. At our next meeting, we discussed the students who are standing up to gun violence. The Change Agents showed their creativity, suggesting that they create a large tree. All members of the student body then had the opportunity to write their own personal note of support to the students at Marjory Stoneman and to attach it to the tree. This project was a tremendous success, and a floor-to-ceiling painted tree hung in the Collins GLC filled with messages of encouragement. Each student could show private support of the students and stand with others together as a community. I stared in awe at the tree.

However, in late March, I looked at the school calendar with panic because such little time was left to plan Kindness Week. The only logical date for it to occur was the week of Teacher Appreciation, approximately six weeks away. We needed to make posters to advertise it, materials must be prepped, and so much more. I emailed the head of the Collins PTA (Parent Teachers Association). To my amazement, almost immediately, a core group of parent volunteers responded, willing to volunteer. Similarly, the core group of Change Agents eagerly came to my room every day at lunch two weeks prior to the event to plan. When Kindness Week arrived, the students were fully prepared, and many of the daily activities were a tremendous success. By the end of the year, the Change Agents had successfully planned three major projects, and the Buddy Bench Group made firm plans to paint the kindergarten bench during the summer. Our dream of a school group where students are the leaders in social change had become a reality!

Conclusion

In the spring of 2018, just days before the last Change Agents meeting, I received an email from Dr. Sethia requesting presenters at a fall conference called Transformative Power of Education: Lessons from Gandhi, King, Chávez, and Mandela. I was eager to share with the assembled educators and community members the fact that my dream, the dream of instilling a passion for leadership and social change in students within my school community, had come true! The Change Agents group was giving students an education in nonviolent activism through direct experience. Like the nonviolent exemplars of the past who planned projects to confront social issues, the Change Agents had taken the lead in confronting problems at Collins school, such as social isolation in students as young as kindergarten.

What might be the best way to share information about the Change Agents at the conference? I remembered that years ago I had been introduced to a valuable tool at the 2011 Ahimsa conference called iMovie that I could use to create a short movie with a strong message. I developed a series of questions and asked Madhvi Kohli, a prominent member of the parent community, to ask the Change Agents themselves pointed questions about the group and what they had accomplished this year. It was in the Change Agents' answers to these questions that I came to fully fathom the level of enthusiasm and understanding within the students themselves. In addressing the question about who the Change Agents are, one student answered, "The Change Agents are a group of students that have been selected by their teacher. We make up projects to try to make our school be a better place. To help students have more compassion." Here the student showed her dedication to taking on a leadership role and to changing the school climate itself.

In leading the Change Agents, I had come full circle. Just as I had taken on the challenge put forth by Dr. Sethia to become a social change agent, designing lessons and iMovies about exemplars of nonviolent social change, the Change Agents were taking on the challenge set forth by Ms. Tapec and myself to become the impassioned leaders of the future.

Reference

Ingram, C. (1990). *In the footsteps of Gandhi: Conversations with spiritual activists.* Berkeley, CA: Parallax Press.

Chapter 15

Voices of Student Changemakers

By Susan Milan

Another school year has gone by. Stacked chairs and tables have been pushed to one side of the room to prepare for summer cleaning. Colorful, bulky student projects have gone home, been recycled, or sent to the landfill. Some have been stored away until next year when they will inspire new students who will be spending much of their time here. The unusual stillness of this room provides the space to pause for a reflective moment on my journey of *Ahimsa*.

A Culminating Event

On Friday, June 7, 2019, I awoke excitedly at 4:00 a.m. to read the early addition of our local newspaper, *The South Whidbey Record*. A group of my middle-school Changemakers had shared news about their action project with the reporter at a recent fundraiser. Although I was present at the event, I was involved in a conversation elsewhere during this time, so I did not have the opportunity to guide the interview. The students wholeheartedly spoke for themselves, with no hesitation. In fact, they communicated so effectively that the newspaper article featured their project, one of several funded and presented at this occasion. The students' ability, courage, and solidity to share, I believe, affirm the work of the *Ahimsa* fellowship program, standing as an example of empowering student voice and action in bringing about positive change in our world. In the article, "Foundation raises a record $35,000 for schools: Annual gala spotlights student projects and grant programs," Patricia Guthrie (2019) tells my students' story:

> A goal of reducing single-use plastic in schools resulted in cool refillable water bottles that were given away free to seventh and eighth-graders of the South

C. A. Bracho and D. Dodson (eds.), *Teachers Teaching Nonviolence*, 207–217.

Whidbey School District. Whidbey Island is outlined in white on the stainless-steel bottles. There's also a tiny globe surrounded by the words, "Be the change." Students behind the idea proudly showed off their action plan and finished product at the South Whidbey Schools Foundation annual fundraiser June 1st at Freeland Hall. Teacher Susan Milan leads a 7th-and 8th-grade class called Changemakers and that's where the refuse-reuse-reduce water bottle idea came from, she said. "The students were asked to choose a topic that they cared about and wanted to make a positive change," she said. Talking about the lessons learned during the project were Ava Ferguson, Audrey Gmerek, Katya Schiavone, Morgan Batchelor, Abi Moss and Sophia Patrin. "We chose water bottles as a way to reduce plastic use in our school," said Ferguson as she gathered with the group that called themselves "the Reducibles." Students researched how to come up with a design, check out possible manufacturing companies and learned the art of asking for money for a cause.

My Journey of Nonviolence

As I hear the agency in my students' voices, I pause to recognize that this year marks a full decade since I received an email regarding a fellowship opportunity to study Gandhi and King and to develop lessons promoting nonviolent social change. I was particularly interested in this institute, having grown up Detroit during the 1960s amidst the struggle for civil rights and racial equality. My parents' values were rooted in social justice, and my uncle was on the frontlines in the fight. He served as an organizer, activist, and attorney in Detroit, working to literally rewrite policy and to change the course of history. As an eight-year-old white girl in what became a predominantly African American neighborhood, I remember being petrified by the riots, fires, and violence that had overtaken news reports. I remember the night I lay awake, wondering if I would see my dad again, since he had to walk home from work in downtown Detroit because of curfews. Although I was very young, I somehow understood the frustration and anger of my friends who eventually directed it towards me and my sister. This prompted my parents to move our family out to the suburbs. We were one of the last white families to leave. Martin Luther King, Jr., made a huge impression on my early development and brought a sense of comfort and hope during this tumultuous time. My journey of nonviolence had begun.

As a teenager and a college student, I was active in the environmental movement. In the late 1970s, while focusing my studies on natural resources at the University of Michigan, I grew passionate about addressing the degradation of the earth due to human activities. During this time, research was beginning to predict how the use of fossil fuels as infinite resources would lead to major global issues. As an organizer and activist in the local environmental movement, I took some of the first environmental education courses in college and worked in the community to raise awareness about solar and other types of renewable energy. My personal path towards sustainable living continued as I eventually moved to the Pacific Northwest, learned the arts of growing food, and began living a simpler lifestyle that was easier on our planet and future generations. As a parent, I volunteered at the local school, where I soon became a teacher. This is my path for making a positive difference in our world.

Although I had exposure to Gandhi prior to the Ahimsa Institute, the opportunity to delve into his texts and learn from experts gave me a deeper understanding of concepts I had grappled with since childhood. Gandhi's insights and actions based on truth, soul force, empathy, and constructive program have been compelling and grounding. The idea of *Ahimsa* as thoughts, words, and actions that permeate all that we do connects social and environmental justice to everyday habits and choices. My ongoing journey continues to be transformational as I learn, grow, and connect with many passionate educators to bring the principles of nonviolence to our youth. During our current time, we are overwhelmed by daily perpetual attacks on social, economic, racial, and environmental justice. Violence founded on racism and bigotry is rampant, as mass shootings and hate crimes take over our hearts and minds. Profit-driven policymakers have reversed years of progress towards addressing institutional racism and climate change. As educators, we are called to propel our students into meaningful, productive, and intentional actions, guided and fueled by *satyagraha,* truth or soul force.

After a decade of putting much of my energy into state, district, and local policy-making entities in attempts to bring positive change and influence, I have returned to fully investing my energy into the classroom. Currently, I feel that my most effective professional place is relating directly with the students, striving each day to be a positive force in their lives. Gandhi (1922) recognized the importance of youth in positive social change: "If we are to reach real peace in this world and if we are to carry on a real war against war, we shall have to begin with children." It has become my mission and my guiding force to provide space, time, and support for empowered youth to envision and create the world we wish to live in.

Educating for a Culture of Nonviolence

In addition to teaching middle school science, I had the opportunity to experiment with a new course during the first semester of the past school year. The following excerpts represent some of the voices of the middle-school students in my weekly "Changemakers" class. The action projects were conceptualized, developed, and led by the students themselves. They were inspired by brief lessons I shared regarding Gandhi, King, and other nonviolent leaders. Several issues percolate in the hearts and minds of these students, including pollution, racism, bullying, and perspectives on kneeling during the anthem. By encouraging and facilitating student choice, I affirm that these students can excel and be productive beyond typical classroom expectations.

One project focused on reducing food waste through exploring possibilities for a school composting system. Led by two 8th-grade students, this idea expanded our district garden program, which has been "growing" for the last several years. I also integrated the science and design of possible systems in my science classes, involving over 100 students. Adeline and Rain, who began by looking more broadly at reducing waste and then narrowed their focus to food waste after lunch, described their project:

> We are working on creating a compost system for extra lunch food that kids don't eat at lunch. Having a system that is used for extra food instead of tossing the extra food in the garbage is important because the food we don't eat can actually benefit our school gardens by contributing to a system that makes all the composted food help our plants and later hopefully use the food in our school lunches. It will ideally be a healthy, earth-friendly cycle. It's also great for kids to grow up in an environment that shows how to reuse food and compost what you don't use instead of throwing it away. Putting food that could be composted in the trash which would later end up in the landfill, becomes methane, which is a part of climate change.

As this testimony reveals, change begins with education about facts.

A humbling reality-check occurred in the second semester when I no longer had Adeline and Rain in class. The compost system idea was delayed. I had hoped they would be invested enough to continue, even without the formal meeting time. I soon accepted that we were all involved in many activities, so it really did require scheduled meeting times to continue such a project. Several students have asked me if we could still make it happen, and they have generated ideas to reduce school lunch waste. Some have returned to visit, to initiate conversations, and to share suggestions for actions. There seems to be a growing awareness and an interest in moving forward. Connected to the Ahimsa Institute, the principles of sustainability, interconnection, and personal responsibility are foundational concepts for these actions.

Another Changemakers' project group consisted of three students focused on creating a school culture of nonviolence. They explored quotes and created art posters with themes of diversity, inclusivity, and respect. As Mimi, Pearl, and Lily related,

> We are a group that makes posters for our school. The posters are about diversity, bullying, and making people feel better about themselves. So far, we have made around ten posters, which we have hung around the school for everyone to see. Our goal is to help prevent bullying. Also, we are trying to help our school community see that everyone is a part of the same human race and needs to be treated with the same respect.

This group worked during first semester, displaying their posters around the school. Most of these posters remain and are now part of the atmosphere of our school.

Students Taking the Lead

The most pressing issue for more than a third of the students in the Changemakers class was the negative impact of plastics on our health and environment. This completely student-led project developed several different branches. Students researched the effects of plastic on health and the environment, and they created a presentation and shared it with all 7th- and 8th-grade students. From concern about the marine food web, to the microplastics in products we use, to the connection between fossil fuel use and climate change, they became well-versed and grounded in evidence as they reached out to fellow students and organizations to support the effort. Through raising awareness and offering reusable water bottles for all students who chose to join the effort, they encouraged the boycott of single-use plastic water bottles sold in school vending machines. These students effectively worked with our building principal and with the community to help with financial support and implementation.

This project generated agency in the students' abilities to voice awareness. One leader of the effort, Audrey, stated,

> Over the past two months our group, the Reducibles, has been figuring out solutions on limiting the use of plastic content in our school. We have noticed people in our school buying lots of plastic water bottles from the vending machines. After seeing the plastic consumption in our school, we wanted to make a difference in our school and community.

Camilla added,

> In Changemakers, my group is trying to get water bottles for everyone
> in 7th to 12th grade. The reason we are trying to get these is because
> our school vending machines are generating too much plastic in my
> opinion. I really do think that our school would benefit from this and
> so would the planet!

Wesly and Myca further explained,

> We are working on a way to educate people on the damage that
> pollution is doing to the ocean. We find it very important that younger
> generations educate their peers because if it is coming from an adult it
> is just another lecture. I really think we're making a change.

As the first semester ended, several students continued to meet at lunch to
sustain their projects. They were inspired and dedicated.

The challenges of implementing real-world, long-term projects for us, as
educators, are many. Continuity and perseverance amidst multiple classes,
sports seasons, school workload, illness, and family events are challenges. I
realized that if this project were to continue, we needed dedicated time and
student leaders. During second semester, I used time in my No Child Left
Inside Class (environmental science enrichment), which met every
Wednesday. This class was initially intended to connect students to the
environment, and several had projects that overlapped with the
Changemakers projects. One of the lead students from Changemakers, Ava,
was also in this class and was willing to provide the continuity, while several
other students eagerly volunteered to be involved. Due to challenges with
funding and continuity, we decided to focus the project on 7th- and 8th-grade
students, our direct circle. The students in the group were leading the way
while truly forming a sense of solidarity with the broader student body.
Fundraising was a bit challenging, as not all the adults in charge embraced
and understood that this was a student-led effort with the goal of raising
awareness and reducing plastic use. It was seen as giving out "free water
bottles" that would just get lost and be unappreciated. Luckily, the team did
not let discouragement slow them down and continued to reach out in a
way that resonated with enough donors to move forward. We also realized
involving the high school would require student leaders in that age range.

When the water bottles arrived, we had new energy and broader
involvement. The kick-off went well, and 180 out of 220 students
participated in the effort. Three of the new student leaders did a
presentation for our school board, which included a video created by an
8th-grade participant. The original leaders and the newcomers shared the

project at the fundraising event covered in our local newspaper. One lesson I learned was that allowing people opportunity to join in the action any time along the way helps to grow and broaden the movement. There have been many moments on this path when I have literally had to breathe deeply and ask, "What would Gandhi do?" Truth, courage, persistence, and focus on each small step helped to guide us. The story of Gandhi's salt march was very helpful. His brilliance to select an issue that affects everyone, such as salt or water, is simple yet incredibly powerful. We received interest from both the elementary and high school, as well as the broader community, about extending the project.

Izzy, one of the students who became involved later in the year after she did an environmental project on how climate change affects national parks, helped create and share the presentations for the public outreach events. She wrote,

> I've always been interested in the environment, but having a class for it has really helped me to think more about it. All around the US, our National Parks are meant to be a way to preserve the wild and natural land. I wanted to learn more about what humans are doing that affects them, positively and negatively. Now I get two hours once a week dedicated to working on my project, which has been really nice, because I still have time for my other homework. When I got involved in the Water Bottle project, I realized just how much students can do. Our Changemakers group and Ms. Milan worked really hard to get environmentally safe stainless-steel water bottles for all of the 7th and 8th grade students who wanted one. It really opened my eyes to what we can do for our community.

Learning From Our Students

The water bottle project taught me so much about the importance of following through and showing up in support of our youth. Our principal, James, made this a priority throughout the school year. No matter how busy he was with a multitude of other issues, he frequently came to check in with the students and me to see how he could help facilitate the project. In public school life, there are so many high-need issues arising daily. It is challenging to discern what the focus should be. Then, once decided, as other things arise of equal or greater importance, it can be challenging to stay focused. For myself, I try to keep coming back to the work of Ahimsa. In this moment on my path, the focus is creating the space for student voice and empowerment.

As I experiment with how to provide space and support for students, I ask my students for feedback to help me learn and grow as an educator. Georgia shared her insights:

> In Ms. Milan's No Child Left Inside class I am able to use my time to work on projects that I feel strongly about, or that will actually grasp my attention, compared to other classes where I get told what to do and what my attention should be on. Her class allows me to have a creative outlet that I can channel into my work. I am currently working on multiple pieces about climate change and plastic pollution, two subjects I have a strong opinion on. I am working on a slide presentation about plastic pollution and a piece about climate change. This time changes the products I buy, use, and how I live my life, for example, I have stopped buying stuff with excessive plastic packaging and stopped using single use plastics, as they are horrible for the environment, I have also stopped leaving unnecessary lights on or keeping my water running for too long. In her class I am able to gather information and produce some arguably good presentations, all the while being in a comfortable setting that encourages me to use my knowledge and voice. Her class and guidance also pushed me to talk to our school's principal about our school handbook and dress code. Her class pushes me to speak out for things I wish would change or at least spark a conversation about. Her NCLI class gives me a supportive and helpful environment, where I feel comfortable to work.

Cathrina, also involved in project action, shared,

> I'm doing a project on how paper affects the world, and how a new kind of paper could be the solution. I was wondering what to do for an environmental project for school. I had a list of ideas, one of which was learning about how paper affects the environment, but it wasn't high on the list. It's such a common topic. I wanted to do something different. That's when my partner, Morgan, remembered a kind of paper, that didn't involve cutting down trees. It was a kind of paper made of elephant poop. I really liked how different it was. I'd never done a project like this before, at least not one that was this student directed. We ran it by our teacher, and started searching how it was made, the effects that normal paper had on the environment, and the benefits of the poop paper. The poop is cleaned out, mixed with non-wood, natural materials, and flattened into paper. No smell. It was nice, though a little weird, to read about how this kind of paper can help the environment. It could be a really good way to save trees around the world. It's really fun, and really nice to be able to have more input in what we get to do during school. I'm glad that we got this opportunity.

Another student, who has a challenging home life and needs extra support at school, added further to the dialogue of action: "I think it's a necessity for kids to have a voice in their community and work. I am one of many kids who wasn't made to sit behind a desk for seven hours of the day cause my ADHD goes crazy, but when I can work on cool things and hands on projects and choose my interest for work it makes school a whole new place."

My work as an educator has become deeply personal as I focus on creating spaces for youth to feel empowered to "create beauty," as Winona LaDuke, indigenous environmental justice activist and leader, beckons us. This partners well with "be the change" and Gandhi's concept of constructive program. The work is inspired by Dr. Bernard Lafayette (2016), who was tasked by Martin Luther King, Jr. to "institutionalize and internationalize" nonviolence. The passionate youth need us, as adults, to serve as facilitators, supporters, and mentors. As Gandhi (1941) states in *Constructive Programme: Its Meaning and Place,* "I have reserved students to the last. I have always cultivated close contact with them. They know me and I know them. I know that they are the hope of the future."

Looking Ahead

As educators, we are exhausted at the end of a school year, but we also reflect and look forward. Next year, I have offered to help expand elective opportunities based on student feedback. I will be creating space for art, singing, and Spanish language classes in addition to life science. Our students are hungry for change and want to be involved, creative, and respected. They need to be heard and supported. Moving forward, I will continue to use the *Ahimsa* filter to help set priorities and contribute to positive change efforts. Having the support of administrators in this goal is vital. For example, our principal James articulates thoughts about the positive impact that the Changemakers have had on our school culture:

> Watching the students become the "Changemakers" has been a humbling experience for me. I think it is easy to focus and react to the pressure of high stakes testing and academics of ELA, Math, and Science and lose sight on providing a well-balanced and holistic educational opportunity. Ms. Milan and these students, through their work and passion, reminded me that our role as an educational institution also incorporates building up the voices of our students. They gain such confidence and resilience when working on projects that create change on a large level. They are beginning to learn what their "footprint" can be on the world and how to positively impact the environment around them. This group has inspired me and as a school leader, I have made it a goal to be more conscious of embedding these types of programs into our school culture.

Making Ripples

On the Sunday evening after the fundraising event where the Changemakers shared their project with our beloved community, I received this email from a parent of a 7th-grade student who was not directly involved in the project. Jodi wrote,

Hello Ms. Milan,

I just wanted to let you know how moved I was to hear your students talk about their Changemakers project. It was so wonderful to see the passion and hard work they put into making a difference.

I thought you might like to hear this story...when I arrived home last night, I asked Hans where his new water bottle was. He responded that he didn't have one. So of course I asked why? He told me that he gave it away. This answer made me curious because it really isn't like Hans to just give something away, most things mean a lot to him. So I questioned why he gave it away and this is what he said, "Mom I gave it to a kid, my friend, that didn't understand how the project worked so he didn't sign up to get one and felt sad about not having one, so I gave him mine."

So here is what I say about the Changemakers...you all probably don't know the full depth and breadth of change you create when doing good for the collective world. Yes, we are a little island, somewhat isolated from the big world, however, big ideas touch many lives in little ways, making what you are doing HUGE in my book!

The reason for me telling you this story is not about my admiration for my son's kindness (although, I totally admire him and am very proud of him), my reason is to take the opportunity to thank you for showing these kids how to open their hearts and minds to make a meaningful life for themselves.

Conclusion

As the days of summer shorten and the new school year approaches, I am preparing for a new Changemakers class. I have received emails from students who are already planning projects and actions to make the world a better place. As an educator, I feel extremely grateful to share my days with our future. Each day brings new challenges along with some successes. The dance of balancing academics with social and emotional growth is perpetual and dynamic. Each day, I work to move through challenges with soul force, compassion, empathy, and justice. This always requires effort and awareness, along with a consciousness of breath and a willingness to reflect and improve. My journey continues, with the support and guidance of our *Ahimsa* fellowship, which provides a sense of belonging. The more we share our paths and humanity with our students in authentic ways, the more we can connect with them and support them to realize potential and to make a difference in our world.

References

Gandhi, M. (1922). *Young India.* Madras: Tagore.

Gandhi, M. (2010). *Hind swaraj.* Delhi: Rajpal & Sons.

Guthrie, P. (2019, June 7). Foundation raises a record $35,000 for schools. *South Whidbey Record.* Retrieved from http://www.southwhidbeyrecord.com/news/foundation-raises-a-record-35000-for-schools/

LaDuke, W. (n.d.). Mission and Values. Retrieved from https://www.humansandnature.org/ mission-values

LaFayette, B., & Johnson, K. L. (2016). *In peace and freedom: My journey in Selma.* Lexington, KY: University Press of Kentucky.

Chapter 16

Navigating Tension to Develop a Practice

How a Teacher Transforms

By Sarabeth Leitch

---

noun
1. the state of being stretched tight.
2. a strained state or condition resulting from forces acting in opposition to each other.
3. mental or emotional strain.
4. a strained political or social state or relationship.
5. a relationship between ideas or qualities with conflicting demands or implications.

verb
1. apply a force to (something) which tends to stretch it.

When I was a sophomore in high school, my basketball coach gave the team a quote at the end of each practice. The daily thoughts about life came on colorful paper, and they were used to help us rise above, show tenacity, and meet a common goal. A quote from basketball legend Robert Horry has stayed with me all these years: "Pressure can burst a pipe or make a diamond." It is a scientific reminder that tension is very natural, but we can also frame it for a purpose. That is teaching. That is living. And that is centering one's life around nonviolence. Often, I have wanted to explode from the fallout of injustice, yet each time I meditate on the beauty that can

C. A. Bracho and D. Dodson (eds.), Teachers Teaching Nonviolence, 219–228.

come from a challenge. As a teenager, I started this journey when I took the meditations home, stapling the quotes to the ceiling of my room. I ended each day in bed, the words of wisdom draped above me, moving me in one way or another. A choice to let tension lead my actions began then.

The Soul of Learning Is Liberation

Ahimsa is one of the most vital responses to tension, yet it is rarely discussed in schools. As educators, we must live it to become internally healthy and outwardly influential. Our own relationship with trauma, and our navigation through it, determines how our students repeat or dismantle the tension to achieve transformation. We are the models for this type of liberation. My experience with ahimsa's connection to education began during my third year of teaching when I first met my new vice principal. I knew her enthusiasm for equity matched both my hope and my raw skill as a young teacher. When she taught radical curriculum and received pushback, she simply shared her well-developed intent, provided evidence of the lesson's impact, and appeared confident amid the naysayers. The more I learned about her path to resiliency through conflict, the more I wanted to emulate her purpose. She saw this desire in me, realized my timidity, and understood my shock that not every teacher entered the field to make a more just world. Thankfully, she forwarded an email from the Ahimsa Center for an upcoming "Journeys of Nonviolence" Institute. Though I had been trained in a graduate program about equity, I was starting to shrink under all the expectations and the tension of school realities. Thus, when the opportunity arose to study how Gandhi and King had the resilience to move the people, I was sold.

As I sat in the institute room with scholars, historians, educators, I knew instantly that my students would have an enhanced experience. The fellowship gave me the language and the fortitude for *satyagraha*. The writings of King and Gandhi illustrated the paths of tension that lead to revolutionary acts, both individually and institutionally. As we delved into what made them stronger leaders, the pain, the wonder, and the courage were there for me to witness. Most importantly, I saw their humanity. Their work evolved as they answered a steady call to action, and it is a call that we can answer too.

As I recall in this chapter how these two models of resilience have emboldened me, I have penned vignettes about my moments of tension. Like other leaders, I have had times when I stayed quiet for fear of pressure, but I gain more strength when I write about it. The following are my stories of releasing materialism for greater graces, marching in the streets with families to mourn their loss, writing letters to administrators about steps to end racist policies, giving speeches at board meetings to advocate continued programs for supporting marginalized youth, uniting with others for the common cause, and processing my own grief as a way to be present with my students and their families. These moments involved substantial tension and deep reflection. Through the brilliance of others, I have learned how to use both my voice and my body as agents for change.

While the institution of education will wear down even the most radical and committed teachers, together we must show devout adherence to the process of ahimsa. The soul of learning is liberation. In acknowledging how one must remain resilient amid the tension, bell hooks (2017) states, "There are times when personal experience keeps us from reaching the mountain top...so we are just there...yearning for a way to reach that highest point. Even this yearning is a way to know" (p. iiii). That is why I am compelled to share in honor of those who came before me, those in solidarity with us, and those whose futures depend on it.

Valuables

The Ahimsa Institute inspired me to contemplate valuables. The classroom is where our values are revealed—in how we both set up the space and show up. Each year I ponder how to establish the most inclusive environment. Relinquishing control is an act of anti-racist teaching, but one must unlearn many prior lessons. I admit that it is not easy for this first-born, bossy Taurus. However, if I don't, what am I reinforcing? I sit in discomfort as I push against what is expected so that I can make our community a more democratic, restorative place.

Because of this, I believe that the teacher must model agreements and establish ways to reconciliation. People will cross boundaries because a need has not been met. How we handle situations exhibits so much about what we value. Gandhi uses a hypothetical situation through an anecdote. If a thief breaks into your house one night, the next night you should leave the door unlocked. If the thief does it again, the next night you should leave the door open, and then the next night you should create a clear path to your door. If the thief returns, you should move all the valuables to the front of your house so that they are easy to access. Through this anecdote, I started to see crime differently. For a country that has a clear school-to-prison pipeline, we need more narratives that examine implicit bias while making room for accountability and healing.

One school year, I was able to apply this transformative learning when money was stolen from my desk. When I discovered this, I was with a colleague. Eventually, I relented to the loss of some dollars and said, "Oh well, I guess they needed it more than I did." She gave me a funny look and said, "How are you not angry?" I shrugged and said, "Well, I mean, I don't really need it. And maybe they do. I am just worried that they are going to feel guilty from stealing it, when if they'd asked, I would have gladly given it to them." She was speechless. Later that day, our principal walked past me in the hallway and grinned. He said, "I heard what happened to you today. What a unique response." I am not sure how the thief spent the money, but today I keep access to snacks, art supplies, and technology in my room. Even when my wallet or my phone are on my desk, they remain untouched. Rather than despair and vengeance, we can assess the situation and respond with heart. It is liberating to both enact and share this Gandhian tale as one example that has had many ripple effects in my life and, therefore, in my classroom.

Marching

This liberating response of heart also is present in my belief in taking to the streets. During the Ahimsa Institute, we talked about peaceful protests and the need to take over the freeways. Though I have never faced the consequences in the same way that many people of color have, when the Black Lives Matter movement arose in my city, I responded, "I'm with them." I joined the movement—first in mind and in spirit and, eventually, in body. Because of tension, it took time to do so consciously.

Even before then, I remember that my first major march was accidental. When I lived in NYC, there was a march against the WTO. As we strolled through Central Park, we were invited to carry signs on the frontline. I was totally chill—until I saw that there were riot police three rows deep lining the route. That feeling of being outnumbered was visceral. Then we were instructed how to respond to various whistle blows. One, stop. Two, link arms. Three, sit down. Four, lie down. This was not a parade. This cause that I stumbled upon was my first test of nonviolent action before I even knew the term.

Fifteen years later, inspired by the Ahimsa Center, I stood with teenagers on a street in Portland, literally facing off with officers in masks, shielding me from any of the faces I might recognize. They gave us commands over speakers, and I rushed to make decisions about whether to step on the sidewalk or to stand side-by-side with the youth who had just lost their friend to police violence. This moment held the artifacts of history in my heart. I thought about the bridges. I thought about the pavement. I thought about the batons. Even though I was the only adult I knew in that crowd, I decided to stay. I didn't want to. But I had to. In this clear example of action, we were holding space—for mourning, for accountability, and for hope.

Speaking Truth to Power

Because becoming a spokesperson for a cause is not easy, we must demystify the effort that goes into truthful living and break it down in parts, steps, and focuses. As a young man, Gandhi had emotional and physical responses to what felt "right." I totally identify with this. Those who know me have seen my stubbornness and anguish when it comes to justice work. Whether I'm writing letters, poems, speeches, or a chapter, my belly will ache until I move toward action against injustice.

During the Ahimsa fellowship, Dr. Tara Sethia and historian Louis Fischer shared that Gandhi's journey led to his legacy. His pursuit of truth was a slow, meditative process. It brought me relief that it took him effort. Fischer (1954) points out that the "real Gandhi" did not come into existence as an activist until young adulthood: "Gandhi was not the student type. He was a doer, and he gained knowledge, confidence, and stature through action" (p. 19). That is what genuinely makes being a responsive educator equally hard and rewarding. You cannot just read about it in books; you must live it.

One moment of tension was a catalyst for Gandhi's transformation; it occurred when he was asked to move cars on a train because of his skin color, even though he had a first-class ticket. When asked to move, he replied that he was not going to do so voluntarily. Again evicted, he refused to leave the platform and contemplated his own duty: "Should I fight for my rights or go back to India, or should I go on to Pretoria without minding the insults, and return to India after finishing my case?" (Gandhi, 1983, p. 97). Thankfully, he allowed this observation of injustice become a call to action: "In the presence of evil he had to act. Mere headshaking and hand-wringing never satisfied him" (Fischer, 1954, p. 22). I have these sensations too.

Once I was reprimanded for not following the disciplinary protocol of locking students out of the classroom if they were late so that they could be swept into the cafeteria for a scolding. I was reminded via email that I should start following this rule. Some of the educators believed that this would help truancy; however, in my gut, I knew it was not right. How was I supposed to simply shrug when I saw the face of a student two minutes late peering through my door to get access to education? I couldn't. So I penned a five-page poem weaving together the stories of students, my family's experience with incarceration, and some lines of Baldwin, like "We can make America what America must become." I have no idea if my principal read the whole thing. But when he walked into my room, told me that he understood, and relayed the message that I no longer had to lock my door, I felt relief. This is an example of tension and resistance in the face of a violent educational policy, requiring us to reexamine what we think we know about schools.

Martin Luther King, Jr. also spoke of moments that pushed him quickly from childlike innocence into a true understanding of the world. Often violence comes from a place of over-confidence, while nonviolence is grounded in humility. King's (1998) internal monologue depicted the truth of struggle and actualization as he sat on a segregated bus: "One of these days, I'm going to put my body up there where my mind is" (p. 9). Reflection must assess the situation to plan for action. It wasn't until the Ahimsa Institute that I learned that the bus boycott was a 380-day demonstration led by more than two people. I want my students to know not only that we can make such dreams come true but also that there is strategy behind the idealism.

In speaking such truth to power, one must understand that tension, conflict, and violence are levels of pressure that are not to be confused with one another. We can be trained to handle each through meditation, dialogue, or civil disobedience. When we recognize oppression, the pure violence of it is striking. Leaders against injustice have had to train themselves to manage the atrocity and pain so that they can reflect to society what is true. Gandhi pioneered—or refined—this approach to social reform. It started with *satya*, which means "the truth." He did not mean simply to seek the meaning of life; rather, he referred to concrete observations about the world in a non-static way. Historian Anthony Parel (2009) speaks to this as well, saying that viewing the truth is like attempting to reach the shore in a boat; you may never see it or know exactly where it is, but you continue to move towards it in hope.

That's exactly how it feels to sit in meetings: calling into question how grading practices impact a student's sense of self, demanding a different approach to discipline, or persuading oneself to stop teaching books that reinforce stereotypes. The journey is one of constant perusal of truth and action to a better end. Gandhi applied this pursuit of truth to the next developmental step: global transcendence, *satyagraha*, or soul force. Tara Sethia (2005) says that "Gandhi's strategy was 'war' armed with a moral force. He called the force 'satyagraha'—an active pursuit of truth through love and nonviolence" (p. 1373). Satyagraha, thus, is the fundamental principle for teaching nonviolence. While Gandhi believed that most humans are good, he acknowledged that practicing satya requires effort. Achieving the path of virtue through truth in one's actions and words allows one to gather both inner strength and outer confidence. This transforms not only individual but also the world.

When students have asked me to sit beside them as an ally or to speak in honor of them in front of powerful people, I have had to stomach my own uneasy esteem. I wish I were able to always perform like an emcee; however, to be honest, I am still working on that. I remember as a youth standing with no script in front of 500 people and talking to them about the most intimate details of my life. However, somehow as a teacher, I have developed a censoring demeanor that makes my hands shake when speaking on a microphone—even when I have everything typed on size 14, Arial font, double-spaced paper that is ready to read to a panel of politicians. Our profession is so public that we are often feel judged.

A few years after the institute, a former student begged me to speak on behalf of a program that was in danger of being cut though it kept him from dropping out. I knew how effective this program was for students who felt excluded. I had never spoken in front of the school board; though my nerves wanted to get the best of me, I couldn't let him or any of the other youth down. They trusted me. I worked for days and days, writing and re-writing. We had recently studied King's speech techniques in the Modern Voices course I taught, so I channeled what I knew about making an appeal. Then on a Tuesday night, I was surrounded by colleagues and students who carried signs that spread the message of the power of the program. I was shaky, sweaty, and ready to disappear. However, when I got my two minutes, I spoke.

Afterwards, a current student approached and gave me a big hug. He said that I reminded him of King. I was genuinely shocked. He was in my class, so he may have recognized some ethos, pathos, logos. Beyond that, it made me feel like he thought there was hope. That was huge. I knew I had spoken up for him and the Options program to which he belonged, I knew that I had spoken with fervor on behalf of marginalized youth, and I knew that I had been called to do so. I realized that King was a preacher who became a revolutionary and that I am a teacher who can do revolutionary things too. I will have different stages, and I will have different topics, but I can invoke a similar sentiment and ability to have folks feel seen, heard, and supported. That student was proud of me, and I imagine the great Dr. King would be too, for the program still exists to this day.

These juxtapositions of internal and external tension act as a propelling force. When teachers can practice these principles in their communities, students witness the individual and society transform simultaneously. The lives of Gandhi and King illustrate that they, at some point in time, were called to put their values into practice, reaffirming their beliefs. These were not mere hunches. Their focused effort allowed both themselves and the people around them to evolve. This is where the world starts bending towards peace and justice. Through satyagraha, the world witnesses—on both the small and large scale—how individuals who choose to become satyagrahis profoundly impact their communities.

Critical Educators Collective

As I began applying satyagraha to my work as an educator, I increasingly realized the need for solidarity. Being an activist for nonviolence in an inherently oppressive system takes a type of resolution that requires reflection, sacrifice, and skill. Moreover, I understand the force within an institution that is driven by competitive monoculturalism. However, it wasn't until my twelfth year of teaching that I truly realized how one cannot do it alone. This isn't to say that I didn't have amazing PLCs or transformative PDs, but I needed a posse. Though I should have known this from what I learned from the institute, sometimes we need reminders. I was feeling ineffective and burnt out when I met a group of teachers just out of graduate school who had formed a collective because they knew that educators need more training for bringing social justice to the forefront of what we do. Having had prior careers from labor organizing to social work to professional art, they knew culture, and they knew leadership. Most importantly, they knew that they needed to know more.

Instantly, I was reminded that one person's truth can connect to what others have in their hearts. This is what creates mass movements of satyagraha. One of the most meaningful parts of Gandhi's *Hind Swaraj* is that it is a dialogue, showing that Gandhi is not opposed to questions or critiques because these build the process. In a similar way, this collective of teachers recruited speakers like Linda Christensen and Dr. Lauren Leigh Kelly, allowing us to collaborate to create curriculum and classroom routines that empowered people in our presence. As we studied other collectives to model shared leadership, we rallied 600 teachers after the 2016 presidential election to come together in solidarity to discern how to best show up for our students. I've seen this modeled in other local organizations that have helped me examine my implicit bias and stay updated about culturally responsive practices. Whether participating in training with the Center for Equity and Inclusion or attending workshops at the NW Teaching for Social Justice Conference, I find other educators who understand that we must sharpen our critical lens just like other civil rights leaders did before us. It's not an option; it's an ethical duty.

One of the most profound things I learned at the Ahimsa Institute was that these honorable exemplars did not work in isolation. That is why my greatest piece of advice to other teachers is always that they must find a crew. One cannot practice nonviolence without feedback, encouragement, support, and multiple perspectives. Satyagraha is a life routine, not a one-time event or a solo mission. King (1998) used many metaphors to highlight this point: "Anyone who starts out with the conviction that the road to racial justice is only one lane wide will inevitably create a traffic jam and make the journey infinitely longer" (p. 49). Relationships pave the way to more efficient and long-lasting change.

The Mountaintop: Crying on Planes

These relationships that we build in commitment to nonviolence in education hinge upon both professional and personal work, as the memoirs of Gandhi and King illustrate. There was horrendous violence that they, their families, and their communities endured. However, they were steadfast in their nonviolence. I, too, have had to—and will continue to have to—make that choice. I have had to rise up when I feel hopeless, to approach trauma with reformation.

The hardest time was when I lost my cousin to gun violence, killed by his own gun at the hands of a friend in a fight. I remember asking the detective if I could talk with the killer to work through a process of forgiveness. The man was taken aback. No one had ever asked him that before. I was taken aback. How do we live in a world with many examples of how to repair harm from great tragedy, yet we rarely use any of the tools gifted to us by our elders? My family pursued all sorts of help with this process, legally and therapeutically. While our hearts were taken care of, a sense of justice and healing will never happen, for we have no structure for it.

That's why I went to school the morning after he was killed, even as my family mourned, for his end wasn't random. It was a product of how we institutionally raise our youth. I knew that as a child. I saw what discipline looked like. I felt the impact of exclusionary practices on my own family. Angry youth—no matter how talented, skilled, artistic, and passionate—are pushed out. Rather than channeled into elevation, they are often trained to be docile. Our schools are instruments, and that's why nonviolence is critical. We cannot keep our youth from rebelling, asserting, and demanding, but we must model those expressions for them in heart-led ways. Sharing my cousin's story at the beginning of the year with my students and their families, I tell them that I will show emotions and will embrace theirs. I let them know that each learner approaches challenges differently, and it's my job to learn how to encourage them. I inform them that I will make mistakes, and that we will repair that harm when I do, showing that I will give them the same grace. By creating circles where we sit and share about ourselves, where we speak about what's impacting our community, and where we work on accountability to our community, it is my hope that we will be teaching the next generation to do what we haven't fully done yet.

I sat for hours the evening that my cousin was killed, making a decision to still have hope. Then I remembered "I've been to the mountaintop." Each of the empathetic lines rattle my core: the dream, the sorrow, the message, and the acceptance. When I recall what King articulated in this famous speech, I fully understood my job as an educator: "Well, I don't know what will happen now. We've got some difficult days ahead. But it really doesn't matter with me now, because I've been to the mountaintop." We get to see the world for what it really is: a place of great harm and a place of great triumph. The latter is why I teach, not as a career choice but a choice to become a part of a revolution. As this chapter shows, this requires both internal wrestle and steadfast commitment. Being deeply immersed in the writings and relationships of Gandhi and Dr. King has graced me with the ability to live in a way that is countercultural to our current learning atmosphere. Their stories have given me tools to try. Through my vignettes, I hope that you, the reader, can glean not just the ways to ride tension but that you also submit to the vulnerability that it requires.

References

King, M. L. (1998). *The autobiography of Martin Luther King Jr.* (C. Carson, Ed.). New York: Warner Books.

Fischer, L. (1954). *Gandhi: His life and message for the world.* New York: Mentor.

Gandhi, M. K. (1983). *Autobiography: The story of my experiments with truth.* New York: Dover Publications. (Original work published 1948.)

hooks, bell. (2017). *Teaching to transgress: Education as the practice of freedom.* New York: Routledge.

Parel, A. (2009, July). *Ahimsa Institute.* Lecture conducted from Cal Poly University, Pomona, CA.

Sethia, T. (2005). Gandhi, Mohandas. In *Berkshire Encyclopedia of World History* (Vol. 4). Great Barrington, MA: Berkshire Publishing.

Chapter 17

DIY Revolution

Arts, Technology, and Nonviolent Social Change

By Vikas Srivastava

Like many educators, I initially became a teacher to support social change, advance democracy, empower youth, and build a more peaceful world. Also, like many educators, I soon lost sight of my idealism in the daily struggle to survive as a public-school teacher, provide standards-based curriculum, and meet administrative expectations. After spending two weeks at the Cal Poly Ahimsa Center Fellowship with forty other educators who had a similar passion for integrating non-violence in K-12 education, I was inspired to make civic engagement and nonviolent social change a priority. During the two-week residential fellowship, we explored different aspects of Gandhi's life, message, impact, and application of *ahimsa* and *swaraj*. We challenged the discourse, voiced our struggles, shared our successes, and developed a vision for change. Our culminating project was a digital storybook.

I returned to the classroom with an urgency to integrate nonviolent social change regardless of the timing, curriculum, or standards. I taught Audio Technology at a very liberal magnet high school that was known for its emphasis on the arts. Our student population was mostly Caucasian, with a small minority of Asian, South Asian, and Hispanic students. The number of African American students could be counted on one hand. Most students came from affluent families, and less-than-affluent students camouflaged themselves well.

One Monday I simply "paused" class and asked the students to sit in a circle and to deliberate the seemingly unprecedented rise of violence in our lives. I did not really have any plan besides holding space to discuss violence

C. A. Bracho and D. Dodson (eds.), *Teachers Teaching Nonviolence*, 229–239.

with the intent to encourage nonviolence and maybe to tie it to the content of the class. I began with a question, facilitated authentic and critical dialogue, and waited until the last 10-20 minutes of class to share my thoughts. Each day I digested the dialogue and planned for the next day.

The result was a five-day seminar that served as the foundation for a culminating project that integrated arts and technology for nonviolent social change. The organic flow eventually settled into a predictable framework that proved effective at different school sites with hundreds of students from very diverse backgrounds and lifestyles. I began with making a "call to action" that resonated the need to address the current state of violence with students' personal lives. This led to a deconstruction and mutual agreement of the definition of violence, which naturally opened the door to discussing nonviolence as an effective means to confront and transform violence. This emphasis on an awareness of violence as the foundation of nonviolence unexpectedly developed into a new understanding of the role and cooperation of privilege and oppression. Communication surfaced as the bridge to awareness, using the arts and technology as the most effective form of communication.

At this point, my students and I realized audio technology had everything to do with nonviolent social change. What was less obvious was the motivation to engage in social change if one did not feel personally threatened by the status quo and, more importantly, if one benefited from the status quo. This led me to reflect upon and share my own personal journey with an expanded consciousness that my wellbeing existed beyond the immediate needs of my physical body. Finally, each semester the template for the culminating project of change was refined so that it was equally effective for anyone with minimal access to technology, regardless of the student's background in the arts.

What follows is a summary of each phase that led to this project. Sometimes a phase ends sooner than expected, and sometimes it continued longer than planned. When I first piloted this curriculum in my Audio Technology class, each period was 90 minutes. In other schools, I often had 45 minutes. As a stand-alone workshop, I sometimes had two hours a day. Often, I had consecutive days, and other times I had one to two days a week. Finding that the best strategy was to be present and to allow for an organic flow with each group, I participated mostly by holding space and correcting false claims. As the truth became more evident and simpler, the sessions became more fluid.

Making the Call to Action: Phase One

The purpose of phase one is to relate to students the urgency to confront violence in their personal lives, their community, and the world around them. The objective is for them to understand that they have a direct (not indirect, distant, or abstract) relationship with violence, so the content is relevant. Through the process of sharing my personal, social, and political relationships to violence as a victim, offender, and bystander, I model the next phase that asks students to share their relationship to an act of violence. Because we are most effective when we teach what we ourselves believe, we must carry a sincere internal urgency to confront the unprecedented acts of violence in our time.

On the one hand, there may not be an ideal opportunity to integrate nonviolence and social change into our curriculum. On the other hand, literacy and test scores will not matter much if we cannot learn to live with each other. Regardless of our personal lifestyles, daily choices, and future goals, violence seems to affect us all. We may be victims, consumers, bystanders, or offenders. We pay taxes to governments that wage unending wars. Though we are no longer surprised that domestic acts of terrorism happen, we are more concerned with where the next act may occur. Children have become calloused to images of violence in movies, television shows, games, and the nightly news. We have accepted social inequity in favor of 1% of the population as the price we pay for free-market capitalism, as if the level of freedom justifies a level of oppression.

The unfortunate truth is that modern consumption is related to violence—if not towards people and animals, then towards the environment. If you don't know the origin of the products you use, chances are they are made in a developing country. Furthermore, they probably were constructed by some form of poor work conditions (if not child labor) and have contributed to environmental degradation. In short, our ignorance and insensitivity are measured by the degree to which we are unable to perceive violence in every aspect of our existence.

I relate to students by asking them to check the tags on their clothes to see their origin. I ask them to consider the story behind the products they consume. We discuss modern abstract consumption of products completely separated from their source and process of production. We imagine if we could purchase shoes from a sweatshop giving the owner $100 and the worker $1. We also imagine what it must feel like as a laborer to live a life of scarcity while others live in wasteful abundance. We ask ourselves whether it is wise to ignore the permanent depletion of natural resources and destruction of the ecosystem for short-term convenience, comfort, and entertainment. Furthermore, we consider whether our relationship with the outside world is related to our relationship with self and others.

Though it seems we can agree that some degree of violence is a matter of survival and the life cycle, there is the unnecessary violence that is fueled by greed, intolerance, hate, and unresolved personal issues. While it is not entirely accurate or fair to blame recreational violence for all the violence we experience in the world, we can agree it does not support, let alone promote, peace and harmony. While violence unfortunately plays a role in everyone's life, privilege seems to be reflected in the degree to which groups of individuals experience and/or feel the effect of systematic violence and oppression. Thus, the effect of violence in people's personal lives ultimately seems to transcend many (if not all) of the characteristics that otherwise differentiate us—regardless of the motivation. When the Twin Towers went down, victims did not fit any single social category. During mass shootings, victims did not fit into any social category. In war, innocent people who lose their lives do fit into any single social category. Global warming is apparent around the world, regardless of the city creating the most pollution, and affects us all, regardless of any single social category. Victims of physical and/or emotional abuse do not fit into any single social category. The truth is, cultural discrimination may affect the degree to which violence seems to directly impact life choices; however, education, privilege, health and/or morality do not exclude violence from one's life. Test scores, literacy, college degrees, and well-paying jobs may prove to be of little value if we do not address the increasing prevalence of violence in our relationship with ourselves, our family, our community, and the world around us.

At the end of "The Call to Action" assignment, students are asked to write about a personal experience of violence in their lives. These written experiences remain anonymous and do not identify any one involved. More specifically, the written experience should include why this was an act of violence and how it personally affected the writer. It is essential that students are made aware that all the written experiences will be collected, randomly redistributed back to students, and read aloud in class. Therefore, students should only share experiences that they are comfortable sharing with the class, even if the process is anonymous. These written experiences will be used in the next phase to create a collective definition of violence for the remainder of the unit.

Defining Violence: Phase Two

The purpose of phase two is to broaden, deepen, and refine students' understanding of violence in a student-centered discussion that transitions content knowledge and ownership to the learner. The objective is for students to discuss and to develop a collective, mutual definition of violence. In the process, they articulate multiple forms of violence, recognize varying degrees of impact, and define how violence can be both a cause and an effect.

With students seated in a customary circle, I collect and shuffle the written experiences (assigned as homework the day before) and randomly redistribute them. The students take turns reading out loud the written experiences they receive. I ask them to refrain from laughing, regardless of the content, because we do not want to risk offending someone's experience. We also refrain from commenting on the experiences until everyone has shared. After all the students read out loud, I invite them to share their feelings about hearing about the violent experiences of their peers. I emphasize the purpose is to be aware that these experiences exist in our class and comprise someone's definition of violence.

As students read the experiences, I take notes on the board of keywords or phrases that we can use later to build our definition. The intent is to highlight that violent events can be personal and/or impersonal, physical and/or emotional, cause and/or effect. Later, I bring their attention to the board and ask them to identify common themes. Then the students are randomly divided into smaller groups and asked to present a definition of violence that encompasses all the recollections and notes.

After 5-10 minutes in groups, I ask for the first volunteer to share a definition, which I write on the board. I then ask for another volunteer from a different group to add or modify this definition. Making visual edits to the definition as students continue to make suggestions, I work with them until we have unanimous agreement, such as "Violence is a conscious or unconscious act by a living being, non-living object or an act of nature that results in physical or emotional injury. Violent offense also includes refraining from confronting violence if and when possible."

The first step is to find common ground based on our experiences and to agree on a single definition. To understand better how we proceed after our foundational exercise, I prompt students with this question: "To what degree are we responsible for violence as we have defined it?"

At first, students will debate whether violence is a natural way of life. Many argue that the effort to end all violence is unnatural because it is inevitable to the cycle of survival. This discussion often includes natural disasters, the natural balance between predator and prey, and the constant conflict between groups throughout human history. This is a good time to prompt students to differentiate between natural violence and unnatural violence. Natural violence is based on basic survival needs or an unpreventable act of nature. Unnatural violence, on the other hand, is unnecessary for basic survival and perhaps is motivated by malign intent and/or selfish gain. This can lead to a discussion about recreational violence in video games, movies, sports, hunting, and the arts. Often students struggle with their participation in a culture of violence. Ultimately, the issue of consciously engaging in a culture of violence, allowing violence to continue as a bystander, or realizing we may be unconscious participants in supporting acts of violence is an open door to the complexity of personal liberty versus social harmony. This discussion can also delve into historical discrimination, privilege, social/political/economic inequity, rape culture, toxic masculinity, and wars in the name of peace.

Knowing Violence: Phase Three

The critical purpose of this phase is to introduce students to the fundamental principles and practices of nonviolence. The objective is to emphasize the awareness of violence as a precursor to nonviolence, highlighting the end goal of transformation. Students begin to recognize what is, as well as what is not, our responsibility as activists for nonviolent social change. It is important to use this discussion to further deepen their understanding by showing that violence often leads to more violence. It is also crucial to illustrate that the emotional impact of violence tends to be more significant than physical injury. The process of knowing violence serves as the basis of nonviolence.

I share with my students that the effect on any victim of any violence is disempowerment. Because motivation behind violence also seems to boil down to self-worth, people can be hurt more by those they know than strangers or natural disasters. As a result, the emotional pain hurts more than the physical pain. Furthermore, people who commit acts of violence are—more often than not—victims of violence themselves. When we begin to understand violence as projection of personal needs and the continuity of experienced aggression, rather than as a random stand-alone event, then we can begin to understand an effective solution. We must be careful not to separate the symptoms from the disease. The important question is "Is there a proven method that confronts and prevents violence without inciting more violence?"

As students discuss violence prevention, they often seem hesitant to suggest that nonviolence can be effective against current acts of violence, including international safety. However, in defining nonviolence as an act of defiance that does not utilize physical violence, they point to the belief that nonviolence takes more courage and strength than violence. Also, while they agree that violence does not provide long term results, they also think that nonviolence did not guarantee any results. When the discussion moves again to the inevitability of violence as a fundamental quality of life and specifically humans, I intervene and refer to Gandhi's thoughts on the perceived frequency of conflict in relation to harmony: "Gandhi referred to history as recorded breaks in harmonious coexistence." Perhaps we feel conflict occurs more often than harmony because we can only record and report on the incidents of conflict and violence. In any given moment, an infinite number of harmonious acts take place, too many to possibly report. In fact, as we sit in the classroom, many such people moments have occurred. Instead of noting each second that the universe works in concert, we report, instead, on the breaks in harmonious coexistence because that is more feasible. For example, we cannot report on the uncountable agreeable interactions between people around the world that occurred in the last twenty-four hours; to the contrary, if there is a major conflict in the classroom or the community or somewhere in the world, it is reported. There is undoubtedly a lot of violence around the world; however, though we appreciate our awareness of it, to say there is more conflict than harmony doesn't seem statistically accurate.

Historically speaking, the wars in human history have not ended and, instead, have created resentment amongst certain groups, even empowering terrorism. To be honest, there are no wars in which the benefits outweigh the loss. Wars have destroyed communities' ability to operate, and war-torn areas no longer have water or electricity or walkable neighborhoods. Also, when soldiers return from the wars, they are unable to lead normal lives. Furthermore, even our representation of history has many gaps and inaccuracies. For example, we do not discuss that in WWII the U.S. responded first to Pearl Harbor and then to Hitler; that Pearl Harbor was a response to U.S. sanctions on Japan; and that Japan had conceded before the nuclear bomb was dropped on Hiroshima. This is the true history of the U.S. violence that we need to accept. We should not expect different results when we do not change our strategy of true awareness of historical violence. Violence leads to disempowerment. Disempowerment leads to resentment. Resentment leads to revenge. Revenge continues the cycle of violence.

Contrarily, it is vital to show students another true representation of history: that the nonviolent revolution in India led by Gandhi convinced the world's greatest empire to grant independence without technically losing a war. The cycle of violence did not continue in India with revenge or retaliation. We see a similar transformation as a result of the independence movement in South Africa and the nonviolent civil rights movement in the United States. In fact, there are countless examples of mediation, restorative justice, and compassionate acts that have reduced violence and increased harmony in communities, families, and personal lives.

In India, the word "nonviolence" is derived from the Sanskrit term "Ahimsa." "Himsa" means violence, and "A" is the negative prefix "non-." It's important to realize that peace is an entirely different word, "Shanti." While peace and nonviolence are obviously related, they are different. Peace is a passive state while nonviolence is an active state. Peace is possible with or without violence; however, nonviolence is active and constant negation of violence. Therefore, one must know violence to be able to negate it. For this reason, in our study and discussion, my students and I dedicate much of our time to understanding and to deconstructing violence before considering how to utilize nonviolence.

The foundation of Gandhi's Ahimsa was to be the change you want to see in the world. Gandhi did not separate the means from the end. Therefore, we practice nonviolence while we confront violence, rather than justify a violent process towards a hypothetical peaceful future. Using violence towards peaceful ends has simply not shown to be true. The first step in nonviolence is awareness of the violence that exists and, more importantly, that we directly or indirectly participate in. The second step is to be the change we want to see. The third and final steps are to utilize nonviolence not only to reduce and to prevent further violence but also to transform the perpetrator. Only by transforming the perpetrator can we effectively prevent or reduce future violence. This is what took place in India with the British Empire.

Understanding that Privilege Is Power: Phase Four

The purpose of this phase of our study of nonviolence is to illustrate the necessary cooperation between oppression and privilege for successful social change. The objective for students is to identify, deconstruct, and utilize privilege as well as to recognize the importance of speaking up about personal oppression. In the process they realize that they can use their privilege to bring awareness to issues of oppression and violence.

There are privileged groups of people that can enjoy greater liberty at the expense of equity, while oppressed groups of people must give up freedom to accommodate the privileged. I define oppression as the degree to which people are not in control of their lives. Privilege is the degree to which there is control of one's life. One way to identify privilege in a culture or community is to notice what is taken for granted and what is given special attention. For example, a Caucasian male who is straight rarely defends his race, gender, or sexuality when running for president. However, we notice the issue of race is magnified when a person of color is involved. Similarly, gender is magnified with women, and sexuality is magnified when the person is gay. Interestingly, a Caucasian straight white male is also not statistically at danger to be arrested, paid less, or told whom he can marry. Privilege is something that cannot be known until compared to what it is like to be without privilege, so it takes someone who is oppressed to educate someone who is privileged. For example, women let men know we're privileged. Gay friends let straight friends know we're privileged. People of color let white people know they are privileged. We even take our eyes and ears for granted until we meet someone who is blind and/or deaf. We don't know we have privilege until someone without privilege makes it obvious. My theory of "Privilege is Power" is that privilege is nothing to be ashamed of or feel guilty for, but rather it should help us realize it is exactly where we have privilege that we have the power to make change. Therefore, the oppressed need to speak up, and the privileged need to listen. When we have a partnership between the oppressed and the privileged, then we have a revolution. For example, as consumers we can make clear what we are willing or unwilling to fund with our purchase so that we are not supporting such things as oppressive labor in sweatshops.

If our privilege is the place where we have the power to make change, then it is critical we identify our privilege. If you have sight, hearing, four limbs and/or a working brain, then you have privilege. If you feel safe right now, can speak your truth, and/or have internet access, you have privilege. If you can for a moment, think beyond your personal day-to-day survival, then you have privilege. If the first step to be nonviolent is to be aware of the violence, then the question is how do we use our privilege to spread awareness about issues of violence so others can practice nonviolence?

Moving the World Through a DIY Project of Change:
Phase Five

The purpose of this phase of the class instruction is to consider how creative expression is a powerful form of communication, healing, and transformation. The objective is for students to connect privilege, nonviolence, and the arts as a historically successful and still potent formula for social change. In the process, students find their own life experiences support this project of change, which I term a *DIY Revolution*.

I begin by asking, "How many of you read the news every day? Digital or paper?" Very few students raise their hands. "How many of you read books on your own every day?" A few more will raise their hands. "How many of you have memorized a page in your book?" Usually no one raises a hand. "How many of you have memorized a political speech?" Rarely (if ever) does any student raise a hand.

Then I ask, "How many of you listen to music every day, on your own?" Without fail, all of them raise their hands. "How many of you have ever memorized the lyrics to a song?" Again, everyone affirms. The medium of nonviolence is communication, and the most effective form of communication will serve as the most effective form of nonviolence. The most effective form of communication is song. The most powerful form of communication is a video with a song. No one wants to hear speeches and read essays anymore, but everyone will watch a five-minute video.

After moving through the four previous stages, students will create this project of change: a digital slideshow that includes facts, statistics, and images to define violence as well as to bring awareness about a form of violence (including the cause, effect, victim, and offender) and the ways that one can stop (or limit) this form of violence. This slideshow has a soundtrack and appears in a format that can be streamed online. As we end the unit by watching three-five projects a day as a class, we offer constructive feedback to improve our work, and then we share it with the world.

I have come to understand that violence is an energy and that energy cannot be created or destroyed. It can only be transformed. We cannot effectively confront the violence of the present if we do not confront the violence of the past. The arts heal the wounded artist and audience through abstract identification in a way that does not threaten the unwounded. The arts speak to people exactly where they are. The arts have the power to speak the truth with grace. The arts leave gaps where we do not completely understand, where we all find our own understanding, and where the deepest understanding is hidden. When we express violence through art, we have the power to transform it without inciting more violence. The artist is blessed with the ultimate power of universal language. Put it in song, and people of all ages will sing along with you. Put your fist in the air, and people of ages will fear you. Put it an academic paper, and people of all ages will ignore you. As Stevie Wonder, Bob Marley, and countless other artists have understood, it is powerful to simultaneously create music and address change.

Though there was a time when technology worked with us, helping us to do things more efficiently. Such things as hammers, drills, water hoses, and typewriters required us to work together. Then an evolution in technology occurred—with dishwashers, laundry machines, and sprinkler systems—making life easier by doing things we could do but no longer had to do. Now technology works beyond us in ways that we could not work without it. It can distribute information faster than any human being is capable of. In a split second I can send messages anywhere in the world to anyone who has access to the internet. When you utilize your privilege to combine the power of the arts with the power of technology to bring about awareness of issues of violence, then you are the revolution. When you do it with intent to transform the oppressor—to transform the violence and to transform the world—then you are the revolution.

Chapter 18

Listening to a Sound Heart

Applications of Ahimsa in Education

By Laura Hirshfield

I never *wanted* to become a teacher. Though I loved reading and writing, I didn't see the value of classroom learning. I understood the game (memorize what the teacher tells you, regurgitate on the exam, get the A), but I didn't really understand why I was playing, aside from the narrative that compliance gets you into college, and getting into college awards you a good life. I wasn't particularly interested in being a part of that system, so I only majored in Education because it was a degree that logically led to a job. But I distinctly recall when I felt that teaching could (and should!) be so much more than that—the moment I realized it was the most powerful pathway to social justice.

It was during my student-teaching experience at Newton North High School in Newton, Massachusetts. In a lesson I was teaching on *The Adventures of Huckleberry Finn*, we were exploring Mark Twain's confession that this novel is one "where a sound heart and a deformed conscience come into collision and conscience suffers defeat" (cited in Railton, n.d.). This statement and the ensuing discussion it inspired radically transformed my perspective on education. As a class, we talked about how a conscience could become deformed. In this case, why was Huck so tortured at the thought of doing the right thing—freeing a slave—when conscience is supposed to lead us? There were countless ways we connected this concept to the real world, reflecting how society has evolved and things once considered "right" are now clearly viewed as wrong: slavery, child labor, racial discrimination, limitations on who can vote, segregation, and the list

C. A. Bracho and D. Dodson (eds.), *Teachers Teaching Nonviolence*, 241–252.

continues. I saw this quotation, and this book, as a call to readers to understand the importance of critical thinking and *constant* reflection on conscience. What is right, and how do we know? How can we listen to our sound hearts?

This is what resonated most about *ahimsa*, or the study of nonviolence. When I first attended the Ahimsa Institute in 2011, I was completely ignorant about Gandhi, ahimsa, César Chávez, and social justice. I grew up in an upper-middle class community on Long Island, New York; to be honest, the community (at least on the surface) was not concerned with these things. Everyone in my immediate surroundings had enough, and poverty and injustice were things you read about in books or saw on television. I knew inside that this wasn't a realistic vision of the world, but it was all that I knew. Therefore, when I had the opportunity to fly across the country to California to study Gandhi, nonviolence, and social justice, it immediately appealed to me—though solely on an academic level at the time. However, what I learned during those two weeks transformed not only my worldview but also my personal and professional life, initiating my own incredible journey of nonviolence, which has continually deepened my belief that the foundations of social justice are rooted in the practice and promotion of ahimsa. Since then, I've worked tirelessly and with endless rewards to bring a culture of nonviolence into my life, my classroom, my international professional development work, and my management of a nonprofit institution.

The very first day of the Institute, Dr. Tara Sethia began with a PowerPoint. I vividly recall taking out my notebook, prepared for the typical class session: listen, take notes, likely zone out, zone back in, repeat until the end of the session. One of the first proclamations was that violence aims to defeat and exploit and to cause harm and hurt, but nonviolence seeks to change minds and hearts by creating compassion and care and healing wounds. My interest was piqued. Dr. Sethia also pointed out that violence affects people negatively by denying humans happiness, whereas nonviolence positively elevates humanity by creating happiness through love, compassion, courage, forgiveness, and gratitude. All this resonated with me, but I never heard any historian, teacher, leader, or mentor say it, and I had never seen any historical figure live it. Though I had always known that the way to a better world is through nonviolence, no one ever tells us it is possible; history class teaches us that social progress comes at the cost of violence. For the first time in my life, I started to see that there was another way.

Hind Swaraj: Reimagining Civilization, History, and Independence

The institute reading that resounded most strongly with me was from Gandhi's *Hind Swaraj,* or Indian Home Rule. While I could write a whole chapter on how this book shifted my entire perspective, four concepts particularly influenced me as a teacher: the reimagination of civilization, the real definition of history, the superiority of passive resistance, and the true meaning of freedom and independence.

People strive to live in a "civilized" way. However, *Hind Swaraj* causes us to reconsider exactly what we mean when we're talking about civilization. While we're in general agreement that it means advancement, are we talking about technology, advanced weaponry, luxury living, and machinery? Or are we talking about living in a way that advances the wellness of the self and others? Gandhi writes (through the voice of *Hind Swaraj*'s "Editor") that civilization must be defined as living in a way that "elevate[s] the moral being" (p. 57). This contrasts with the traditional view of civilization, which focuses more on bodily comfort, often at the *cost* of morality. This reflection brought me back to 2005, talking with Newton North students about Huck Finn's deformed conscience; Huck was living in a world largely considered civilized, but it was the civilization that had deformed his conscience, making him see wrong as right, and right as wrong. Gandhi's encouragement "to find out what is right and to act accordingly" (p. 72) deeply resonated with what I had been striving to understand for years: what is the purpose of education? To me, it is to encourage people to grasp Truth, listening closely to what their hearts and consciences know to be right, despite what the world might be saying.

Part of the challenge in holding firm to Truth is living amid the bad that happens in the world. We are usually taught that when there is injustice, we must fight it. History class involves studying war after war, ingraining in us that the only way to defeat injustice is with violence. This is what I grew up believing, though reluctantly; I saw the hypocrisy in retaliation, but I just didn't know another way. Gandhi's Editor describes two different ways to resist injustice: "the force of arms" or "soul-force" (p. 68). These words awakened something in me; before this, I had only seen violence as a means to fight injustice. Here was a more effective way that aligned the means and the ends: the way of nonviolence and the power of soul-force. However, I never had heard of anyone in history achieving peace with "soul-force." *Hind Swaraj*'s "Reader" regarded this similarly: "No instance seems to have happened of any nation having risen through soul-force" (Gandhi, p. 70). History, instead, "is a record of the wars of the world" (p. 70).

However, because history most accurately should refer to everything that has ever happened, to reframe it sheds light on "tens of thousands" occurrences of love, soul-force, passive resistance, and ahimsa that sustain the peace of many nations (Gandhi, p. 71). What an incredible awakening! If we view history in this way, we're overwhelmed at the number of instances when conflict was resolved nonviolently. When violence erupts, *that's* the anomaly. However, the fact that violence is what we record distorts our consciences, telling us that the world is inherently bad, and that the only way to fight evil is with more evil, an incredibly dangerous belief. I left the institute with a profound sense of responsibility to reframe what and how I taught, to ensure that I don't further such an inaccurate and problematic view of the world.

What became most important to me was understanding and bringing to my students a teaching philosophy that avoided deforming the conscience and that encouraged listening to the heart. Connected to this goal is Gandhi's meaning of *swaraj*, self-rule or independence. Before the institute, I understood the term "independence" to mean that no one was controlling you. For a country to be independent, the entity "ruling" must be expelled; for an individual to achieve independence, whoever was controlling him/her needed to be driven out. Gandhi argues, to the contrary, that swaraj occurs with self-rule and that true independence involves acting in accordance with one's conscience, even at the cost of personal suffering. This means living fearlessly in alignment with one's values and ethics. Thus, swaraj means disobeying rules that go against what one believes is right; to do anything else is slavery. To do anything else deforms one's conscience, confusing what the heart knows is right. This basic idea of swaraj was critical to my process of unlearning what the world had taught me and of contemplating what I needed to do differently when I returned to the classroom.

Gandhi's Editor states that he does not assume his readers' sudden acceptance of his views but feels that in time they will one day understand (p. 58). This, to me, is the heart of teaching. As teachers, we do not tell young people anything they do not already know; if what we are teaching is Truth, it will resonate in the heart. I left the institute hoping to bring these new understandings home with me to more deeply understand myself and to become a stronger, more open-minded, compassionate educator for my students.

Returning to the Classroom

Firmly rooted in the belief that education of the heart is more important than education of the mind, when I returned from the institute, I constantly sought ways to create experiences in my classroom that would enable reflection on what swaraj meant to my students, even if I never used that term. I worked at a competitive high school with high expectations of both teachers and students; I needed to make the work both relevant and rigorous. The challenge renewed my love for teaching and allowed me to create engagement in new and inspiring ways.

One of the first units was centered on the book *Siddhartha*. Traditional curriculum asked students to analyze passages and ponder this work as a coming-of-age novel. After the institute, I saw both the character Siddhartha as well as my task teaching it in a different light. When reading about Siddhartha, a wealthy man of privilege, choosing to leave his wealthy lifestyle and pursue greater happiness as an ascetic, I asked students to reflect. Drawing upon the institute's discussions about "modern civilization," and about how becoming more civilized has led to immense violence in the world, I talked about materialism, consumption, greed, and Gandhi's decision to renounce wealth and only take what was required. Though he had the means to live a comfortable lifestyle, he, instead, *chose* a life of simplicity, much like Siddhartha. This choice was one I thought worth pondering. These two men questioned what the world told them and listened to their hearts. Many students thought this was an admirable but outdated choice: "Siddhartha lived in 2000 BC! Gandhi lived in like 1900!" How could this be relevant, or even possible, today? To be honest, I didn't have an answer, so I did what any teacher would do: I sought one.

I had heard that Jains were committed to a minimal lifestyle, so I literally Googled "Jain community center near me" in the hopes of finding someone who could speak from an authentic place about what it could mean to live minimally in the United States in 2010. A series of emails and phone calls with the Jain Center of Greater Boston led to a guest speaker, Yogendra Jain, who spoke to our class about the Jain philosophy of *aparigraha*, or non-possession. While there are some who live as Gandhi once did and as Siddhartha lived after leaving his comfortable village, Mr. Jain shared that to live modestly in 2010 could mean something as simple as donating a shirt each time you buy a new one. It could mean pausing before buying an item that isn't really a need and being mindful of its cost, from production to consumption. This was my first reminder that living a life committed to nonviolence does not mean one has to be perfect; it's about minimizing violence and maximizing care. Mr. Jain also spoke about meditation, a quieting of the outside world, and led students in a short practice.

After Mr. Jain left, we reflected. What did we think? Was it relevant? The talk inspired a class challenge: for one week we would practice meditation daily and make one significant change to our daily routine that would allow for more mindfulness. Afterwards, I was blessed by such reflections as this:

> This was definitely a worthwhile experience. It is fascinating how something just as simple as focusing on your breathing and laying down can feel so amazing and refreshing. In addition, not having my Xbox made me more productive and creative in finding other ways to occupy my time. I even picked up my guitar and played more without having Xbox to play...Just camping out and being with nature and myself seem extremely therapeutic and self-refining. If there is anything I took away from this experience, it is that meditation can serve as the ultimate de-stressor—something I have needed in my life for a long time.

Reading this affirmed what I had experienced myself at the institute; if we give students the chance to experience something different, in this case the chance to feel that more does not necessarily mean better, the truth will ultimately reveal itself.

Studying Gandhi, Martin Luther King, Jr., César Chávez, and nonviolence as a strategy left me feeling cheated by my education: I wondered both why I had I never learned any of it and how society could expect to develop peacebuilders when all we studied in school was war. Though I wasn't a history teacher, much of the literature involved war, so I reframed those texts to be studies of violence. We read *Beowulf* through this lens, asking important questions:

— What is the recorded version of war and how is it different from war's reality?
— What is the impact of war on combatants and on society? Is the cost worth it?
— "Wars are poor chisels for carving out peaceful tomorrows." Is war an effective method of building peace?

Throughout the unit, we discussed these questions, concluding with persuasive papers. It was interesting to watch nearly all students say the same thing: that war is an absolute evil. However, the subsequent comment and question echoed the very same one I had at the Ahimsa Institute: Yes, violence is bad, but what alternative is there?

At this point in the unit, students were exposed, most for the first time in their lives, to nonviolence as a strategy. We watched *A Force More*

Powerful and discussed the Dandi March, and we read the chapter on Passive Resistance from Gandhi's *Hind Swaraj* and discussed the meaning of civilization and soul-force. Eventually, groups of students were explored different nonviolent movements in history: India's Salt March, Malala Yousafzai's fight for female education, the Green Peace's anti-whaling campaign, the Argentinian Mothers of the Plaza de Mayo, Ruhrkampf and Nazi resistance, the various campaigns of the American civil rights movement, and more. The most frequent comment was "Why don't we learn about this in history class?" The same question resonated with me for years to come, influencing both the curriculum I taught and my involvement in professional development.

Teaching for Peace: An Indian Immersion Experience in Practical Nonviolence

My work with professional development was anchored in my remembrance of one of the first things I learned about nonviolence at the Ahimsa Institute: nonviolence must be an inextricable element of our being. A teacher and lifelong learned by nature, I sought coursework that would lead to this end; I couldn't find anything. I contacted Yogendra Jain, the guest speaker on *Siddhartha*, who suggested that I contact the International School for Jain Studies (ISJS) in India. While the ISJS did not offer a course specific on ahimsa or for teachers, it was willing to collaborate with me to *create* something. From November 2011 through May 2012, I actively worked with ISJS to build a program for teachers to visit India in an immersive experience to study nonviolence: *Teaching for Peace: An Indian Immersion Experience in Practical Nonviolence.*

This class was located not only where nonviolence was born but also where a teacher's commitment would truly be tested: three weeks in India in the heat of summer. The goal was both a mental exercise in learning and an experiential practice because nonviolence is easy to talk about but not as easy to live. It's easy to be kind, generous, compassionate, forgiving, and patient when you are comfortable and have all that you want. It is not so easy when you're in a new environment with no familiar faces, no WiFi, or no amenities that provide the comfort of home—when food, language, and culture are unfamiliar; when you're hot, ideas are new, and language barriers exist; when you are constantly navigating different territory that challenge worldviews. All these pieces were critical components of the program. In India, each year I deepened my understanding of *ahimsa* and the Jain principles of *anekant* (multiplicity of truths) and *aparigraha* (non-possession).

I came to see the combination of these three principles as keys to Truth; any conflict I faced, when viewed through this lens, could be seen more clearly. As the program evolved, I began to realize that its value was not so much the development of lessons but the personal reflection it inspired. What do I project? To what extent do I practice compassion? How do I unintentionally commit acts of violence? What can I do to minimize harm and maximize care? I continually revisited these exercises and reflections with a new cohort of teachers each summer from 2012–2017.

Working at YouthBuild: Rebuilding Lives and Communities

Building upon the transformation of the Ahimsa Institute and the program in India, in 2014 I moved to Los Angeles to begin my teaching career in a community and a school vastly different from anything I had experienced before. I accepted a job teaching English at CCEO YouthBuild in Lennox, California, a small community between the larger neighborhoods of Inglewood and Hawthorne. YouthBuild is a national nonprofit organization that supports a network of over 200 local programs in low-income neighborhoods around the country and the world. These programs serve 16 to 24-year-old "dropouts" who were pushed out of traditional schools; they come to YouthBuild to get their high school diploma, earn a construction credential, assist in building affordable housing, develop as young leaders, and rebuild their lives and communities. Lennox, where our program is located, is 93% Hispanic or Latino, and about half of residents were born outside of the U.S. The average household income is below the national and state averages, and the high school graduation rate in 2017 was 49%.

Though these demographics are unique to Lennox, they largely represent the population that YouthBuild programs serve around the world: communities that are often marginalized and young people who are too often underserved. John Bell (2013), one of the co-founders of YouthBuild, writes the following about participants:

> They have tremendous talents and gifts, have shown courage and resilience in handling their lives, even while sometimes making mistakes. But by the time they get to YouthBuild, they have been pretty beat up by life—by racism, poverty, abuse, oppression, poor education, violence, family trauma, broken communities, broken homes, broken promises, broken hearts. (p. 142)

This being "beaten up by life" manifests in the classroom in many ways: mistrust of people (especially authority figures), defiance and disrespect, drugs and alcohol to self-medicate, lack of sense of agency over their lives and decisions, and the inability to confidently imagine a future as an objectively happy, healthy, successful adult. Young people come to YouthBuild looking for a second chance, acceptance, and a safe place. YouthBuild seeks to restore their natural love of learning, engage them in community service, create agents of change in the spirit of social justice, and provide the nurturing environment necessary for this transformation. This is nonviolence in action, and thousands of lives have been transformed through the power of love and opportunity.

Stepping into this community and program required constant applications of *ahimsa*, love and compassion; *anekant*, the understanding that my truth was not the only objective truth; and *aparigraha*, the willingness to simply let go. While I had studied these concepts in India, YouthBuild offered me the opportunity to practice them daily because the purpose of this program is to assist youth in recovering "as much of their inherent nature as possible" (Bell, 2013, p. 142). This is anchored in the creation of a safe emotional and physical environment that includes "caring and skilled adults who can balance kindness and acceptance with accountability and discipline" (Bell, 2013, p. 142).

What usually happens in schools when students are defiant and disrespectful, use drugs or alcohol, or show apathy and lack of caring? Adults are angry and resentful, demanding some sort of punishment: scolding, shaming, suspension, and sometimes expulsion from the community. Before the Ahimsa Institute, these practices were all that I knew. However, YouthBuild does things differently. "Accept, Correct, and Move On" is a mantra that is heard daily; in fact, this phrase is written on the back of participants' t-shirts and embodies our programmatic philosophy. The response to any misbehavior is to accept the perspectives of the young people in the program, to work with them so they understand the harm that may have been done (to themselves or to others), to assist them in developing a plan to repair the harm, and then to move forward together as a community. I was exposed to this restorative approach to discipline at the Ahimsa Institute, and it is infused into all that we do at YouthBuild.

Concluding Thoughts

To say that this has been a journey would not accurately describe the detour my life took after the Ahimsa Institute. Exposure to Gandhi, Ahimsa, and compassion has transformed me personally and professionally, giving me a compass to determine what is *right*. To me, teaching nonviolence means showing learners that there is *another* way, allowing their hearts to decide. As the Editor in *Hind Swaraj* optimistically shares, swaraj is not simply a dream; it is a conscious, daily commitment that begins individually and then subsequently propels one to work "to persuade others to do likewise" (Gandhi, pp. 58–59). This speaks to what I felt in 2011 as a calling, and it is what I have sought each day since. Ahimsa does not have to be a dream. It merely requires exposure. If it's right, it will flourish. I trust this truth, and I'm endlessly grateful for the opportunity be a part of rewriting (and teaching) history.

References

Bell, J. (2013). *YouthBuild's north star* (2nd ed.). Somerville, MA: YouthBuild USA.

Gandhi, M.K. (n.d.). Hind Swaraj or Indian Home Rule. Retrieved July 20, 2019, from www.mkgandhi.org

Railton, S. (n.d.). "Second Twain Lecture." Retrieved from http://www.people.virginia.edu/ ~sfr/ enam312/lects/feb4.htm

About the Editors and Contributors

THE EDITORS

Christian A. Bracho is an Associate Professor of Teacher Education at the University of La Verne, where he is a Co-Director of the Center for Educational Equity and Intercultural Research. He received his Ph.D. in International Education at New York University. Dr. Bracho's research areas include teacher identity, teacher movements, LGBT communities, and nonviolence education, and he has been published in *Politics & Policy, Education Studies, Journal of Homosexuality,* and *Forum for International Research in Education.* A former high school English teacher, Bracho was a 2005 recipient of Ahimsa Center Fellowship and subsequently served as a Curriculum Facilitator at the Ahimsa Center K-12 Institutes. He has served as a professional development consultant/facilitator in Los Angeles County, Europe, and Africa, and was awarded faculty fellowships by the Center for Minority Serving Institutions, the Transformative Teacher Education program, and the American Association for Hispanics in Higher Education.

Danita Dodson is an English, Spanish, and Humanities teacher at Hancock County High School and Walters State Community College in East Tennessee. She holds a Ph.D. in English from the University of Southern Mississippi, specializing in 20th-century women's and postcolonial literature. Dr. Dodson's published scholarship has centered on utopian and dystopian fiction, including a published interview with novelist Margaret Atwood. Loving to combine professional work with travel and cultural competence, she has been a Fulbright-Hays scholar in Turkey, a university professor in Nicaragua, and a five-time National Endowment for the Humanities fellow. A recipient of a 2015 Ahimsa Center fellowship, Dodson teaches and promotes nonviolent social change. She also is the Guest Editor of the *Ahimsa Center Newsletter.*

C. A. Bracho and D. Dodson (eds.), Teachers Teaching Nonviolence, 251–254.
© 2020 DIO Press. All rights reserved.

THE CONTRIBUTORS

Elizabeth Benskin is the Director of Teaching and Learning at The Baltimore Museum of Art. She has worked extensively with K-12 audiences throughout her 18 years in the field of museum education.

Jode Brexa, Ed. S., has facilitated Digital Storytelling projects for youth voice in the western United States, Tajikistan, and South Africa. She lives and creates digital stories in Santa Fe, New Mexico.

Shara Carder is a second-grade teacher in the Cupertino Union School District in Cupertino, California. She has taught elementary school for twenty years.

Adam Dennis has been an English teacher for 17 years. Currently he teaches sophomore and junior English classes along with a Mindfulness elective in a small public school just outside of Portland, Oregon.

Andrew Duden teaches World History, US History, Civics, and The Luscher School to Farm Internship at Lake Oswego High School in Lake Oswego, Oregon. He has taught for 23 years. He earned his Masters of Arts in Teaching from Lewis and Clarke College.

Esteban Hernandez teaches English at Los Altos High School in Hacienda Heights, California. He has also taught English in Chile and in China.

Donna S. Hill retired in 2012 after 33 years teaching for L.A.U.S.D, but she has maintained an active role in Cleveland High School Humanities Magnet as a substitute and mentor.

Laura Hirshfield is the program manager at SBWIB YouthBuild in Lennox, California. She taught English for ten years before moving into nonprofit management. She is also the co-founder/program coordinator for Teaching for Peace: An Indian Immersion Experience in Practical Nonviolence.

Sarabeth Leitch is a language arts teacher and basketball coach at Madison High School in Portland Public Schools. She has been an educator for thirteen years.

Susan Milan has taught for the past 22 years in the South Whidbey Schools in Washington State. She currently teaches 7th grade life science and empowers young people through connections between human and environmental health.

Danielle Mizuta, MEd, taught special education in Hawaii for 13 years. She has served as a State Level Lead Mentor, a Hawaii Hope Street Fellow, and a Regional Teacher Fellow Coach with Hope Street.

Quixada Moore-Vissing is a civic researcher and a public engagement designer. She earned her PhD in Education at the University of New Hampshire.

Tazeen Rashid teaches AP/IB Economics in Florida. She received a Master's in Social Policy from the London School of Economics. Winning the Governor's Award for Excellence in Teaching Economics, she has a passion for equity in teaching.

Karin Rose recently began teaching English at Doherty High School in Colorado Springs, Colorado, having taught elementary and middle school the previous 12 years.

Tara Sethia is Professor of History and founder and Director of the Ahimsa Center at California State Polytechnic University, Pomona. Under the auspices of the Center, she helped establish an interdisciplinary program in Nonviolence Studies at Cal Poly. She directs the Center's summer institutes for K-12 teacher-leadership on nonviolence and social change. Dr. Sethia's books include *Gandhi: Pioneer of Nonviolent Social Change* and *The Living Gandhi: Lessons for Our Times*. She received her Ph.D. in History from the University of California, Los Angeles.

Eusebio Travis Sevilla is an educator in San Diego, California. A lifelong artist who uses various mediums, he incorporates the outdoors and the environment into his work whenever possible.

Peggy Sia teaches elementary school in Los Angeles County. She has served as a mentor teacher for the Ahimsa Center Summer Institute for K-12 educators. She is also a member of Education for Global Peace, serving as lead teacher for Classroom Connect.

Vikas P. Srivastava is Director of Mindfulness at Legacy Early College Charter School in South Carolina. He specializes in educational design with an emphasis on nonviolence, creative confidence, entrepreneurial mind-set, and sustainability.

CPSIA information can be obtained
at www.ICGtesting.com
Printed in the USA
LVHW081908021221
705096LV00005B/228